prayer
and the art of
volkswagen
maintenance

Donald Miller

HARVEST HOUSE PUBLISHERS
Eugene, Oregon 97402

Cover by Left Coast Design, Portland, Oregon
Interior photo courtesy of Adams & Faith Photography, Portland, Oregon

Prayer and the Art of Volkswagen Maintenance
Copyright © 2000 by Donald Miller
Published by Harvest House Publishers
Eugene, Oregon 97402

Library of Congress Cataloging-inPublication Data

Miller, Donald, 1971–
    Prayer and the art of Volkswagen maintenance   /   Donald Miller.
      p.   cm.
   ISBN 0-7369-0160-4
    1. Christian life—Miscellanea.   2. Miller, Donald, 1971–
Journeys—United States.   3. United States—Description and travel.
I. Title.
BV4501.2M4733   2000
277.3'0829'092—dc21
  [B]   99-41916
                                   CIP

Printed in the United States of America.

00 01 02 03 04 05 06 / BC / 10 9 8 7 6 5 4 3 2

for my Mother,

...sin has learned a fear of thee and goodness found a home.

Based loosely on a true story.

Contents

Author's Note

Long ago I dreamed of writing a book. A novel that would move and woo like a symphony. This is a task for a genius, though. A task for folks like Emily Dickinson: dressed in white and locked in her father's house, angrily, crazily scratching her restless pen against her notebook. I want no such life, for I have always thought to write of true love a man must know the emotion firsthand. So my novel will be more like a pops concert than a symphony.

This is simply a story about an adventure of discovery; of how I came to know a fellow named Paul, one of my best friends to this day; of how I wrote poems and watched God scratch messages in the clouds and adjust the stars so they were as He wished; of how I came to know God and believe in Him with a way that was all new to me yet ancient time to the world.

Travelers' Song

A fire lit, its embers sigh
like voices quiet in the night.
Over these go Angel's eyes
Or blinking stars on endless skies.

Peering down through time's bleak bend
The angels blink and blink again
At travelers lost but all in gain
For grace and peace the heavens send.

Their echoes rattled desert spaces,
Green and Mountain made their stage.
An enterprise surmounts the pages
Of the tale these travelers made.

And you are too invited hither,
Pack your gear and boarded go.
For we upon the globe shall dither,
Our Maker having us in tow.

1. Travel

Houston, Texas, at night, as seen from Interstate 45, is something beautiful. The interstate approaches and collides with the city's center in a tight, second-level loop that hugs skyscrapers three-quarters around downtown before spinning off north toward Dallas and south toward the Gulf coast. It is, as you know, an enormous city; its skyline brilliant with architecture and light. A landlocked lighthouse on the flat surface of south Texas.

Tonight she shines. The towers are lit and the road is ours alone. A bank sign marks the time at 2:20 A.M., alternately flashing the temperature at 73 degrees. Houston has an empty feel to it at such an hour. Her size demands traffic and noise. But this is a southern city and people sleep at proper hours, leaving the landscape to changing street signals with nobody to obey their commands.

Night travel is best. Mild, thick air pours through the windows like river water, flowing in circles around our heads. Paul and I are quiet; our thoughts muffled by the tin-can rattle of his 1971 Volkswagen camping van. We are traveling north toward Oklahoma and then, perhaps, the

Grand Canyon. After that, we have no plans except to arrive in Oregon before we run out of money. We share a sense of excitement and freedom. Not a rebel freedom, rather, a deadline-free sort of peace. There is nowhere we have to be tomorrow. There is no particular road we have committed to take and, I suppose, if one of us could talk the other out of it, the canyon itself could be bypassed for some other point of interest. Tonight we are travelers in the truest sense of the word; a slim notion of a final destination and no schedule to speak of. We are simply moving for motion's sake.

Our plans were shared with friends, but few understood. "Going off to find yourself," was the standard interpretation. I don't think that is really our point. We are shaped by our experiences. Our perception of joy, fear, pain, and beauty are sharpened or dulled by the way we rub against time. My senses have become dull and this trip is an effort to sharpen them.

"Does it snow much in Oregon?" I say to Paul in a voice loud enough to be heard over the wind and the engine.

"Snows a couple feet every winter. Some winters it snows a little more."

"Do you think there will still be snow on the ground when we get there?"

"I doubt it; most of the snow melts off in March. We will catch it a couple of months too late. The mountains will have snow and there may be snow on Black Butte, but Bend and Redmond will be dry."

My mind has been swimming in imaginings of mountain landscapes. Paul has lived in Oregon most of his life and he's told stories of its terrain. I know the look and feel of the Three Sisters, Jefferson Park, and Smith Rock; all of them stitched together by a Pacific Crest Trail going from Mexico to Canada. They've got trout the size of sea bass, bars thick with pretty girls, a cliff-bordered ocean, waterfalls, canyons, and just about anything Ernest Hemingway ever put in a novel. In Oregon, men live in the woods and let their beards grow. I know it all happens the way Paul says it happens because he doesn't shift his eyes when he talks and his stories are never long, the way liars' stories are.

Paul came to Houston to entertain thoughts of starting college. He shuffled himself around and got his thinking straight, but never looked at a school. He stayed long enough to fix his van and earn gas money home. While here, we accepted him into our small group of friends and enjoyed his stories about life in the Northwest. We'd sit around a fire and prod him to talk about the wilderness. He'd talk a little and then get to missing it and just as soon shut up, passing the talking to someone else. We knew he wouldn't stay.

Houston is no place for Paul; he doesn't fit. Time moves quickly here; people are in a panic to catch up. Paul exists within time but is hardly aware how it passes. I check my watch every ten minutes out of habit and I don't think he's ever owned one. He is a minimalist. Everything he needs is in this van. His gear includes a tool box, camping stove, backpack, and about ten Louis L'Amour books. I think he has a pair of jeans, some shorts, and tennis shoes stuffed behind the seat. Not much more than this except the clothes he is wearing. He is living proof that you can find contentment outside of the accumulation of things. The closest I've come to his sort of thinking is in the writings of Thoreau. Walden Pond sounds like a nice place.

We haven't known each other very long. We met several weeks ago at a beach house on Crystal Beach, just east of Galveston Island. A friend rents the place every year when the phosphorus in the water dies. At night the waves glow bright green. It is the closest thing Texans have to the Northern Lights. The phosphorus gets less attention because it too closely resembles radioactive waste. Last I checked, this natural wonder hadn't made the pages of the *Texas*

Travel Guide. We who know, celebrate the waves annually, filling a rented house with as many guys as can sleep on the floor. Paul, introduced to me as a friend of a friend, was included in this year's festivities. He was doing pull-ups on a cross beam beneath the beach house when I arrived. Who's the surfer? I thought to myself. Paul is Oregon at heart but California in looks. He has wild blonde hair and a smile that endears him to women. He's framed tightly with muscle, carrying his mid-sized stature in efficient, able-bodied strides. A swimmer's arms, not bulky with excess, but efficient, thick, and sun-weathered.

There were old friends to catch up with, so we didn't talk the first day. Night came and I slept in a hammock on the porch. I was awakened shortly after sunrise by someone dragging a kayak over the dunes and onto the beach. I watched as Paul lifted the kayak to his shoulder and stumbled fifty yards to the shore. He dropped the kayak into the water, pulled the two-sided paddle from the inside of the boat and lowered himself into the opening. The water was still that morning. He slid quickly, pacing the beach. He turned away and paddled into the ocean until I lost him in the horizon. Several minutes passed and he didn't return. Concerned, I rolled out of my hammock and stood against the railing. Still no sign of him. I decided to wait before waking the guys. Paul had operated the boat with such confidence; he obviously knew what he was doing. Several minutes passed and he appeared again, a speck on the horizon growing larger and more defined.

That evening, around the fire, Paul told us about his morning ride. He said he had found a school of dolphin and ridden above them as they criss-crossed beneath the kayak, playing with him, surfacing less than ten feet from the boat and then diving into the deep. "It was as if they wanted to race," he said. "They were gliding beside me the way a dog runs beside a moving car."

He quickly earned our admiration and, once assured he was not interested in our girlfriends, we included him on road trips. Paul was welcome company and his van came in handy. We made weekend runs to New Bronsfels and Central Texas. Soon we began talking about an extended trip; one that would have us living in the van for months, meeting new people and discovering new places. We plotted hypothetical routes up the east coast or north to the Great Lakes. We bought a map and traced back roads connecting Civil War battle sites. We considered the Bible Belt and the Florida Keys. We pictured ourselves in New York and actually made a call to inquire about Yankee tickets. Paul and I began to consider the trip seriously. We spent days at the library and flipped through glossy pages of mountains and rivers and cities at night. When our dreams gave way to plans, our other friends faded back into thoughts of responsibility and comfort. They became apprehensive; it would mean leaving their jobs or taking a semester off from school. Soon, Paul and I were the only ones willing to go.

There were, in our goodbyes, feelings of permanence. Some goodbyes were more substantial than others. Kristin's last embrace was difficult. Our relationship had come to an end because of this trip. I could not ask her to accept a half-hearted promise of returning soon, so, a few days before we left, I called it off.

We parted with dignity. In our last hours she had asked, again, my reasons for leaving. I told her of the need to travel, to gain memories, and to be, for a while, completely free. She could not understand, but accepted my explanation without losing self-respect or a commitment to our friendship. It is this sort of strength that I admire and will miss.

Our time together ended too soon. We were to be at a friend's house where our close-knit group had gathered to say goodbye. Paul's van was already there when Kris and I arrived. We could hear people talking inside so we walked in without knocking. The room was filled with familiar faces. Paul was on the couch with Bob, Jim, and Kyle. He was vaguely answering a question about our itinerary. Tia, Heather, and Kurt were standing in the kitchen. Jeremy, who was sitting on the stairs playing his guitar, was the first to notice us.

"You know, I never took you as the hippie type," Jeremy said.

"Good," I replied. He took his hand off his guitar and reached out for mine. Gripping my hand tightly and matching my eye, he said, "I'm gonna miss you."

"I'll miss you too, bud," I replied.

Within seconds we were surrounded and Kristin slid off into the kitchen to avoid the reality of the moment. There were sincere goodbyes, tones of loss were in our voices. It felt good to be in the spotlight. We were vagabonds, drifters, Republican rebels setting out to see America. There were stories and laughter and promises to write, promises I will keep. Fred gave us silver crosses on leather straps and Dan gave us wool blankets he took from his Coast Guard barrack. I sensed an innocent envy from the guys. We wished they could join us and they wished likewise, but school and work owned their youth. Trips like ours are greener grass left unknown for fear of believing trite sayings; sayings that are sometimes true. But theirs is an existence under the weight and awareness of time; a place we are slowly escaping; a world growing fainter by the hour and the mile. Our letters will arrive like messages in bottles from shores they may never know.

———— ———— ————

Each mile driven lessens the weight in my chest. Our friends are back in their homes, long asleep. And we are fading from the familiar into the unknown. The glass towers have given way to suburbs and darkly lit shopping malls. We are in that part of Houston where the sons of the sons of cowboys live in master-planned communities and play golf on weekends. They married their high school sweethearts and exchanged horses for Volvos; each of them Southern Baptists who aspire to be politicians.

The van moves slowly. I am able to focus on a reflector mounted to the concrete barrier separating the north from the southbound lanes. As we approach, I turn my head to watch its white brightness dim as we pass.

"At the rate we're going we may not reach the North-west till next winter," I observe.

Paul leans his weight into the gas pedal. "At this rate we may not even get out of Houston till winter."

Paul is more comfortable with the slow progress than I am. We are cruising at a sluggish fifty miles-per-hour and, when ascending an overpass, the van chugs and loses a few notches on the speedometer. From the passenger's seat, I can see into the console where the miles are clocking at a snail's pace.

Paul has nicknamed his van "the road commode" and it's a fitting name. The box-shaped van barely passes state standards. Throwbacks from the sixties, these vans are mobile intimations of the Woodstock era. Volvo-encased couples pass us on the street, look into each other's eyes and remember when. They understand why this is the hippie "vehicle of choice." The van can comfortably sleep four (five if you lay a board across the two front seats). Paul has reconstructed the sink cabinet with wood scraps. It sits directly behind the driver's seat. Beyond the sink, parallel with the back window, there is a bed folded in a bench. Another bed can be created by turning a crank which lifts a tent-like contraption on the roof. There are two boxes of books on the floor between the sink and the bench and another box of groceries and utensils in the open space beneath the sink. Several blankets are folded and sitting on the bench and both of our backpacks lean against the side wall. There is a small, open walkway between the two front seats where a person can easily get through to the back. The interior is a black, wax-like plastic and rubber. They built it when plastic was new material so it's more rigid than they make it now. A working stereo hangs out of a hole in the dash and there are a few lights and knobs here and there. The gearshift is long and comes out of the floor. Volkswagen vans have rear engines, so we are sitting at the absolute front of the van. A glimpse over the dash allows me to see the headlights and the front bumper with the road passing underneath.

—⁓— —⁓— —⁓—

Stretched before us is an endless system of interstates, highways, and back roads. Every intersection passed is an artery leading to workplaces, schools, and homes. Small towns dot the interstate for more than fifty miles north of Houston. Each city its own world; high school football games, church picnics, and Boy Scout meetings keep lives moving in a comfortable rhythm. Tonight they are but clusters of street lights strung from neighborhood to neighborhood. Each neighborhood with its homes, each home with its family, and each quiet soul sleeping one thin wall from another. Charles Dickens tells us that every heart is a profound mystery to the heart beating nearest it. I am starting to understand him. Watching the dark towns pass gives them a new significance. During the day they connect with cars and people. Tonight the thick dark lines separate one neighborhood from another. These homes house families we don't know. So many sleeping people; all of them spirit, bound by flesh, held together by bone and trapped in time.

Rarely do I question the mystery of it all. We are atoms connected together to create big, awkward, intelligent animals; animals complex in construction, equipped with minds, hearts, and the like. Spinning secretly around us is an intricate system of interconnected physical laws, completely dependent upon each other for effectiveness. And we are in the middle of it; actors on Shakespeare's stage, madmen in Nietzche's streets, accidents in Sagan's universe, children in God's creation.

Paul and I agree on the latter view. We are part of creation by natural birth and Christian by rebirth. Many of my questions about life have been settled by the words and deeds of a Jewish carpenter from Nazareth. Part of our agenda is to deepen our faith during this trip. Paul and I have talked time and again about our desire to spend time in prayer and study. Now, with ample time and a fellow spirit in Paul, this will be a priority.

But this new pursuit of God will be different from ones past. I am approaching from a new side: the rear. I was raised in a family that attended church on Sunday. It has become such a part of my life that I am no longer certain if it is real: Do I possess a personal faith, or just my own learned behavior? I have passed through what modern Christianity has to offer and am standing at the other end, questioning, "Is this it?" Years of Sundays stack end to end on a calendar marked with church camps, youth group, mission trips, concerts, seminars, revivals, and retreats. All of them add up to the chasing of an elusive emotional fulfillment, one that slips in and out of my consciousness like a ghost. Still, and despite my weariness with this chase, I am looking for fulfillment in Christ. Something inside keeps me in pursuit. There must be something more. Something authentic. I feel that I have only passed through the shadow of the Christian faith and eluded its consequence and substance.

I know enough about Christ to realize that He focused more on action than on persuasive words. He spent little time convincing and much time proclaiming. His willingness to take the cross captured my attention. Further investigation led me to believe His claims. He was, in fact, the Son of God. And this is where I find my dilemma. Having believed and experienced life change in the newness of my faith, I am left now, having passed considerable time since my rebirth, with a faith that feels as empty and arid as a cavern. I've memories of joy, but nothing to quench the present thirst.

Maybe my relationship with Christ is like any relationship. Time wears newness out and I am left with discipline and will. Occasional thoughts, poems, songs, or sermons revive the spirit, but they are few and far between. In short, I do not feel fulfilled by what I know or experience of God. The idea of Him, His word, His commands, His footprints on the planet, no longer stimulate my mind. I am not, as the church-goers might say, *walking with the Lord*. I've made efforts to revive this numbness by reading books, listening to tapes, and feeding on ideas about a soft Jesus healing the sick and riding off into the sunset, sharing the horizon with the Lone Ranger and Tonto. But He seems a Sunday school character, no more substantial than Daniel in the lion's den or Noah in the ark. He fits snugly in the toy box between Big Bird and Humpty Dumpty. He is a cloth cutout on a felt board. A name in a song. A prayer on the lips of a politician.

Somewhere, however, beneath my childish, immature perception of God is His true identity. I consider this trip a stepping away from myself, from my comforts and from my weak understanding of meaning, purpose, and faith. I want to grow beyond my childish understanding of God into an adult reality: A faith based on the facts of Scripture and the knuckle-grinding reality of a day-to-day existence. I need more than a bedtime story. I need more than a youth group God. I am looking for a savior. A guide. An existential answer to my questions about purpose and meaning. I want true fulfillment in my Christian faith. I am looking for joy.

"You feeling tired yet, Paul?" He is looking groggy at the wheel.

"I've been tired for a while," he says.

"Why don't you pull over the next time you have the chance. I've got to use the rest room and we can switch."

A few miles pass and we see a rest area sign. Paul slows the van and coasts down the entrance past some trees and into the parking lot. A dozen or more tractor trailers are parked in long spaces. We pass them and pull into a spot near the rest rooms. Paul turns off the engine and we are immediately enveloped in the whistle and hum of a million crickets. Texas silence. I unbuckle my seat belt and stretch my back. Stepping out of the van, we move slow and road-travel weary toward the rest room. "I don't think I remember how to use my legs," Paul says, walking in an exaggerated wobbly motion.

"I'm pretty sure you just put one foot in front of the other, but it definitely doesn't feel right," I joke.

The temperature has dropped and a layer of moisture soaks the ground. Brainless june bugs make loud, fast dives at a street light. One broken-winged bug struggles on the side walk. I squash him under my boot and say softly, as if to myself, "I hate those things."

Paul hears me and replies, "You and me both." He swings the heavy bathroom door open and we are mugged by a foul stench; a smell unique to rest area bathrooms.

"People really should eat better," he says, and we laugh while trying not to breathe—a difficult task.

I beat Paul back to the outside world and gasp for air like a diver finding the surface of the ocean. Making my way across the lawn, I stretch out on a picnic table to flatten my back. The stars in Texas are distant and faded. They are grouped together in patches and encompassed in a hazy, humid-gray darkness. There are a few dark patches that I recognize as clouds. They are stationary at first sight, but watching, they engulf twinkling stars one at a time.

The road from Houston to Dallas cuts through the heart of the big thicket. We are encaged in a fence of tall pines. A blanket of pine needles and scattered cones shields the ground. Behind us, an island of trees is surrounded on four sides by the highway, the rest area, and its entrance and exit. Before us, across the parking lot, a dense forest, dark with shadows, extends perhaps as far as Nacagdocheous. Save the choir of crickets, the air is silent and still. The truckers are asleep in their trucks and the rest area is quiet and peaceful. The weather slows its roll and glides high and slow like a crow with a full stomach.

"Should we sleep here?" Paul asks.

We've not driven more than four hours and that we did slowly. We've not made enough progress to stop, regardless of the hour. "I'm good for a few more miles. I could prob-ably take us through Dallas. Why don't you fold out the bed and sleep while I drive?" I say.

"Sounds good." Paul stretches his back and walks aimlessly around the picnic table with both hands in his pockets. His jeans are faded and torn on one knee. They look like they've been through a cement mixer. I notice that one of the rips on the inside of his pant leg is patched with a red, patterned cloth. "Is that a bandanna?"

Paul looks down and pulls his pant leg around so that he can see the patch. "Sure is."

"You patched your jeans with a bandanna?"

He gives me a defensive look. "These are my favorite jeans."

"Did you do that yourself?" I ask.

"Yeah, so what?"

"Nothing, just wondering, that's all." Paul comes back to the table and sits down. There is a short period of silence then I speak up. "Hey, Paul."

"Yeah."

"I was wondering."

"What is it?"

"You know, it's gonna get a little cold on the road and stuff and I was hoping maybe you could sew me a little quilt to keep me warm."

Paul pushes me. "Shut up, dude."

"But it's gonna get so cold and you're so good with needle and thread and all."

He leans into me, pushing with his elbows till I am off the table. The grass feels cold, but it is a refreshing change from the plastic, fixed-position seats of the van. I lie against the coolness and watch a cloud take another star. My thoughts return home, to my bed, to my warm room, to my truck parked lonely in the driveway with a black-and-orange "For Sale" sign taped to the sliding rear window. We hear the hum of an eighteen-wheeler through the trees, soft and distant, gradually louder until it roars by on the interstate. Another truck approaches more slowly, gearing down.

Headlights sweep like searchlights through the trees as he rolls into the rest area. The truck is behind us, not visible through the dense woods. Brakes squeal and hiss as he maneuvers into a space.

"I suppose we should get moving," I say, sitting up.

"Yeah, I'm about to fall asleep. Are you sure you're okay to drive?" Paul asks.

"I'll be fine."

I climb into the van and adjust the seat. The clutch pedal offers little resistance. I pin it against the floor with the weight of my foot alone. With the shifter in neutral, I try to start the van. It turns several times before I let off the ignition. No start. I pump the gas and try it again. Still no start. I once had an old Datsun that gave me the same trouble. The carburetor would flood every other time I went to start it. Remembering a trick I used on the Datsun, I hold the van's gas pedal to the floor for a few seconds to drain the carburetor and then pump it once. Turning the key, the engine fires immediately. With the shifter in neutral, I move it over and back. The clutch grinds as it finds reverse. The engine whistles and ticks as I back out of the parking space. Pulling out of the parking lot, I enter the on-ramp. With the pedal to the floor, there is no surge of power. The van feels gutless and old. It is creating a hiss-like whistle and there is a steady, quick tempo to the valves as they click. We enter the highway at a slow pace, like a semi pulling a full load. There is a large-winged, yellow-blooded insect stuck in the driver-side wiper. One wing shakes in the wind and the other is mostly steady as it is fastened to the wiper itself. I hadn't noticed it from the other seat.

The interstate is laid across slight, long hills. A lone truck's red tail lights glow in the distance, disappearing and reappearing as we rise and descend. My headlights cast a ghost-like glow on the blurry road. White, striped lines approach from the distance, slow at the outstretch of my headlights, then quickening as they near until they fire like bright lasers at my left wheel. Stately pines, keeping a careful, untrusting distance, slide by on the left and right. I half roll up my window as the air is coming in cool.

There is a solace in night travel that is absent in daylight. Daylight is broad and exposing. Gas stations, factories, and billboards are all brought to life under the sun. Night covers them. It is as if God has draped a cloth over the cares of the day, pouring them into our memories for meditation and reflection. There is much to think about; much we have left behind. The smell of freedom is as sweet as air through the windows. There is a feeling that time itself is curtained by darkness.

2. Hill Country

Sunshine whispers through the windows and I slide deep into my sleeping bag. Warm and dark in my cocoon, I position the pillow above to block the light. Car doors slam in the distance and I hear the sound of children laughing. Sleepily, I wonder where I am. Fresh, but fading in my mind, is a dream that had me on a horse being chased by men with guns. All of it was so real...the safety of the here and now comes back slowly.

"Don." A muffled voice speaks softly. I lay silent...

"Don...hey bud, it's nine o'clock in the morning." I am not sure whether I am imagining the voice or the one speaking.

"Don, you awake?" Like a turtle from its shell, I take my head out of the bag and open my eyes to the brightness of late morning. I close them again as the flood of washed-out color and light is too much too soon.

"Yeah, I'm up." I cover my eyes with the pillow.

Paul is sitting with his head turned, pressed against the ceiling. He is pulling a boot over his foot.

25

"What time is it?" My voice is smothered by the pillow, my warm breath absorbed by the cotton.

"It's nine o'clock. How long did you drive last night?"

"We're close to Dallas," I respond. "I didn't make it to Dallas but we're close, I think."

I slide back into my bag and mumble empty words at the bright morning sun. Last night I had caught myself thinking too fondly of sleep and pulled over to give in. I am a sleeper by nature. Eight hours allows me to function but I am better with nine or more. I can function on less sleep for a week or so but require a strong hibernation period once my tiredness sets in.

"I'm gonna get us moving again," Paul says. "Do you want to sleep some more?"

"I'm up," I respond, rolling over and burying my face in the pillow.

Paul maneuvers out of the bed and between the two front seats. "I'll be right back; I'm gonna use the rest room." The van door opens and closes and the space around me has a sudden quietness to it. Pulling my head out of the bag, I see Paul walking down the sidewalk toward the rest rooms. Outside the back window, I notice the headlights of an RV. They are high, broad apart and tainted brown with road dust. It is parked so close that, were it not for the glass, I could reach out and touch it with my foot. The small rest area looks less significant than it did last night. What I thought was a thicket of trees is only a weak scattering of saplings mixed with shrubs. It is more of a roadside pull out than a rest area. There are rest rooms and picnic tables. A trash can is mounted at its top to two rusty poles with a large, lazily placed trash bag hanging off its rim. I change my position to lay on my side, stretching my back. Still in the sleeping bag to my neck, light illumines floating, rolling, falling particles of angel-bright dust meandering ever so lazily down morning beams, filtered through a dirty window.

Cars pass in quick, colorful blurs. Yawning, the van air comes in stale.

Outside the window, somewhere behind me there are children laughing. I catch their small frames in the corner of my eye. Turning over, I find two red-haired kids staring into the window. Surprised by my sudden turn, they step back and release a sudden spurt of laughter, covering their mouths and pulling close to each other in one motion. There is a boy and a girl. They look like brother and sister. My reflection in the window is unshaven and disheveled—my thick hair standing in the front like a wave frozen in the ocean. Allowing my eyes to fall back to the children, they release another giggle. The girl, in an act of bravery, steps forward and knocks on the window. The boy pulls her back by the sleeve of her sweater. I play the part of the hippie and hold up two fingers to make a peace sign. Another spurt of laughter erupts and they become red-faced, not looking for long but taking short, split-second glances, followed by a gasp and a laugh and a pulling close to each other. I can't help but smile. Suddenly two women walk by and the children attach themselves, disappearing behind the RV.

We are one day out and home seems an ocean away. My watch ticks inside my boot. I don't need it. I'm not late for anything. There is no disgruntled friend waiting for me at a coffee shop or office. The people I used to be surrounded by are getting along without me. Somehow, that really bugs me.

What if the feeling of freedom I felt last night turns to boredom? Maybe the very thing I am trying to escape is that which sustains me. I am becoming irresponsible.

Paul opens the door just as I am thinking this through. "You up, Don?"

"Yeah, I'm up."

Climbing into the seat and pulling it forward with a shift of his weight, he turns the key and the engine offers several slow revolutions before bellowing out a loud, unsteady start. It runs only for a second and then stalls. I reach for my boots, throw them to the space between the seats and then follow, climbing out of the bed to the passenger's seat. Meanwhile, Paul is pumping the gas and fiddling with the key. I'm struggling with my feet and my boots and the small space I have to work with.

Just as I begin to tell Paul about the trick with draining the carburetor the van gives a sudden start. Paul lays into the pedal and the engine screams uncomfortably and cold at 4000 RPMs. He holds it there for a moment, then releases the pedal and pumps it again. The cold sleeping metal rubs against itself and wakes in a grumpy, old dog growl. Normally you wouldn't rev an engine which has been sitting all night, but with an old wreck like this, there is no other way to wake it. You've got to put something explosive in the carburetor and light the plugs.

"How are we on gas?" I ask.

Paul looks at the console. "We've got a quarter of a tank. We should stop soon."

"Coffee would be nice too."

Paul nods in agreement and backs the van up slowly, no more than a few inches, and then pulls forward, tugging the steering wheel with both arms, hand over hand, easing us only a small space from the bumper on the car in front of us.

Light reflects in sharp points off windshields in motion. Stripes of gray asphalt, two lanes in each direction, are banked and separated by grass and trees. Weeping willows hang depressed limbs low, sweeping the ground and rolling slowly around themselves in a light breeze. Shapeless clouds bring the bright sky close and cast an eye-squinting reflection off a sign that marks Dallas at 47 miles.

From the south, there is no industry to indicate a great city is near. Soon we will crest a hill and beneath us will rest a modern skyline complete with a towering cluster of buildings, factories, and freeways in a grand display of the new south. Dallas is the Seattle of Texas. It is what Chicago used to be and wants to be again. Every mayor of every growing city wants their town to evolve into a replica of Dallas. But no single man built the coming town. Dallas blew in on the wings of a Gulf Coast hurricane and rained glass and steel onto a field of bluebonnets.

We crest a hill and there she stands, just as I recalled, puffed up and proud of herself, all bustling with activity and shining in the late morning sun. Cars line the distant freeways thick and slow, bumper to bumper, moving together as if they were connected like an endless train. The highway rolls straight toward city center, through suburbs, past parks and soccer fields.

There is but one Texas, and for Texans there is need for nothing more. A country within a country, these people believe they have found the promised land. Businessmen wear $1000 suits with $100 Stetsons. They drive king-cab trucks to their office jobs while their wives drive minivans filled with kids in transit to and from school, band practice, or soccer games. Texans are good people; always on the go but slow enough to offer a "Howdy" or a "Where y'all from?" I am glad that Paul got to know my neck of the woods. I am as proud of my territory as he is of his. Who needs mountains when you've got the Dallas Cowboys, the Houston Astros, and the Alamo?

As the city passes we fade from metropolitan landscape to farmland, bound slow but sure for Oklahoma. The air is cooler today than yesterday. These clouds were brought in from the north and soon they will pass and leave a deep-blue sky that will blanket the state with, quite possibly, the last cold front of the season. The temperature tints the air with cleanness.

I pull my Bible from my backpack and flip through the thinly-sliced pages. Lately I've been drawn to the Old Testament. It has something the New Testament lacks. There is more sex and violence in the first 39 books of the Bible than in all of Poe and Wilde combined. It is a wonder Christians didn't rip their Old Testaments out years ago and burn them with Charles Darwin and Karl Marx. I cannot believe I ignored the first half of the Bible for as long as I did.

This morning I will spend time in Ecclesiastes, a book I read long ago and have been hungering for again. My study Bible tells me the book was probably written by Solomon, the son of King David and a king himself at the time of authorship. The book is painfully realistic and cuts deep into the question of human meaning; a question that has darkened the wits of many great thinkers.

At first read, the book carries a melancholy tone. Solomon talks of emptiness in all his pursuits. He finds satisfaction nowhere. Wisdom, accomplishment, pleasure, wealth, and labor are all given equal time. Nothing surfaces as a source of contentment. I am picturing Solomon at his candlelit desk, head in hands and struggling for the words to convey his ideas; a king, having had all that a man could desire and yet not satisfied, and so troubled by his discontent that he would leave a testimony for ages to come. Tried this, tried that, so to say, and all of it vanity, all of it chasing after wind.

I read further to find, and remember, that Ecclesiastes does not simply contain a message of complete hopelessness. Solomon finds meaning, but it is only in the awareness of God. Contentment can be found in endeavors only if they are seen as gifts from God and not accomplishments gained for and by one's self.

"Not much left for humanism," I mumble.

"What's that?" Paul looks over.

"Nothing, just talking to myself."

He shifts his eyes back to the road and returns to his thinking. And I return to mine. I remember a few years back, watching the Braves play the Indians in the World Series. As the camera panned into the audience it found Ted Turner, who owns much of Atlanta and the Braves along with it. He was slumped low in his box seat, nodding his head, struggling to stay awake through the latter innings. Meanwhile, a boy in the bleachers behind him, riveted with excitement and wide-eyed at every play, sat on the edge of the wood, hand in glove, short of breath, clapping hands and stomping feet. And if polled, most men would choose to walk in Turner's shoes, rather than the boy's.

Solomon, as if standing atop his tomb, looks back on a life of accomplishment and pleasure and counts it loss, all loss. It occurs to me it is not so much the aim of the devil to lure me with evil as it is to preoccupy me with the meaningless. And the consequence of either temptation plays out the same. Some men are lost to the brothel, others to the workplace, but the two differ only in deed; the heart of the matter is the same. Both lives wasted; one to earthly nobility and the other to immorality, but neither shedding light through and beyond the grave. Funeral after funeral offers music with no spirit, words with no answers, unfounded ideas of goodness in the hereafter, and no sure strategy to get there ourselves. Could we, with human reason, process the finality of death, we would be very different souls, giving more than we take, forgiving easily, and listening with all that is in us for answers to questions we would not have otherwise asked.

I think that Solomon would be pleased with Paul and me, having pulled our worldly anchors and exchanged lives filled with possessions for an inexpensive journey to the center of meaning. And when we arrive at the gate surrounding significance, we will tell the guards we have come from afar, and I suppose we will have to spend a great deal of time explaining that we are not, in fact, hippies, but rather good Republicans just like they are. They will let us in on the condition that we shave and change into our best clothes. Or perhaps it will be nothing like that at all. Maybe meaning is a place where there is no need for guards because no one wants it anyway. The more I think about it, the more that sounds like God; choosing a manger over a crib, a stable over a hotel, and fishermen before Pharisees. It gives me great confidence and pride to think that, had the Israelites been influenced by German engineering, Paul and Timothy might have journeyed in an old Volkswagen camping van. But the timing was all wrong and they were left with foot travel and...

"What in the world are you thinking, bud?" asks Paul.

"What's that?" I respond.

"You're just staring at the dash like you're in a trance." Paul has a smile on his face. He has been watching me for a while.

"I guess I was just zoning a little." I sit back and hang my arm out of the window, making a cup with my palm to feel the air against my hand.

"Are you homesick already?"

I simper and give a slight, defensive chuckle. "Not quite yet. It's gonna take a little longer than this."

The van is moving slowly, even slower than normal. We are ascending a hill that is significantly larger than anything we have yet seen. The road is straight and narrow and there is a good quarter-mile of concrete between us and the summit. The shoulder of the interstate passes slowly. I can make out the gray and green definition of small stones and broken glass.

"You want me to get out and push?" I ask.

Paul begins to rock back and forward in his seat. I can feel his weight sway the van. I place both hands on the dash and begin to push, clenching my teeth and wrinkling my forehead as if to be working hard. Paul looks down at the speedometer.

"It's no use we're down to 42!"

I sit back and bend my legs to set my boots against the dash. Again, I push and grit and wrinkle my forehead. In an exasperated voice, still pushing against the dash, I ask if we are moving any faster.

"Bud, this isn't good." Paul is looking frustrated. "We are down to 35."

I take my boots off of the dash and lean over to look at the console. "What do you think it is?"

"We're not getting any power. I should have adjusted the valves before we left."

As we crest the hill, two trucks and an RV pass us quickly and loudly on the left side. From atop the hill I can see the road dipping low into a ravine and then rising through trees in a four-lane bend toward another hill of greater size.

"We've got to get some speed on the downhill," I comment, just above a whisper, as if talking more to the van than to Paul.

Paul has the pedal to the floor and the van is gaining speed. He announces our progress in increments of five. Fifty feels like 90 compared to the 30 we've been doing. The van rattles and whines and enjoys the slope of the road like an old man who has been given a youthful burst of energy. Showing off, it lifts its shaky needle to 55 and then 60, before steadying at 62. We roar through the bottom of the hill, begin to climb and the van slows. This time there is no rocking or pushing and what was funny only seconds ago has lost its humor. We crest and descend five or more hills at turtle then rabbit then turtle speed. Each ascent frustrates us to the point of silence. Paul voicelessly expresses his concern. His hands are tightly gripped on the steering wheel and his slightly wrinkled brow frowns toward the noonday horizon, as if to wish he were there and not here.

An hour into our trouble we meet with Oklahoma. The welcome sign is of no consequence as we are preoccupied with the trouble and the van. What would have exacted a "Yeehaw," or a stirring and not quite accurate chorus from the state's own musical has been deluged by our circumstance.

Having talked of solutions, and Paul having brought up the valves, I ask, "Do you think we should pull over and try to adjust them?"

"Well, we'd have to wait for the engine to cool. That could take several hours and the more I think about it, I am not sure it's the valves. It could be the carburetor. It feels like it's not getting enough gas. I can hardly feel it when I step on the pedal." As he says this, he deepens his foot into the gas and there is no thrust. We crest another hill, descend, and begin upward. These hills are long hills; they are several minutes to the bottom and 20 minutes to the top. At common speeds a road looks small and thin, but at van pace it is broad-shouldered, wide-laned, and dashed with long, distantly spaced lines. We have slowed to an embarrassing speed of 23.

As we crest a hill and turn a bend, we see a small store and pull into the dusty, roadside parking lot. A few weathered pickup trucks are parked outside. Paul kills the engine. As we get out of the van, two young boys exit the store with small paper bags filled with candy, each holding a cold bottle of Coke. They notice the van and strike up a conversation.

"Where y'all com'n from?"

Paul, slightly surprised at their friendly interest, answers in a soft, withdrawn voice. "We drove up from Houston."

The boy who asked the question leans into the other and they both speak at the same time.

"Jessie's been to Houston..."

"I been there. My uncle lives there and we went down fer Christmas. That's a big city too."

The other joins in before Jessie finishes his sentence. "I've been to Dallas, to Six Flags too. You sleep in that van?" The boys walk to the side of the van, looking at it in wonder. The nameless boy speaks before we can answer his first question. "Ben Bonham had a van like this but he sold it and got a car." Jessie, disagreeing with the other, starts at him with a childlike arrogance.

"Nu-uh, Ben still gots it. He gots two cars. A van and a car."

"He did too sell it. He ain't got but that one. I bet you a fireball he ain't got it."

"I know he still gots it. I seen him day 'fore yesterday."

The boys trail off, across the parking lot and back through some woods, all the while talking about Ben and his car and how he does and doesn't have a van like ours. Paul looks at me and shrugs his shoulders and we walk into the store. As we enter, my eyes adjust slowly to the dim light and for a second everything is covered in gray. Deeper into the store, past the counter and the large woman behind it, things begin to sharpen. Part quick-mart and part grocery store, the shelves are half-empty and in disarray. A layer of set-in dust covers the floor and the place smells more like a feed store than a grocery store. We pace the short aisles, past the chips and candy, around the endcap of styrofoam coolers and then back, down the cat food and aspirin aisle, toward the woman at the counter.

"Can I help y'all find something?"

"Yes Ma'am," I respond. "We're looking for carburetor cleaner."

"Car stuff is behind you."

We turn to see a small sampling of motor oil and pine-tree air fresheners. There is one can of fix-o-flat, but no carburetor cleaner. A plaid-shirted, red-faced man, who has been standing at the counter talking to the large woman all this time, walks toward the door and stands in the bright light, looking out at the parked cars. "You boys having problems with that van out there?"

Paul answers as he walks down the aisle, toward the man. "Yes, we think it's the carburetor."

"What's it doing to ya?" The red-faced man asks.

"We get no power when we're going uphill. It slows down to about 25 or so."

The lady behind the counter speaks up, addressing the plaid-shirted man. "I don't think Michael Johnson's place is open today, is it?"

"He's out of town. Won't be back till Tuesday," the man answers, not looking at her, only staring out at the van and picking at his teeth with a toothpick. He is thin and weathered from a lifetime in the field. Layers of sun on his gray-brown face add ten years to his aspect.

"Ben Bonham could help you boys. I think ol' Ben is home."

The lady joins in, as if to remember, and agrees with the man. "Ben sure could help. He knows about those vans. He used to have one."

"Yeah, Ben could help you boys. Ben's as good at fixin' them things as Michael Johnson is. He's just up the road a bit if you wanna go out there."

"Does he have a shop?" I ask, toward the man but glancing at the woman to include her in the question. The man and the woman begin together but she quiets to his response. "He works out of his home, just over yonder." The weathered man takes the toothpick from his mouth and points, in a sudden, general motion, across the road and toward a side street. He puts the toothpick back in his mouth and goes to the counter where the woman hands him a pencil and a piece of paper. Writing and talking at the same time, he begins his directions.

"Go on out across the street there and head up Dagg road. That's Dagg right there" he says, as he points with the pencil to a dirt road just out the door and across the paved street. "Head on out Dagg till you get to Midland, and Midland ain't marked but Dagg dead ends there so you'll know it when you come to it...."

The man goes on like this for a while, carefully writing down each street. As he finishes, Paul thanks him for his kindness. The plaid-shirted man accepts our handshakes and farewells in a removed, masculine, country way. We climb back into the van and edge slowly across the parking lot, rough and rattling, kicking up dry dust.

—·— —·— —·—

A dot on the highway, this town is all mobile homes and pickups. Each trailer differs only in fencing and color. Families with money have built carports and fence-like trimming to cover the tires or their trailer hitch. Paul navigates us through streets long given to potholes and sections of shell and dirt. We arrive at what looks to be Ben's place. The trailer sits at the edge of town and backs up to a piece of land that is raised in the front and dips down to a man-made pond and a squab of wiry berry-bushes and woods. A large toolshed sits between the trailer and the pond. On its doors are hung ancient, rusted tools. It occurs to me that Ben, compared to his neighbors, is a wealthy man. He is, as we learned from the people at the store, known and admired.

We turn up the drive and notice a Volkswagen van, abandoned and surrounded by a tall mesh of weeds. Paul cracks a smile and I make a comment about how someone owes someone else a piece of candy. Around the front of the trailer is an enclosed porch, complete with floor-to-ceiling screens and a thin glass door. Aside from Ben's van, there are no cars and we begin to wonder if anyone is home.

It is an uncomfortable position to burden a stranger with your troubles. Doctors, lawyers, and mechanics are constantly queried for free advice and labor. The expressions on our faces note our disdain for our state and there is an uneasy, brief moment of stillness as one waits for the other to approach the door. Paul goes and I follow at his shoulder, through the glass door, into the porch. He knocks and there is an immediate stir. As we step back, the door opens and then draws closed, leaving only a crack of darkness. A rotund, female figure is outlined in shadows through the dim opening.

"Yes?" Her voice is small and secretive. Paul, standing in front, takes the conversation.

"Does Ben Bonham live here, ma'am?"

"He is my husband."

"The people in town told us that he might be able to help us with our van. We were just passing through and the mechanic in town is away."

The door opens a little more and a friendly, round, elderly face claims her voice. "Ben is out right now, but he should be in soon. Where are you boys from?" Taking advantage of the broken ice, I involve myself in the conversation. "We've come up from Houston and are heading to the Grand Canyon."

Our conversation goes on for a while about the Grand Canyon and her twice having been there; once with Ben when the kids were young and another time only three years back. The dialogue never stales as brief moments of silence are quickly absorbed by another story or bit of trivia about the canyon and her two trips there. Several minutes later, Mrs. Kate Bonham still standing in the doorway, a long, old car pulls behind our van. Kate's gentle smile tells us it is Ben. She slips back into the trailer.

We meet Ben at the back of our van and I explain to him our dilemma. All filled with kindness and pride, Ben sets his coat and lunch pail on the hood of his car and opens the engine compartment. His hands are aged 80 years or more. They are stained with grease and time.

"I got one like this myself, boys. Put it out to pasture a few years back, but liked her while she ran good. I blew a piston trying to turn my tractor over when I rolled it. What seems to be the problem with yours?" Paul and I are both silent, imagining a 77-year-old man rolling a tractor and then attempting to right it again with a Volkswagen.

"I say, what's the problem with yours?" Paul shakes off his daydream and answers quickly, making up for the inattentiveness. "It doesn't have any power. We do about 25 when we're going uphill. I thought maybe it was the valves..." Paul is interrupted by Ben before he can finish his sentence.

"...Valves wouldn't do that to ya. It's a gas problem. Sounds like the carburetor." Ben rolls up his long, stained sleeves and leans under the hood, over the engine. He is a short, pudgy man whose size gives him an advantage leaning into the low compartment. His overalls are long and extend past the heel of his steel-toed boots. "I never did like these dual carburetors. Did you know that you can get you a kit to change her to a single carb? I did that to mine and had it for the better, that's fer sure."

"I didn't know that," Paul responds, hands in pockets, peering behind Ben's shoulder and watching his hands shake wires and work levers.

"Do it chug when you give it gas?"

Paul, hesitating as he considers the question, speaks softly and reserved, inches from Ben's ear, "It do...I mean, it does."

Ben barks a command at me, "Start it up, boy."

I round the van to the driver's side, wait for the signal, and turn the key. Without pushing the pedal, the engine revs fierce and loud. Ben releases the lever and it dies. "Start it again, son!" His voice comes muffled and distant from within the engine compartment. I turn to see Paul twisting his fist and fingers in a sign to start the van. Again, Ben controls the RPMs from the rear and the engine whines loud and inconsistent. He releases the gas and it dies.

"You're miss'n some linkage here." Ben shows Paul the lever on the right carburetor. Two holes in the lift are empty. "You boys are working off of one carburetor. See this here..." Ben moves aside, still holding the lever with his right hand, "...this connects to this other and gets a tug from the gas pedal to give gas to the carb. It's a wonder you got to 25 miles-per-hour with just one carb." Paul, looking relieved to know that the problem is a simple one, crunches down and pulls at the lever. Ben disappears behind the van and reappears in the distance, walking toward the toolshed. He returns with a small piece of bailing wire. "Let me in there for a second, son." Paul moves aside and Ben's efficient fingers go to work twisting the wire to link the two levers. Upon Ben's signal, I start the van, pump the gas, and the van gives a loud, dual carburetor wail.

"She sounds all right to me. I think that might do her."

Ben's proclamation is met with gratitude and an offer to pay. He will have nothing to do with that and changes the conversation to earlier-neglected introductions. After telling him where we are from and where we are going, we listen again to stories of two trips to the Grand Canyon; several years ago with the kids and a few years back with just the wife and the dog which "ain't around caus'n it got run over just last month." It was a good dog. Named Bear and was hit by a truck. Had three legs to begin with.

"You boys should take a like'n to that canyon. Amazin' thang she is. Deep as hell herself with a river at the bottom

to boot! We never went to the bottom, but seen it in the pic-
ture-cards and the Calarada runs right thru the thang. Folks
go a boat'n thru her too. You boys gonna go down?"

"We hope to," I answer. "We're just sorta playing it by
ear. Hey listen, give me your address and I'll send you a post-
card when we get there."

"I will," Ben answers, smiling and huffing toward the
trailer for a piece of paper and a pencil. He returns with an
opened, scrap envelope from a piece of junk mail and a dull
pencil. Paul and I are silent as we watch him write his name
and address next to the same name and address printed on
the envelope. Ben's eyes are lit like a boy at Christmas. He
hands me the envelope and reminds me again what it is for.
"A picture-card will do. Kate and I really liked it there."

"Ben, are you sure we can't pay you? You've done so much."

"Get outta here boys, I gotta get washed up." Still
wearing a giant smile, he shoos us with his hands as if we
are chickens being scurried through a gate. Paul locks eyes
with him as he turns to go. I close the door on the passenger
side and give a soft three-fingered wave and grin. Paul backs
out of the drive, going off into the worn grass to pass Ben's
car. The old man watches through the glass, inside the
porch, and waves as he sees I am still looking at him.

We weave back through the dusty streets and onto the
road that will take us to the interstate. "Ben has the life,
doesn't he?" Paul comments, breaking a minute or so of
silence. I nod my head in agreement and sit with my hand
against the glass in thought. Paul continues on about Ben.

"Works all day, comes home to the woman he loves.
You couldn't ask for a better life." Paul's last statement is
spoken rhetorically. He looks over and sees me staring out
the window, not paying much attention.

3. Thin Ice

We move with new and appreciated quickness toward a sinking sun that sets to flame the backs of close and distant hills, causing clouds to flare in violent strips and tall trees to lay their shadows across the road like night clothes across a bed. Oklahoma has no better show than evening.

Our conversation has lulled from praises of Ben Bonham to comments about the sunset to silence. Out the passenger-side window the blur of green opens and closes with each passing red-dirt road. My mind focuses on life beyond the trees and the hills and this road cutting through them. It is there I imagine a small home surrounded by forest and a man sitting by a fire, reading the pages of a book he has read before and will read again. He is tired and nodding and, though his eyes still brush the words, he has long stopped reading. The fading light through the windows and the warmth of the fire soothe him into a sleep from which he will not wake till morning, finding himself still dressed with a book across his lap. Miles from the cabin, in another home, still in the here and now (albeit in my imagination) I see a family at evening supper, perhaps saying grace. And at that table there is a woman who is glad to have her husband home as he has been to such-and-such a place to do business. And that same man is thinking he prefers no other company than that with which he is blessed tonight. Ever nearer, and perhaps in a home just off this interstate, down a dusty driveway weaving through maple and pine that spread March over these rolling hills, there is a young girl at her desk, constructing a letter to the boy who has earned her heart. And just outside my window, 100,000 voices fire through the phone lines that parallel this road, each voice carried swiftly to a listener who trusts his response to broad-shouldered poles and sweeping lines marking the miles from home to home and business to business.

It is something sensational to consider that there is, far and close, vague and defined, separate but intertwined, a God who watches all and is not confused, but sets the sun to its course, frames the trees with symmetry and, with like precision, judges each man's heart as quickly as it beats. No poet, in the greatest of his imaginings, could conceive of anything greater than the real; this great plot pitting us against our deaths, this spinning sphere of color and smell giving flesh to the story God is slowly telling Himself; a story growing nearer and nearer to its dramatic conclusion. It does not escape me that I am blessed to be included in this tale of a billion human conflicts and singular resolution.

We are in the part of God's story where the sun is swallowed by the hills, leaving ample room on left and right for blood-red glow and backlit clouds. To the east, darkness and shadows. Our headlights press softly against the oncoming road.

In the glove box I find a few tapes. Secretly I scold myself for not bringing music of my own. I had decided this trip would be given to God and that music and other depravities would be foresworn for the sake of silence and meditation. Sometimes I think these self-righteous labors are attempts to impress myself rather than sincere strides toward God. Amidst thin scraps of insurance papers and part-shop receipts, my fingers find a tape.

"Lynyrd Skynyrd?"

"You can't beat Skynyrd," Paul defends.

"I could if I had a bat."

Other tapes include U2's *Joshua Tree* and a fellow named George Winston. "Who's George Winston?"

"He's a piano player. That's a great tape."

"Is it classical?"

"Not really, its just kinda mellow. Like Enya without all the voices and instruments and stuff."

"Enya without music you mean."

Paul smirks, "Exactly."

Music is the sound track of life. The absence of it is unforgivable on a road trip. This is a James Taylor moment and we are stuck with a piano player who wants to sound like Enya and a southern funk band that, somewhere along the line fell into thinking Alabama is a sweet place to call home. Catchy meaninglessness. A more thought provoking, smooth desperateness is in order. Lyle Lovett would hit the spot right now. Rich Mullins or David Wilcox would make fine background music for a sojourn such as this. But I am without, and silence being the next best thing to noise, I resolve to myself to listen to that which is so commonly called nothing. Tonight's silence is road and tires, engine and wind. Each so well-composed and rich and made for each other. All that thumping beneath the van and the whistling from the wind against the mirrors. Each resonance rivals for the lead, taking it one from the other and in no specific order. There is a faint squeak that, when focused upon, becomes great and overbearing. It is best left beneath the noise of the road and the tires and the wind and the engine. All this silence is thick and buzzing and it takes some effort to break it. "Maybe later," I comment, placing the tapes back in the glove box.

Paul is the kind of traveling companion who will go along with anything. He has few desires of his own and even those are willingly sacrificed for someone else's comfort. Yet unlike most who fit this mold, he is not easily walked on. He is stout in build and no different in character. Back home, we all wanted to be like him. Paul is the guy who gives up both armrests in a movie theater, reads books from beginning to end, and listens more than he talks. He's not perfect, but he's a heck of a lot better than the average guy. I look forward to figuring out the mystery sitting next to me. We hadn't gotten to know each other that well back in Houston, and Paul is the kind of guy you have to prime to get something out. Noise being the next best thing to silence, I start him off.

"So what are you going to do with your life, Paul?"

The mystery leans his shoulders forward, placing both hands on the wheel. "This and that."

"Sounds like a good plan."

"Well, you know, get a degree, a dog, a job, a wife, and a kid," he says.

Paul had dated a girl back in Houston named Lynette. They seemed to hit it off. I know he didn't promise her anything when he left, but I never really got a feel for how serious they were.

"Is Lynette in your plan?"

He pauses before offering an answer.

"I'm not too sure about that. She's a sweet girl, but I don't know. There's a girl I dated back in Oregon. We went out for a couple of years. She might be the one, but I'm not sure about her either."

"What's her name?"

"Michael Ann. I met her in junior high and we dated off and on through high school. She's pretty cool. We've had some good times together. We used to hike down to the head of Jack Creek and catfish till sunup. She's a girl you can take fishing."

That last statement tells me as much about Paul as it does Michael Ann. There are two types of men in this world—one is looking for a woman to make his life complete and the other is looking for a woman to join his complete life. Paul continues with his stories of fishing, rock climbing, hunting, and hiking. Michael Ann has small roles. She fell in a stream in story two and beat him to the top of Smith Rock in story three. It becomes obvious that Michael Ann is not the one for Paul. It is one thing to have a woman join your complete life and another to have her tag along. As he winds to the end of story four, I keep him talking with a question.

"Describe the perfect woman."

Paul sighs and sits silent for a second. "In 50 words or less, right?"

"As many words as you want."

"That's a tough question. I think I'll know her when I meet her."

"But you must have a general idea. What does she look like? How does she act?"

"Okay, now we're on to something. She's got a great smile. She doesn't have to look like a model, but I've got to be attracted to her. That's a given. She's going to be an athlete and likes the outdoors. I plan to do a lot of camping, so she should probably look good when she hasn't showered for a month."

"Good luck, bud!"

He continues, in a voice louder than my laugh. "She loves God and wants to pursue Him with me. I want to have that in common for sure."

"Oh yeah, she'll fit right in down at the church. People will smell her from the front pew."

Paul ignores me. "I also want to travel, so she'd have to be willing to live on the road. I'd like to hike Europe sometime, living in youth hostels, never knowing what we are going to eat the next day. And when we hunt, she has to help carry the deer back to the truck."

"Well, Paul, she sounds like quite the woman. Do you think that she will ever give up professional wrestling to settle down with the likes of you?"

He eases back into his chair, pauses, looks down at the console and then out onto the dark road. "You know I'm not being serious, don't you?"

"I hope not."

His tone turns mellow. "I guess I'm looking for what any guy is looking for. I want a companion, you know. Just someone to share life with. I want her to be my biggest fan and I want to be her biggest fan, too. I want us to raise kids in a home where they know their parents are in love with each other, with them, and with God. I guess that's all I want."

Realizing he had taken the question seriously, I offer a penitent comment, just above a whisper, loud enough to know he can hear me, "That sounds like a pretty good want."

"How about you, Don? What are you looking for in a woman? What gets the fires burning for you?"

"Oh, you know, this and that."

"No way. I answered, you've got to answer."

The van chugs a good quarter mile before I speak up. "Well, she's going to have to love to sleep."

"Sleep!" The driver's eyes light up.

"Yeah, I like to sleep. That's my favorite thing to do. Do you have a problem with that?"

"No, I mean if that's your thing." He tries to speak without laughing but his voice comes distorted through a grin stretched from ear to ear. He half covers his mouth. "Sleep is a good thing, Don. I sleep almost every night."

"You bet you do. Sleep is entirely underrated. All these Tony Robbins wannabes talk about how the early bird catches the worm. I'd like to see them go one week without sleep and try to function."

"Preach it, brother!"

"All I'm saying is I don't want a girl who's going to wake up in the morning and expect me to be mowing the lawn by ten o'clock."

Paul's laugh is a silent laugh. A teeth-showing grin and a light gasp. His head is down on the steering wheel and he's holding his stomach with his free hand. The right side of the van drops onto the shoulder and he pulls it back to the pavement, managing his laughter now with eyes on the road. "I can just see you, Don. The sun is in mid-sky and there you are mowing the lawn in your pajamas!"

Making sure I don't lose face with my new friend, I switch moods on him. "Now you know I'm kidding, don't you?"

Paul doesn't easily lose his mood. Several miles of silence and spurts of laughter pass before we are back to my response.

"You know what I want in a woman, Paul?"

"What's that?"

"A friend. A true friend; someone who knows me and loves me anyway. You know, like when I'm through putting my best foot forward, she's still there, still the same. I meet

these people and it's all conditional. They are in it for themselves. They are friends with you because you fit the image
they want to portray. It's a selfish thing. Do you know what
I mean? I'd like to get a girl who doesn't think like that.
Don't get me wrong. She's got to be proud of her husband,
I know that. I don't mind trying to make it easy on her in
that way. But all-in-all, there's got to be some sort of soul-
mate thing going on. That's gonna take work, I think. There
are some people in this world who love their spouse because
they provide them with the life they want, and there are
others who love their spouse just because they've chosen to.
Something way back endeared one to the other and they
made a decision to lock into it."

Paul gives an understanding nod. "You hit on a fear of
mine," he says. "It's like I don't want a girl to get too wrapped
up in me because she'll just get let down. Living with a
woman is going to be tough. They tend to be really domes-
ticated, you know. They fold things and clean things and
know what they are going to have for dinner several hours
before it's time to eat. Sometimes I wonder whether I'm cut
out to live that way. I don't know whether a woman is going
to put up with me. Is that what you're talking about?"

"Maybe. I'm not sure where you were going with that
folding clothes thing. I'm just saying I want her to love me
at my worst. I don't know if that's a low self-esteem thing
or something else."

Paul tilts his head and motions out a slow *no*. "I don't
think so. I mean nobody's perfect. We can't be perfect."

I think of Solomon who had all the women a man could
desire and yet concluded that the fulfillment of these pas-
sions was meaninglessness. Outside of God's perspective,
even romance loses its significance. Not in riches or in
romance do we find fulfillment, but in God. But then there
is the same catch as before; I have God and do not feel

completed. Perhaps there is no fulfillment to be found. If fulfillment is an emotion, then it would have to depend heavily
upon mood and climate. It doesn't seem like God would give
us an aim so temperamental. Following Christ surely must
be more than a roller-coaster ride of emotional dryness followed by bliss.

It has been my habit to ride this roller coaster for most of
my Christian life. Monumental sermons and church retreats
are that great height which leaves me breathless, and then,
headlong into the depth of the everyday, with the mornings,
the busy hours, and the coffee and then going to bed and
repeating it over and over and over; each day a short distance further from the faith to which I assign to my Sundays
and my occasional Wednesday nights. A roller coaster it is.

"You never answered my question, Don."

"What's that?"

"A woman. What are you looking for in a woman?"

"Your guess is as good as mine." My mind returns
slowly to our previous train of thought. "I like to read, so
maybe she will too. I don't know exactly. Sometimes I catch
myself thinking God is a genie in a lamp and He's going to
grant me this perfect woman someday. I don't think it works
like that. He will grant me the woman I need to go about
His calling for my life. It will be the same for her, I would
imagine."

"So what is your calling?" Paul asks.

"That's why we're on this trip, remember?"

"You're going to have it all figured out by the time we
reach Oregon, is that it?"

"If I don't, I want my money back!"

Paul is humored and cracks a smile, all the while rolling
up his window as the air snaps with a dry coolness.
Reaching around the seat, I grab my jacket and push my
arms slowly through the sleeves. No glow now on the
horizon. We have ventured one more day on our journey.

Time moved quickly today. It passed like a whisper. The days go that way sometimes.

Time is like thin ice. Our days are spent living like ants in a mound, collecting our substance to survive the winter; to retire in comfortable plaid pants, blue socks, and golf shoes. All the while, the ice is melting, thin and slick. We don't notice it until struck with tragedy. We or a friend are mangled in a car wreck, and we reflect on how fragile the whole thing is. Our wives and our children become beautiful again. Our priorities change as we realize we are temporary beings. It is with this in mind that Solomon writes his book. Here is where aged couples renew their vows.

But not all of us are granted such severe mercy. Death is a difficult thing to process when no hint of it is at hand. We may never hear the ice crack. Mark Twain was right in assessing that the two elements of success are determination and ignorance. Success being the six-figure salary and ignorance being a blindness to its temporal capacity. Beyond the gravity binding us, our souls travel alone. We ascend without the anchors of material possessions. We ascend empty-handed; our shells, neatly dressed in pressed suits, set snugly into caskets. The graves are all silent. The caskets are vacant. Stalin has no more wisdom for us. Nietzche is preserved in books, having forgotten to lift his casket lid and tell us he was right. Muhammad gives us the slip. So does Buddha. It is Christ alone who defeats the grave. He came back from death. Nothing left in the tomb but echoes and cobwebs. And so we do well to listen to Him with the ears of dying men.

The hills have completely buried the sun. We pass roadside houses, windows aglow with the flame of television and the ten o'clock news. Paul is quiet and has been that way for miles. With the road atlas across my lap, I follow the thin line of Interstate 35 with my flashlight. She runs straight into Oklahoma City. My thinking is that we will cut there and head back into the Texas panhandle, crossing into New Mexico, Arizona, and then north toward the canyon.

"What are you getting on the map, Don?"

"Looks like Interstate 40 from Oklahoma City. That should take us right to the canyon. Would you rather take back roads?"

"No, let's head straight there. I'm looking forward to seeing Arizona and we should be able to make it by late tomorrow. Do you want to drive through the night?"

"Sounds good to me," I say.

Paul's face shows a red reflection from a light on the dash. Leaning over, I see that the engine light is lit. "Did you notice the engine light is lit, bud?"

Paul looks down at the light. He looks out the side window. He doesn't want to answer the question.

"Paul, did you notice the engine light?"

"Yeah," he says. "It's been bugging me."

"How long has it been on?" I ask.

"Twenty miles," he says.

"Twenty miles?" I say.

"Twenty miles," he says.

"Twenty miles?" I question.

"Twenty miles. Ten times two." He lets on that he is agitated by my questioning.

"That light has been on for 20 miles?"

"Yeah, 20 miles. It'll be 21 by the time you stop questioning me."

"Twenty-one miles," I respond.

"Right in there somewhere. Yeah."

"Did it ever occur to you we should pull over and check the engine?"

"It did."

"It did?"

The driver breathes deeply. "Do we have to do this again?"

"Help me out here. Why aren't we checking the engine?"

"I've had it with this van, Don. It wouldn't bother me to see the thing go up in flames."

"Are you serious?"

"Yeah. This van has given me more headaches than I care to recall. I figured we'd just drive it into the ground."

"Paul, what are we going to do when the van breaks down in the middle of nowhere?"

"Don't worry. I have a plan."

"Fill me in, would you?"

"You won't like it."

"Try me," I say.

"Well, see those train tracks? They've been running alongside the road for a while. I figured we'd just jump a train heading west."

"You want to jump a train!"

"I said I had a plan. I didn't say it was a good one."

"You're being serious about this, aren't you?"

"I've always wanted to jump a train, Don. Imagine it. Riding the rails. Setting out across the painted desert, legs dangling off the edge of a boxcar."

It is my tactic in moments like this to remain silent. The agitator sits and meditates on his foolishness. Anyone can convince themselves an idea is logical but when that idea is spoken, when it's out in the air like his is, and it rests in the ear of a being more rational, the instigator is forced to reason. I don't argue his point; that would suggest there is merit to it. Not a lot of merit, but enough to justify a response. My silence speaks louder than anger. It forces him to sit alone in a room with his own foolish thoughts and know I am not willing to join him.

His plan, although outrageous, isn't bad. It doesn't anger me as much as I let on. I'm not going to tell him, but I grew up near a train track and have always been fascinated by them. Still, it frustrates me that he didn't include me in his thinking. How could the guy who gives up both armrests in a theater fail to mention that the rest of this trip would be provided by Santa Fe Railroad? After giving him his due silence, my calm voice comforts. "When were you going to tell me about this?"

"Soon. I promise. I didn't know how you'd feel about it."

"Isn't jumping trains a little dangerous? What if we run into some hobos?"

"Wouldn't happen. Hobos don't ride trains anymore," he says.

"They don't? Well, that's good, I guess."

The lunacy of my friend's plan is beginning to dilute. I imagine the painted desert passing before my eyes, the rocking of the slow-moving train.

"Why don't hobos ride trains anymore?"

"It's too dangerous."

"Oh," I say with a grunt and a sigh while looking away.

"They don't do it anymore because the gangs have taken over."

"Gangs?" My voice gives a hint of surprise.

"Gangs."

This is hard to picture. Bank robbers ride trains. Hobos ride trains. Cowboys ride trains. Gang members ride around in low-rider cars and shoot indiscriminately at stray dogs. They don't ride trains.

"Paul, gang members don't ride trains."

"They do."

"How do you know this?" I ask.

"I read it somewhere."

"What, you subscribe to train jumpers magazine?"

"I don't remember where I read it, alright? But I read it somewhere. It's how they get around. They ride trains from city to city."

I have no idea why I am allowing myself to be suckered into this plan. Part of it is the fact that I want to disprove Paul's theory about the train-riding gangs. Another part of me wants to see the painted desert from the open-holed boxcar. For whatever reason, I sit silently, listening for the engine to give. She doesn't. Miles pass and she doesn't. I look over to see Paul. He's calm and withdrawn. I can tell by the look on his face that he wants the van to die. It's like a vengeance thing. This old heap has been kicking him around for months and now he's killing it. Slowly but surely, driving it into the ground. The glow of the engine light casts a demon-red glare in his eye. He's possessed. Calm and possessed. What a nut. Reaching into the glove box, I slide a stick of gum out of its wrapper. "Would you care for a stick of gum, Paul?"

"No thanks."

"Minty fresh."

"No thanks."

The possessed man drives, looking down at the engine light and then over at the tracks. He's thinking of the van's suffering and remembering all the times he pulled over to save it. Not this time. No sir. This time it's the junkyard.

Taking the moist gum out of my mouth, I lean over and press it tightly against the round, glowing plastic of the engine light. "That should solve our problems, Paul. It's like it never came on."

—·—   —·—   —·—

Clasping my hands together and rubbing them for warmth, I ask Paul if his fine automobile comes equipped with a heater. Without answering, he reaches over and pulls a lever from blue to red, turns a switch and the van delivers a modest, cold breeze, more from the floor than the round, adjustable vents in the dash. In an attempt at efficiency, the Germans engineered these vans to be air cooled. Two wind vents stand out in the rear of the van. They catch wind and funnel it through the engine compartment. That same air (at least in the mind of the engineer) makes its way through shafts to the van's cab, having been warmed by the engine. So goes the Volkswagen heater. I would imagine if one is traveling through the desert in mid-day, that technology might make sense. Not tonight. The heater is being defeated by the elements.

"Doesn't work that well, does it?" Paul concedes. "Grab my fleece, would ya? It's on the bed." Stepping through the seats, I enter the cave of blankets and scattered clothes. Paul's fleece rests in a wedge between the bed and the side panel. The warmth of the blankets and the softness of the pillow allure me. Tossing Paul's fleece at the back of his head, I lay my mind on a pillow and watch the road pass outside the cold window.

4. Discovering George Winston

While I was sleeping, Paul drove through Oklahoma and into the panhandle. The yellow light from a truck-stop street lamp fills the van. Trucks grind gears and turn like elephants into the parking lot. The lights and the noise quicken my waking. I toss my nose into the window and follow with my elbow, all tangled in a net of blankets and clothes.

"Where are we?"

The van rocks as Paul drops his weight on the bed, rolls himself over and kicks one foot against the heel of his other, a struggling attempt to remove his boot. "Back in the Lone Star state, my friend. Can't you smell the manure?"

"We're in Texas?"

"Where the stars at night are big and bright."

Another truck grinds, hisses, and illumines. Its light swings shadows through the van, moving their focus through and beyond us, through the truck stop complete with pumps, a store, and restaurant.

"Did the van give out?" I ask.

"She's purring like a kitten."

"Why did you wake me? I was dreaming about this great girl."

"You were cheating on me!"

"Shut up," I say.

"I can't believe you, Don, how could you do this to us?" Paul says this with an annoying grin.

"Shut up. Don't make me hurt you!"

Paul covers himself in blankets and rests his head against the side panel. "So what was this girl like?"

"You'll laugh."

"I won't. I promise."

Sitting up and throwing my blankets off, I begin, "She was a cowgirl." Paul covers his laughing face with a pillow.

"You said you wouldn't laugh."

"A cowgirl," he says into the pillow.

"Her name was Cheyenne. I'd appreciate it if you would call her by her name."

Paul slips the pillow down his face and looks me full in the eye. "That's a beautiful name, Don. I'm sure your dream was influenced by the smell of the pasture across the street." His heckle is delivered with a straight face but changes to a grin as he anticipates my response.

"It is a beautiful name for a beautiful girl. You'll never get one like that."

"It was a dream, Don. Let it go."

"She needed me. We were running from the bad guys who killed her father on a ranch outside of Little Rock."

Paul slides himself down on the mattress and tucks the pillow under his head. "I'd like to go to sleep now, Don."

"I'd like to still be asleep, Paul."

With that comment, I belt him with my pillow. He lies motionless. Lying back down I continue my story. "There were three of them. Chasing us on horses. All of them had guns. We had ducked behind a rock and I was telling her..." Better not tell Paul what I was telling her. It seemed appropriate in my dream but... "I was telling her she would be okay. They were coming with guns and she was worried."

"Didn't you have a gun?"

"I had a bull whip."

"A what?"

"A bull whip."

"That's great. Indiana Don rescues the girl from Little Rock. Can I have the movie rights to this?"

Despite my friend's harassment, I desire my dream again, and am disturbed at its abrupt ending. I resolve I will not finish rescuing Cheyenne tonight, so I leave Paul in the van to walk across the parking lot toward the truck stop. Gray pebbles and patches of oil, dripped from long-removed trucks, pattern the lot. A wind, slidden off some distant Canadian glacier, presses against the parking lot with frigid hands. It builds strength in treeless pastures and pelts the dimly lit station and store. Texas hasn't seen a colder night since Ann Richards was elected governor. Tom and Huck never had it so bad as we do tonight.

Four coins in my pocket, no five. Three quarters, a dime, and a nickel. Or perhaps the last coin is a dime, too. It is, in fact, ridged and so a dime. Ninety-five cents. One cup of coffee. Money is an issue on this trip. I have $300 sock-wound in my backpack and most of it will convert to gas. My half of the fuel bill will reach $200 in 3000 miles. That leaves little to spare. More money will come when my truck sells. After retiring the car loan, I will have another $1000. The strategy is to not deplete the $300 until the truck is sold. It's a gamble. Coffee is a worthy expenditure, though, and intending to drive the night, I consider it a necessity. Besides, if I don't get something warm my insides will freeze.

"Where's your coffee?"

The store clerk motions with her eyes toward the wall that is closest to me. Two glass pots sit on brown burners.

One is labeled decaf and I reach for the other. "How much is a cup?"

"Fifty cents," she shouts across the aisles. I pour the black liquid (it looks likes it's been stale for hours) into a styrofoam cup and search for the lids. Rounding the aisle toward the counter, I meet face to face with the shouting voice. She is keeping company with a man standing no less than three inches my superior. I am tall by most counts; about six foot and an inch. And so this is a large man. He leans against the counter, muscular and dirty. Dirty with grease on his fingers which wrap around the brown cup he brought with him. Truck drivers own their own cups. The look on her face and the shy grin on his tells me he's hitting on her. Blonde, fair complected, she's used to it. They come in at all hours for a shave and a shower and haven't seen a woman in a thousand miles.

"This man isn't giving you a hard time, is he?" Stunned, she looks at my size and at his and back at me as if I were crazy and then silently punches in the code for a cup of coffee. "I didn't bring my own cup. You'll have to charge me for the cup."

"Cups are free," she says slowly, watching for the reaction of the towering truck driver.

He leans in at the side of my face. "You got a problem with me, hippie boy?"

There is a thick silence now. A portable heater sits behind the counter at the woman's feet. It rattles as it turns, glowing with strands of heated steel. "No problem. I got no problem here," I say.

"You what?" His breath reeks. He is so close, I imagine him biting my ear. "Why don't you get in that van of yours and head back to Austin?"

"I'm not from Austin."

"I don't care where you're from, boy, so long as you go back."

Angry people are stupid people.

"Look, Buck, (his name is embroidered on his shirt) I was just making a joke. It was supposed to be funny." The man pulls his head back, glances confused at the girl, looks back at me, quiets his tone and reveals his ignorance. "How did you know my name?" The girl smiles as she notices the tag across his heart.

"We hippies know everything, Buck."

"I don't know you. How did you know my name?"

"I know a lot about you, Buck."

I drop two coins on the counter, turn my back to the confused giant and walk toward the door. Buck gathers his meager senses and realizes how I knew his name. His hand slaps the name on his shirt and he starts after me. Out the door and into the cold wind, every nerve longs to check shadows over my shoulder. I hear the door close, but make a quick pace and would not hear it reopen if it did (due to distance and the sound of wind). So I walk and do not look back. My mind pictures him coming up quick and throwing his fist against the back of my head. Still, I keep pace and don't turn. The van sits seemingly miles away across the parking lot. The distance from store to van seems twice that of van to store. As I near, I whisper a prayer for the van to start quickly. *Lord God, that was stupid. I will never try to impress a girl if You let me get to the van. Make the thing start for me. Make it start the first try. I won't pull another Tom Sawyer stunt like that if You do.*

Turning at the far side of the van, the corner of my eye finds no presence, and through the driver-side and passenger window (standing outside the van looking through) I see the giant watching through the glass door. No rabbit has felt more refuge in his narrow escape from a fox than I do at the escape of the evening's conflict. No quick-paced heart has been more suddenly soothed.

The van starts at first command and I let it idle as I watch the man leave the door and resume his position against the counter. He is mumbling his pick-up lines through an embarrassed grin and coffee-lacquered throat. Minutes pass as I allow the van to idle. The place has a stillness, save the howling wind.

With Huck Finn asleep in the back, and with one last look about the place and a sip from the coffee which is warm enough to stage a dance of steam, I release the boat into the river of distant taillights and eighteen-wheeled shadows. All shadows set against the dark, dark sky with stars that wander at will.

In this mood, and against this night, I reach with my free hand for the tape in the glove box. Turning the knob, the radio bleeds light across its face and George Winston begins his private concert. Less than a minute decides for me that he is good. I have started him only a few moments into a variation of Pachebel's Canon; a piece I never thought possible on a piano (not impossible, but certainly not possibly done well). He is positively surprising, and great travel music. Winston works his fingers across the keys and just when you think he is falling asleep, he crescendos to something very much awake. *December,* if I remember correctly, is the name of the album. And he does right by the season.

Distanced to the left, across the oncoming lane and across a field, or perhaps several fields on end, rests a collection of lights. Too small to be a town, it is likely another truck stop with a neighboring farm or grain tower. One red light blinks atop a taller building and the other lights are white and yellow, resting on the ground like smoldering ashes. And slow to my notice come other collections, in similar form. Two clusters are up and to the right (many miles) and another ahead by ten miles at least. Winston serenades them through a weak speaker on the driver's side and a strong speaker in the door panel of the opposite seat. And so go miles and miles. The tape flips sides automatically so it keeps music going in an endless loop. The wind is cold; thick like ice and dry like dust. No lights on the road ahead, save the soft yellow faded lamplight of the Volkswagen on the asphalt. Novels are written about country like this.

I want to be a great writer; a great American writer. Better, a great Texan writer. Dusty in the closet of my Houston home are scribbled more than 300 bad poems in spiral-bound notebooks. They are kept secret, too closely favoring high-school poetry to be taken seriously by their author or any literary mind. Bad poetry makes for good poetry though. The ratio, for me, is about two-hundred to one. I have two I consider prize and countless that are rubbish. Thin, weak, senseless words, flat on a page and lyrically stale. I am a victim of slow, confusing rhymes. Still, poems come as they wish, and the pen presses against the page more in the form of a capture than a release. Winston and cold weather, dark horizon, and fields of black begin the words.

Had we known

Slow the words roll.

And how I wish that I had known
What is known and will be known

Poetry is a lost art. Poets are poor and unappreciated. And should I be published, professors would use my work as an example of bad American poetry. They will counsel their students to stay away from easy rhyme. "Think outside the box," they will chant. "Think more deeply and beautifully or you will end up writing like Miller."

> *And how I wish that I had known*
> *What is known and will be known*
> *How flowers suffer...*

I need a word that rhymes with known. Blown, sewn, owned, toned. Snow! How flowers suffer beneath the snow.

> *And how I wish that I had known*
> *What is known and will be known*
> *How flowers suffer weight of snow*
> *to pass their lives and gently go*

Over and over I repeat the first fragment in my mind. The brevity of life as paralleled in the life of a flower. Flowers don't grow in snow, though. Ah, but this flower is dying at the onset of snow, so it fits. It is the end of spring? Perhaps the flower never thought it would end. It has never known winter and now it comes. An end to a dream. A beautiful, beautiful thing that is subject to the throes of coldness. It has no control. It lives and dies as it is instructed.

> *And how I wish that I had known*
> *What is known and will be known*
> *How flowers suffer weight of snow*
> *to pass their lives and gently go*
>
> *And how I long for truth to tell*
> *With open throat to loudly tell*
> *the way the flowers gently go*
> *and choke beneath the winter snow*

The poem is too long now to commit to memory. They fade quickly, these poems. They come and go like comets.

Better to have a pencil and paper in my pocket at all times. No memory is good enough to commit a long poem to memory on a sleepy night. The thing will need to be wrestled like an animal and then forced onto paper to tame it in the coming months. Poetry is my praise. I do not prefer song to verse. Song, in corporate worship settings, is something beautiful. But it is easy. And I feel that I am getting more from it than God is. That is to say, there is a level of emotional gratification that comes from singing that I cannot definitively attribute to true worship. Whether I am singing "As the Deer" or "Rocky Mountain High," the same emotion is present. So worship becomes an opportunity to gratify myself. That isn't all bad. Perhaps God intended worship to give pleasure to the worshiper and worshipee alike. Poetry is long-suffering praise. It is work. Michelangelo and Rembrandt worked diligently at their worship. They painted scenes and labored endless hours in thought and strain. A poem, like a painting, can take a week or a month or a year to complete. When I finish, I can give it to God and it feels more substantial then singing a catchy tune with an organ backdrop. If worship is sustenance, then modern worship is fast food. We've canned the process and covered it in plastic wrap. We microwave it for ten minutes and swallow it in time for the sermon. I think that long-suffering worship is more beneficial. Whether it is running a mile, memorizing a passage, building an orphanage, or writing a poem, worship can be found in all sorts of art and service. Worship is not just something we feel. It is something we sweat. It is an editing of the soul.

Ahead on the horizon is a truck-stop sign. A Waffle House maybe. I could get the poem down on a napkin and never wake Paul from his sleep. Miles go backward and slow, and the poem turns like churning dough in my mind. *A napkin. A napkin and a pencil.* I creep up on the truck stop from behind. It is on the opposite side of the highway.

Turning off at the exit and crossing the overpass, the road gives to gravel. The familiar yellow light of a parking lot welcomes the poet and his sleeping passenger.

Inside are napkins with orange "Flying J Truck Stop, Your Home on the Road" logos printed on the top ridged portion of the delicate tissue. With a handful of these, a borrowed pencil from the lady at the counter, and a hardwood seat with a table, I begin the first draft, stopping twice to buy coffee.

December

And how I wish that I had known
What is now known and will be known
How flowers suffer weight of snow
to pass their lives and gently go

And how I long for truth to tell
With open throat to loudly tell
the way the flowers gently go
to choke beneath the winter snow

December's hand like Poe with Pen
writes haunting tales of God and sin
that choke the heart that beats within
the flowers in the snow-cave den

Had you and I and flowers known
in dim-lit dens we would not grow
nor break the chilling winter snow
and die beneath the drifts of woe
that cover us with flowers

5. Church Culture and Other Painted Deserts

With the van behind me ten, now twelve, now fourteen steps, I stop to breathe cold air. Rich neon blue outlines the horizon; each hill black and jagged. "This is going to be a good one," I mumble. My breath makes no mist though the temperature is certainly cold. Perhaps it's too dry for that. Looking back, the white van is gray. It sits on the shoulder of an empty highway. No cars for miles. No trucks and no noise. No buildings visible. The interstate slices through a field of sand before climbing into a distant pass. The desert floor, still dark with night shadows, lays flat before giving rise to sleeping peaks. Too early to be called morning, this is the blank page before the poem is written. This is the sudden silence in the theater when the lights dim and the projector engages.

"Those clouds around those hills. Watch those light up. She's gonna light up like a Christmas tree. You show me a good one, God." My expression slightly louder now, "I didn't drive all night for nothing. Show me a once-in-a-life-time sunrise. I could use one of those this morning." Still pressing into the desert, I aim for a spot to watch the sun break. The further from the road, the better. Every ten steps I check the east and it changes as I walk. Black gives to blue and it is a blue like no blue on any painting or picture. This is living blue, changing from one beautiful hue to another, shifting slowly the way color does.

The landscape is a circle of vacant miles. Spilled on the brown are dry and shadowy lakes of deep, rich darkness. My tracks lay out to mark my path, and looking back, the van is a small form beside a black, thread-like strip. To the east, the first tint of red arrives in weak shades through over-powering blue. The clouds establish greater form; tall clouds with 30,000 foot lifts. They are coming or going, I do not know which. Though tremendous in size, they are guarded by the length and depth of a black-blue sky, held back by mountains.

Morning lifts with her fingers first, stretching her long bones into the clouds. Engaged, I set myself down on the cold morning sand; my hands beside me and half buried in the desert dirt. The black hills ghost to gray, revealing crags and tall cliffs. I remember when I was a child hearing the story of Noah. How desperately I wanted a rainbow of my own; a personal message from God. I wanted so hopelessly I decided on my own sign: sunrise. Sunrise was mine. God's promise that dark would be followed by light, that sweaty shadows would be lifted and He would break the horizon to take me home.

Suddenly, breaking into my reflective mode, I hear my name called. Standing up and wiping my hands against my pants I see Paul at the front of the van, looking in all directions. I call but he does not turn. Cupping my hands around my mouth, I force my early morning voice, "Paul!" He turns, not completely toward me but into the desert. Waving my arms I secure his attention and he begins walking, barefoot (evidenced by his stride). His feet start left, then right, and his head is down, eyes on the painfully cold sand. He drops a pair of sandals to the ground (he had been carrying sandals, but I did not notice) and steps into them; one foot, then the other. The noise of Paul quietly precedes him. He is coming slowly, keeping an eye on the horizon. His arms are folded tightly and his shoulders are lifted to warm his neck. Unfolding his arms he wipes his eyes, lets go a yawn, and turns his head toward the mountains. He lessens his stride as he nears, takes a place ten feet from my side and watches the silent swirling of color.

The van is a rattletrap. It echoes through the desert with odd ticking and muffler thump. The asphalt is long and twisted. Each passing range opens to the same view as the valley that prefaced; each mile looking precisely like the last. And here is a place in the mind where odd thoughts gather. I haven't slept for hours, but am not tired. Morning passed as Paul and I stood for some half-an-hour, letting the sun have its time. Brown came slowly to the desert, led by dark and then uncommon color before donning the ugly blandness it wears in daylight. Endless brown. My wakefulness is a heavy wakefulness. Not a tired heavy but an aware heavy, as if not truly tired but wondering whether I should be.

"Did you realize it was Sunday?" Paul asks, breaking an hour-long silence.

I grin, looking over. "It hadn't *dawned* on me."

Paul misses the pun. He lays a wrist over the wheel and rests comfortably in his seat. "Right no..." This he says in a contemplative haze, "right now I would be driving to church. Late for the second service." This he says with a smile.

Defeating the lazy braggart, I confess a greater example of sloth. "I'd be getting out of the shower. Late for the second service. I like to show up in the parking lot when people are deciding between Luby's or Mexican food."

The driver licks his lips. "Mexican sounds good."

"It does, doesn't it?"

No amount of famine or flood will stop the south from eating together on Sunday. We eat once a week in the south—after church. Large groups gather difficulty around small tables, give waiters trouble, and leave tiny tips with a four-point message from Bill Bright.

"Do you miss home yet, Don? Is the road getting to you?"

"Not really. I was homesick a little last night, you know. But not really." Not wanting to leave the word homesick hanging in Paul's ear, labeling me a sissy, I speak quick words without thinking. "I wouldn't mind seeing the guys again." Dumb thing to say. Same as being homesick when you break it down.

"You and me both." Paul's comment sets me at ease.

"Did you go to church much when you lived in Oregon?" I ask.

"Sure. I went to a Foursquare Church."

"Foursquare? Is that a town or something?" The actual image in my mind is a group of people in Sunday clothes playing hopscotch.

"No. Foursquare is a denomination. They've got them in California and Oregon and there are some in Washington but I don't think they've got any in Texas."

I should say not. A church with a name like that wouldn't make it in Texas. Churches have to have names like *Southbrook Community* or *Grace Community* or *First Baptist* or *Second Baptist*. There are some called *Southbrook Baptist* or *Clear Lake Baptist* but the only Baptist churches that really make it are the ones with a number in front of them. Now that I think about it, I don't know of a *Third* or a *Fourth Baptist* so I guess the first two get the lion's share of the Baptists and the others have to pick different names. Anything with the word *community* behind it does well also.

"What's a Foursquare church like?" I ask.

"Oh, it's pretty good. I go to one in Redmond. My pastor moved to Oregon to witness to rock climbers at Smith Rock. He worked his way through seminary and they gave him a church. I enjoy him."

"Pretty big church, is it?"

"Yeah, it is. We've got about 200 people there."

A smile comes to my face as Paul's definition of large collides with mine. "Two hundred people would make for a good Sunday school class in Texas. I hate to break it to you, but unless a church has a gym and a bowling alley, they're really not fulfilling the work of the Lord. A church has to have a gym and a bowling alley because people play basketball and bowl and if they do it at a church they are more likely to accept Christ. Widows and orphans especially, they play basketball a great deal."

"Is that right?"

"Sure it is. Listen, let me tell you what I'm gonna do for you." My inflection is that of a used-car salesman. "I'll set up an appointment with this rock-climbing fellow and lay the whole thing out for him. How does that sound? He'll begin to understand what true ministry is."

"I'm sure he'd be grateful, Don." His grin is an understanding grin. Paul and I talked briefly about our frustration with the institutional church when we were in Houston. We never called it the "institutional church" but it was understood that we were talking about the church as a whole, not just the church where I had been a long-time member and Paul a passer-through.

Church doesn't stimulate me the way it used to. It is most often the same as the week before. The worship lyrics are presented on a screen that has all but the little bouncing ball over the words, then the pastor gets up for a ten-minute sermon that could be understood by a group of third graders. It is as if the church is ashamed to present the Gospel for what it is. We've got to water it down and tiptoe around the complicated passages. It is one thing to be seeker-sensitive and another to be silly.

Here are my frustrations with church culture. It is said that a church will emulate the most respected institution in society. That used to be the family. And churches used to be like family. It is not that way today. The church emulates big business. We take our cues from Microsoft and IBM. Entire staffs are sent to time-management seminars or corporate-structuring conferences. Sermons sound like press releases and all of it reeks of politics. I don't like it. Still, and shamefully, such strategy works. I mean, it builds churches. Big, sloppy, useless churches. But who wants a big, sloppy church when they could have a scrawny one with some muscle to it? There must be great pressure among pastors to have a big church.

My second frustration is like the first; we have exchanged entertainment for art. I would rather attend a church with an art gallery than a bowling alley. We have eroded the long legacy of remarkable Christian literature with books containing little thought or originality. Many of our books are arrogant and self-centered, seeming to be centered around this message: I am a hero and you should be like me. The text is then spit-shined with false humility so as not to offend the reader. We've no paintings in our corridors. The stained glass has been covered by a new and unnecessary sound system. There is a difference between entertainment and art. The church doesn't seem to know the difference sometimes. Beauty hurts. It hurts to look at it and it hurts to hear it. I cannot remember the last time I left a service with the ache of beauty in my chest. We need more of that in the house of God.

My third frustration is penetrating and critical, not cosmetic like the first two. Churches have forgotten what it means to care about people. We are endeared to each other, as we should be. We do well with those who wander into our congregation. There are pizza parties and potlucks. We've got mission trips and banquets and workshops and concerts. But poor people don't wander into churches. They don't have the clothes or the social skills to make it through the foyer. I am looking for a pastor who has the pluck to stand before his church and beg. Beg for money, beg for clothes, and beg for food. "There are hungry people in the shadow of this church," he might say, "there are people in need and I want to give them your money. I want more than your money, though. I want your time. We need men with tools and women with a desire to give. We're going to stop doing all the ministering around here. It's your turn to get involved! The kingdom of God will be built by men with callused hands and soft hearts." I have only once heard a pastor take a stand like this. The oration moved me to tears. Ed Young, at the Second Baptist Church of Houston, an enormous and wealthy church in the heart of affluent west Houston, stood before his church and declared his congregation poor in spirit. He was angry as he'd overheard a conversation belittling a destitute, hungry woman who had come through the door in search of food. He said with a booming voice, "I will tell you who is poor. If you think like those I heard in the hall, you are poor. You are the poor in spirit. I don't care how much money you have. I don't care how many companies you own. There are people in this city who are in need, and we will never close our doors to them!" Here is a man we can call a hero. And Ed Young is not alone. There are countless who know, love, and disseminate true compassion. But I fear men like these are losing influence. Too many of us are in competition with the neighboring church. Too many are selling their time to a public righteousness and a private sloth. There is little benefit to the style of preaching that has overtaken our churches. Stories are important. Feelings are important. But there is so little call to action that I wonder how applicable the teaching is?

Ok, so am I trying to be the same kind of "hero" with all the answers? No, certainly not. But Paul, James, Peter, and John, in their writings to churches of the New Testament, were bold to reprimand. I have not thought words so penetrating as "You foolish Galatians," or "You have left your first love." This sort of rebuke comes from God, and these men wrote for God. I do not. Mine is opinion only, and is in that way tainted by bias and rebellion. Do my arguments have merit? I believe they do. But cynicism is a deadly cancer and if we have not love, we have not God. And God, after all, is the aim.

There has been reform in the past, and perhaps we are in need of reform again. Have we truly developed a capacity to make disciples of all men? Are we visiting orphans and widows? Are we salt and light? Possibly, but in my mind it is difficult to find the needle in the stack of wood, brick, and bowling alley. Our efforts are largely to impress each other; an offense against which God gives stern warning: *Beware of practicing your righteousness before men to be noticed by them; otherwise you have no reward with your Father who is in heaven.* We have true need of Christian heroes, but must we continue to fake successful faith? The temptation to impress our brethren sends true growth, as well as honesty on issues of struggle and accountability, into the closet. Church is that tool of God to bring us near to Him. My fear is we are living the Christian life from church-generated habit and not from sincere want. We may know church well, and well we should, but the haunting question, the echo from the pulpit on high, thunders off brick and stained glass: Do we know God?

No offense meant. The positive qualities of my personal biography can largely be ascribed to church life. My history is 21 years. Of those, the bulk has been enriched by the persons, the teachings, the culture that is evangelical Christianity. A church is a fitting playground for a small boy. Turning quick corners on polished floors to meet, at rapid pace, a towering pastor or elder, not to be bludgeoned or receive a blow for my wrong, but dealt courtesy and a smile. What better gift to give a child, a young human, than learning that life, at its very core, has a quality of redemption; this evidence, taught not so much in the boring lessons forced on we children, but rather on the countenance of church members. Forcing myself into objectivity, I must confess that the volume of my criticism is not so much directed at the church as it is at my own despondency, having realized that to know church is not necessarily to know God; that they are two separate institutions and one is the agent, or rather an agent, that takes a person to the other. And at this realization I began to consider, in the throes of dejection, that perhaps I do not know God.

The knowing I speak of is not that benefit of salvation, of this I am assured and I do know, or am known by God. I have, in the training of the church, acquired the proper language, the gestures, the utterance of Scripture which carries a young man to his perceived success. I am "a fine young man," "an anointed child." God's hand is "on me" and He will "use me to do great things." All of this swells the head and develops a lust for more and more. I read C.S. Lewis and quoted him in a Bible study. I was then asked to lead the next study, having been thought an intellectual by my contemporaries. So I read more of Lewis, and of Paul Johnson and Calvin Miller, and then finally elevated to Kipling, Herbert, and Thompson. This branded me as more than literate; I was an appreciator of beauty and of the higher elements in life. All this in complete contradiction to the truth. I rarely felt what I read, only reading to pull quotes and have it appear I resonated with such noble ideas. Still, pushed by my contemporaries, I precipitated further into the ranks of church culture. Having developed an ability to communicate with a degree of drama and insight, I was acquisitioned as a staff member. I led a college group and taught twice each week. Twenty-one being an early age to bear such responsibility, my aspect was that of leader, but my heart was empty. I led, not in obedience to God, but for the reward that comes with the position: the comments and the looks and the shaking of hands and admiration that accompany a "man of God."

I was the one who was asked to pray when eating lunch with friends. I was asked advice on subjects I had never thought of nor experienced. I studied, not for the joy of learning, but to pass myself off as a man of books. I read and memorized lengthy passages of Scripture, not for the feeding of my soul, but that I might repeat them in public. Upon analyzing my behavior, I became despondent. In the midst of knowing about God, the very being I studied, to me, was evasive, was invisible, was no one I knew. I decided my efforts to impress my friends were misleading. I likened my position to a boy who gains a slight romance with a girl then boasts this relationship greater than it is, all to convince himself that what he wanted so desperately to be true, actually was. And when this boy's friends carry on in support of his new-found love, they help him believe it to be true. All the while, the girl is a mere acquaintance and this poor boy is not enjoying a romance for what it is: a secret thing, a sharing of souls, a passing of notes and poems and names on his notebook and long conversations on the phone and thinking endlessly about her beauty and slowly, ever so slowly building a lasting, private, personal love.

Our God is not a romantic figure, but the relationship, as any relationship, works the same. My knowing God will not come through convincing others that I know Him, it will come in seeking, in the effort and in the joy that increase with my familiarity of His goodness. I was convicted by Christ's words, *"And when you pray, you are not to be as the hypocrites; for they love to stand and pray in the synagogues and on the street corners, in order to be seen by men. Truly I say to you, they have their reward in full. But you, when you pray, go into your inner room, and when you have shut your door, pray to your Father who is in secret, and your Father who sees in secret will repay you."*

Do waves lap upon the shore to dazzle neighboring waves? Do mountains lift their summits to endear other mountains? Do birds command the sky to transcend their flock? If it is the whole of life to bring glory to God, have I not wasted my efforts in ill motive? And how does one revive sincerity on its deathbed? And how does one become something never practiced? How does one begin to love God? This is, after all, the goal of my journey; to find a Joshua Tree within this desert, hang a rope from its limbs and do an end to my old self, never again to impress with false righteousness; to become something new, a new creature whose heart beats sincere.

"Maybe we could go to my church when we get to Oregon," Paul says.

"What's that?" I reply.

"When we get to Oregon. Maybe we could go to my church and you could meet my pastor. I think you'd like him."

"That would be nice," I answer. "I'd like that. That would be nice."

6. Trouble

The van swallows dust. It chugs and has the old, arthritic feel that wants and perhaps deserves sympathy. To have been formed by caring Germans, all around green and mountain, and now, after so many years of service, not to retire, but sold to rough brutes who travel dry desert like cowboys. How the thing must loathe its masters.

"I figure we've got another three hours before we get to Albuquerque, and then several more before Flagstaff." Paul's voice comes half coherent through the slapping of wind. The air swirls through the van and has the gritty feel of beach sand. Metal shines in bright, bleached-out glimmers.

"It's another planet out here, you know," I say. "I've never spent any time in the desert. It's just empty. Miles and miles of empty."

"I don't mind it that much," Paul counters, talking loud over the road noise. He steadies the wheel with his knee, pulls his shirt over his head and throws it over his shoulder. "We've got pretty good desert back in Oregon. It's not quite this dry, but it's similar."

"I thought it rained all the time in Oregon," I say.

"It rains on the other side of the Cascade Range but not in central Oregon. Portland and Eugene get all the rain. During the winter, the Willamette Valley is like a rain forest, but go 100 miles east, over the Cascade Range, and it's all desert."

"I never knew that. I pictured tundra during winter and rain all through summer."

"Oh, Don. You're gonna love summers in Oregon. They are perfect. Eighty or ninety degrees, dry, blue skies and clear streams. It's like living in a Mountain Dew commercial...Hey, did I ever tell you that a friend of mine was in one of those?"

"A Mountain Dew commercial?" I disbelieve.

"Yeah. My friend Henry. Have you seen the one where there's a bunch of people on a dock and they swing on a rope over the water?"

"Yeah, I think I've seen it."

"Henry is in that commercial. They filmed it up at Blue Lake. Right near Black Butte."

"No way. How did he get in one of those?"

"They just brought a film crew into Sisters, pulled off the side of the road and started looking for people for the commercial. Henry was at the Thriftway and they stopped him coming out the door. He said he had a candy bar in his hand and when he finally understood what they were asking, he squeezed the candy bar till chocolate busted the wrapper. He shook the guy's hand and got chocolate on it. They gave him two hundred bucks to come swing on the rope. He said it took them all day and then they had dinner and hung out with the film crew. One of the guys on the crew had met Robin Williams on the set of *Good Morning, Vietnam.*"

"That is sweet," I say. "Two hundred bucks to swing on a rope and hang out with people who know Robin Williams.

That's the high life." I ease back and rest my arm out the window. "I'm pretty sure that is what God is calling me to do with my life. I'm pretty sure he wants me to be a rock star or an actor."

"Is that right," Paul says. I knew he would say that.

"Yes sir, it is," I say, even before he finishes his comment. "A rock star or an actor. Me and this Henry are going to have to get together when I get to Oregon. I figure a Mountain Dew ad will be a pretty good place to start." I've got a sly grin on my face and am pulling in about 20 pounds off my gut, tensing my muscles and snorting like Barney Fife.

"I could just see that, Don. You would make a great Mountain Dew guy. They could pan the camera across the girls on the beach and focus right on your hairy back, just when you turn around to address the camera."

"Exactly. You're seeing it now. People dig hairy backs," I say.

"Is that right?"

"Yes sir, it is." I stop him, snorting like Barney Fife. "Hairy backs are the next thing. Chicks know a man when they see one."

"You're making me a little queasy, Don."

"Don't get jealous on me, Paul. This is going to be a long trip and I don't need that kind of conflict."

"I hear you, man. I'll try to stay cool. It's just tough, what with your hairy back and all. Knowing you are going to be a shirtless rock star or Mountain Dew guy and I will probably end up a nobody." Paul makes a pouty lip.

"Don't let yourself think like that. I'll never forget the little people. The little people are the ones that make it happen. When I get my first movie award, you know, the little gold trophy thing, I will stand and say, 'I want to thank the little people. Little people like my old friend Paul. And I want to thank God for calling me into this ministry.' "

"You would do that for me? Stand up there and mention me by name?"

"Sure I would, man. You'd do the same for me."

Paul sits in quiet for a while. Sly grin on his face.

"Actually, Don, I probably wouldn't," he says. "I probably wouldn't mention you by name if I got the award."

"You wouldn't!"

"I don't think so, man," Paul says. "I mean, you've got to thank the producer and the director and other actors and Regis and Kathy Lee and family and all that. I would probably just say 'I'd also like to thank the little people' and leave it at that. Just a blanket statement that would cover everyone. That way nobody gets offended."

My mouth is open a bit, an expression as if to scratch my head. Turning to look at Paul, I offer agreement. "I see what you're saying. If you thank one guy, you've got to thank them all and if you leave someone out, you'd hurt feelings. I guess I'd do the same thing as you in that case."

"What do you mean?" Paul says.

"I'd just thank the necessary people and not list any of the little people."

"You can't take it back," he says.

"Can't take what back?"

"The fact that you'd mention me by name. You can't take that back. You're just doing that because I wouldn't thank you. You already said you'd thank me and you're just ticked cause I wouldn't thank you. Bottom line, you can't take it back. You said you'd thank me and that's as good as doing it for real. So you've done it already and I appreciate it. Still, I wouldn't thank you except for the blanket statement about the little people."

"I take it back, Paul. I wouldn't thank you," I say, looking at him straight.

"You can't take it back, man. You thanked me. It's done," he says.

"I can take it back if I want and I'm telling you I wouldn't thank you by name." I'm somewhat passionate about it now. An exaggerated sort of passion. "In fact, come to think of it, I wouldn't thank anyone. I would just thank myself. I'd just go 'thank me for this award. I really appreciate it' and then I'd go sit down next to my supermodel girlfriend. I doubt I would even remember you at all. I'd be a big star and wouldn't remember any of the little people."

"No. Nope. You thanked me and I appreciate it. Thanks, Don. That was nice of you to remember me."

"I'm telling you, Paul. I take it back. I absolutely would not thank you. No way."

"That was real nice of you to thank me."

"I wouldn't."

"Thanks for thinking of me."

The van slips a funny nudge forward and then suddenly slows. Paul hits the pedal and, nothing. We are coasting. In the middle of nowhere, we are coasting slower and the van is obviously going to roll to a stop. The pedal squeaks as Paul presses it to the floor. Though the engine is running, there is no register in the RPMs.

"You upset the van, Don. You were being selfish and upset the van. Now look at what you did."

"I had nothing to do with it," I laugh. "You didn't move the gum, did you?"

"Didn't touch it." The wad of gum sticks firmly against the plastic light. Paul steers the van onto the shoulder. Rolling to a stop, he kills the engine and it ticks with heat. Several cars buzz by and rock the van with a gust. Apart from the highway, the desert is silent. There are a few cactus and scattered smatterings of rocks and red boulders.

"I've got an idea," I say, very calmly, with melancholy. "Let's jump a train. You could be *Big Pauly Paul* and I'll be *Smack Daddy Pop on the Fly Drop*. We'll meet up with some Crips and Bloods and make our way to Niagara Falls for a campout."

"That's real funny, Don."

"That's what we'll do." I continue, "We'll head back to Los Angeles after the campout and start a riot. We'll smash store windows with bricks and get caught on the ten o'clock news carrying a microwave across the street." Paul looks away, across the highway at the flat, distant landscape. I continue to needle him, half in jest and half satire. "Wait a second *Big Pauly Paul*," I'm looking around, really exaggerating my body language. "There doesn't seem to be a train track anywhere." My voice is sarcastic. I speak slowly, as if stupidly realizing. "Whoops, where did the train track go? Maybe the gangs stole it and took it away. It's a shame. That train jumping was a great idea. Those bad gang guys went and ruined your idea, *Big Pauly Paul*."

"It's the linkage. That's all it is," he says.

I keep talking. "Maybe if we hike across the desert we'll find a train. I want to ride in the caboose."

"It's the linkage, Don. No big deal. Lay off it."

Paul leans in and checks his side mirror for an oncoming car. He opens the door and rounds the front of the van, walking toward the back of the van, past my door and not meeting my eye. I open the door and follow. His look is somewhat frustrated as he jerks open the engine compartment and makes grunt noises like inner cuss words.

"It's just the linkage, man. We just need to tighten it up a little." My words come as something of a condolence.

"Yeah, it looks like that's the problem."

I don't answer. Just nod my head. He leans down on one knee and has his hand in the engine. He pulls it out abruptly, shakes his fist, and blows on it.

"Needs to cool down," I say.

"I can get it." He puts his hand back in. I lean down with him. The linkage has loosened considerably. Both carbs are loose. We weren't getting any efficiency out of either one.

"I can fix this one. Ben left enough cable to rig it. But the other is worn pretty good. The wire is too short." Paul points to the other linkage and he is right. The original cable is fastened at exact length, and the attachment is loose. We are going to have to rig it like the last. New wire and all.

"Should we just clip the old one off?" I ask.

"Probably," he says.

"We'll need more wire," I say.

"Look around for a piece of cable, would you?" he asks. I stand up to look down the long highway. It goes back several miles before it disappears.

"I'll dig around in the van," I say.

The van's got a broken feel to it. It's as if it wants us to appreciate it when it runs, so it stalls on purpose, forcing us to stop and think about the bad treatment we've given it. I mostly ignore the vibes as I look for some wire. I've got the big door open to let some air swim around.

There's no wire in this van, I say to myself. No wire here. The glove box has all the same stuff as before, and no wire. I search the floor, and under the seats, and under the sink, and around all the boxes of groceries (which are beans and rice mostly, with about seven or eight little bottles of Tabasco sauce. Paul bought the groceries. He must have got the Tabasco free somewhere).

"I'm gonna walk the shoulder a bit. See if I come up with something," I say.

"Yeah. We are definitely going to need a piece of wire for this other one." He's behind the van and I can't see him.

The shoulder is as clean as I suspected. Hot and glistening. Vapors swirl in the distance. The shrubs are loose looking, as though you could pull them up and they'd break and give easily. They are few and scattered, dotting the cracked sand for miles and miles. There's not going to be any wire out here, I think to myself. I break a piece of sagebrush in my fingers. It's got that pine tree smell. Smells good and clean, like bottled-up Colorado. Not going to be anything out here, I think again. A semi rolls in from the distance, comes in like wind and blows its horn as it passes. We're parked tight on the shoulder, but no reason to blow a horn, save a man disrupting his own boredom. The gust blows past. Stirs up dirt. Another semi and then a car, and I see, out a bit, a little something glimmering that doesn't look like glass or road. Finding it, it's just a strip of plastic and I toss it back to the shoulder.

Paul's hands are tight around the linkage connector. He's got one hand pushing it in close to the carburetor and the other, working the linkage tight, threading it and wrapping it. He's done it twice now and pulled it out a third time to start over. He looks at the other carb and sees it loose, and sort of blows a little sigh and shakes his head. He lowers his head, presses with one hand and begins to thread with the other. Hearing a semi come up, he tilts his head into his arm and closes his eyes. The truck bellows past and spits some stinging sand across his back and all around the engine and his arms. He shakes it off and goes back to his work, taking notice that his armpits reek.

Looking back, I see the van and notice that it is closer to the road than I thought it was. Paul is invisible behind it. A car comes up and slows a little, making his way half into the other lane and then quickens to pass me at full speed. Trouble is a troubling thing. The stuckness of our situation dumbfounds, causes me to think lethargically. The shoulder is uncommonly clean, as though fate had swept it, knowing that we were coming to a stop right here. Three days ago, there was probably a lot of trash along this road. There was probably a good piece of wire too. Some street sweeper, or more likely a collection of prisoners with yellow jackets and garbage bags, cleaned the place up. Just our luck. Broke down in the middle of nowhere.

I think trouble leads to question and question leads to prayer. I think that without trouble we wouldn't pray. Trouble reminds us we need Him. So I pray a little. Twisting my sagebrush and having the smell of pine sticky on my fingers, I pray. *God, we've got trouble. And You've got peace and hope and calm and we could use some of that.* I'm funny when I pray. God gives and gives and gives and when He slows his giving, I go "Unfair, unjust. What kind of God could allow this and what kind of God could allow that." Here's a good time to break a bad habit. *God, Thanks for the sunrise this morning and thanks for making life so we're always on the edge of our seats, wondering what You're going to do next. Thanks for doing things on Your terms and not ours. You know what it takes to get through to Your creation, and I guess You're doing it right now. Here with our trouble. I guess I have to learn to understand that. So here goes my request. I'll work and think through it and You show me or Paul the answer. Show us what we can use to fix the van. All good things come from You; Your word says so. So, we could use some good things right now. We could use some wire, specifically. God, the sum of it is, again, we need wire. I guess that is my prayer request. Wire. Got any?* (I laugh a little, twisting my sagebrush.) *Dumb request,*

God. Sounds funny praying so specifically. Got any wire? Sounds funny.

There are times when I feel silly about prayer. Most of my requests tend to be trivial. Feels like I'm taking a traffic-ticket argument to the Supreme Court. We've got children starving in Africa and entire ethnic groups being "cleansed" in Bosnia, and here I am asking for wire so we can fix our van and keep on our trip; keep having fun. I get the feeling that God is lowering his reading glasses and giving me a look like He's being put out. Still, the Bible says we should come to Him like children. And heaven knows Christ was asked some pretty stupid questions in the Gospels, yet most of the time He answered with kindness. He must like it when we come to Him with the trivial stuff. It must make Him feel like a dad when we do that.

I get an idea, a fix for our trouble. The idea puts a little jolt in my step and I head back toward the van at a good pace.

"You fond of that stereo?" I yell out.

"What's that?" Paul says.

"How much do you care about that stereo in there? Can you live without one of the speakers for a while?"

"Good thinking, Don."

I get to work ripping the paneling off the passenger door and disconnect the speaker from its wire. Removing the stereo from its hole, I'm able to pull the wire all the way through and I've got a good four feet wrapped around my hand when I round the van. Paul has the first linkage fixed pretty tight and together we manipulate the other. I cut the wire and he connects it and begins to thread an end through the linkage connector. "You ought to stretch it out first," I suggest.

"Yeah." He undoes a little of his work and pulls the wire to stretch it. I hold the connector firm and he threads it through again.

"Work the pedal, would you," he says.

Working the pedal shows Paul's fix is good. He has me hold it and rock the gas so he can test the strength. He wants it to hold for the rest of the trip. "Looks good," he mumbles.

"What's that, Paul?"

"Start it up!" he shouts.

The van starts. The gas that was in the carb quickly fires. New fuel funnels through. It moans, backfires, and drinks gas like lemonade—through two mouths. Pressing down the pedal revs the engine louder and louder. I get the thing screaming and hold it. Paul closes the engine compartment and comes around to the driver's window. He's standing out in the road and giving me a look about revving the engine.

"Sounds like it works," he says with the same look.

"What's that you say?" I've got the engine so loud I pretend not to hear.

"Sound's pretty good. Maybe you should lay off the gas," he shouts, with a smile.

"Give it gas?" I say and press down the pedal.

He thumps me on the side of my face. "No," he says. "It works. No more gas."

"Bugs," I say and begin to roll up the window. "Bugs are biting today." With the engine revving even louder, Paul opens the door and gives a good punch to my leg. He grabs at my shin and tries to get me off the pedal. I punch him and yell out, "Bugs. They're huge. Everywhere," and hit at him until I can get him pushed back and the door closed and locked. He stands out in the road with a defeated smile and I rev the engine and move the steering wheel like I'm driving.

"That's very funny!" he shouts. "You're hilarious, Don!"

I let off the pedal and roll down the window. "Hey. How's it going?"

"It's good, man. You know, just standing out here in the road."

"Need a ride?" I ask.

"That might be good," Paul smiles, grabbing at the lock so he can open the door. Each time he reaches I slap his hand.

"How do I know you're safe," I say. "There's a lot of dangerous people on these highways. How do I know you're safe?"

"You don't," he answers.

"Well, then, I'm not giving you a ride."

"Open the door, dude." Paul's smiling but he doesn't want to. He's trying to intimidate but the situation is too funny, and he's too tired.

"You'll get a ride cowboy," I say as I roll up the window. "Show some leg. That might help."

With that, I end the banter, unlock the door and slide across to the passenger's seat.

"You drive," I say.

"That's right. You haven't slept, have you?" Paul climbs in and places the toolbox between the seats.

"No. I haven't slept in a long time. I'm fading too." The stereo is up on the dash so I stuff it back into the hole, poking the wires back behind it. "That other speaker should still work," I say.

"Maybe time for a little Skynyard." Paul's got a grin and he's reaching over to the glove box. I quickly raise my feet so they're firmly against the dash, blocking the glove box.

"I see how it is now. I see." Paul grins and nods as he forces the gearshift into first and releases the clutch. He checks the rearview mirror and pulls us onto the highway. "I see how it is," he says again.

7. Simplicity

When nearing the city in evening, falling stars dive and duck behind tall buildings. Flagstaff rests on the side of a mountain and so it is serene. You can see the dark peak rise like a thunderhead. We are on a dark stretch of road that enters Flagstaff from the east. Streetlights stand guard like old Roman soldiers. Fire engines are chasing smoke signals from someone's tragedy and the light at the end of the tunnel is slowly flickering out. This city is cut from the same cloth as every other city: people living in community for need of money and companionship.

I come to Flagstaff with presuppositions. Without having been here, I can say with confidence that half these people believe in UFOs. One in one hundred have been sucked into spinning-sphere ships and carry vague memories of little green men taking skin samples from their buttocks. They have scars to prove it and will show you if they've had enough beer, and the bar is nearly empty. There is also a growing college crowd who've bought into the idea of simplicity. They drive fashionable jeeps, wear the same khaki pants every day, and have dogs named Sigmund or Maslow. In each of their apartments you will find, somewhere, a painting by Georgia O'Keefe. They curse cement and consider New York and Chicago a thorn in the side of Mother Nature's flesh. They are tan, good-natured, and don't wash their hair.

I don't know that this town would accept me. They would know by my aura that I am a good Republican and would politely ask me to leave. Paul, however, would fit just fine. As far as I know, he has never been abducted by aliens, but they would forgive that. He is courteous and would look long at their Georgia O'Keefe paintings, nodding as they pontificate about her use of color and form. I, on the other hand, would simply say she uses too much brown and makes me thirsty.

Paul is better than me in this way. He can appreciate the person inside the persona. To him, people are more important than ideas. He does not laugh at jokes that deprecate others. His is a true, empathetic, kind character. We've similar histories, Paul and I. Both of us are from broken homes, both encountered Christ at an early age, both share enthusiasm for taking chances. Still, he is advanced further in his Christian maturity. Or at least he acts more advanced than I do. I've thought long about the reason for this. I know Scripture better than Paul. I've studied it more, and have taught it too. Everything leads me to believe that Christ should reveal more of His character in me than in Paul. But this isn't the case. In terms of kindness, patience, forgiveness, and so many other fruits of the Spirit, Paul has me beat. Scripture tells us that knowledge puffs up.

Perhaps this is the reason I often come off as a know-it-all. I tend to count every good thing I do as credit in the eyes of God. Paul, however, truly understands the idea of grace. He knows and lives the fact that he has been forgiven. I know it as well, and can point right to the scriptures that prove it. But knowing and realizing are two separate things. Perhaps Paul has the ability to realize things when I simply learn them. It is one thing to read about Europe and know where Paris is and where London is and what the temperatures average in all seasons. It is another thing to go to Europe and experience the look and feel of the place. Know the people and the traditions and the art. Paul experiences God and I simply learn about Him. I am not confessing my paganism here. I truly know God in the same way that Paul does. I think the central difference between his faith and mine is sincerity. When he prays, thanks, or studies God, he means it. I simply work to accumulate knowledge. Knowledge is important. Solomon tells us that. But knowledge and relationship are two different things. A Christian can invest in knowledge without investing in relationship.

After all, we learn about the character of God by studying His word. To the New Testament church, Scripture is where He reveals Himself. Without a knowledge of Scripture, we can never be sure what is and isn't God's handiwork. So the point of divergence between Paul and me is this second step of relationship. The step that follows knowledge. For me, everything seeps through an intellectual filter. For Paul, it goes directly to the heart. My ideas about God may be more sound, but his ideas have a greater impact on the way he lives his life. Both approaches have strengths and weaknesses. Paul's approach to faith, in my mind, will often lead him to believe ideas without checking them against Scripture. A preacher can say that the five smooth stones David threw represent faith, hope, love, forgiveness, and selflessness. Paul will take the bait hook, line, and sinker. In response to a sermon like this, he will begin to work on this list of virtues. His life will improve with his efforts. I, on the other hand, will leave the sermon huffy-puffy because the pastor turned a perfectly good story about courageous faith into an analogy. He made a metaphor of an Old Testament passage that God never intended to be a metaphor. So who is in the wrong here? Paul, because he did not think about the proper interpretation of Scripture, yet changed the way he lived his life to please God? Or am I wrong, for not letting the innocent sermon slide and recognizing that the virtues presented were, in fact, biblical, and should be adhered to regardless of whether the pastor chose the wrong passage to make his point?

Another difference in the way Paul and I approach God is in our realization of need. That is, Paul really believes he needs God. I don't. I know I need God, but the knowing does not filter down into the needing, or the realization of the needing. There are times when I don't think about God at all. What I mean is that He doesn't, in any given moment, have any useful purpose for me. The Bible says to pray without ceasing. I'm not sure how to do this. And moreover, I can't, for the life of me, figure out what it is we are supposed to spend so much time talking to God about. If we are at the grocery store, are we supposed to ask Him to direct us to this week's specials? I'm not sure. There are people who seem to be in prayer, or at least thinking about God, all the time. I mostly pray when I'm in a jam.

Paul really tries to be a moral person. I've noticed that about him. There is a characteristic in Paul that you won't find in the average Christian. He is real about obeying God. What I mean is, he actually wants to obey for the sake of obeying. He isn't trying to fit in with his church friends, he's not trying to be a holy roller, he just wants to obey because that is what God wants. It feels good to him. He doesn't talk about it, he just does it. Prayer is a big part of his success, I suppose. He can spend time with God in just about any circumstance. He's comfortable being alone with Him. Meanwhile, I don't feel like I'm in church unless I'm in church. My spiritual life and my regular life are separate. I cannot seem to distinguish the idea of church from the idea of God.

I do right things because my friends at church do right things, not because God would have me do them. My faith has become something of a cultural faith. A Bible Belt, good-ole-boy faith.

My pursuit of God is going to have to start on the inside. I've got to be brutally honest with myself here. No pretending. No playing the role of hero. There are so many things that I know about God, but I am not sure where I accumulated all this knowledge. Maybe in Sunday school or in books I've read. But I need something personal, an authentic faith I can call my own.

It is a hard thing for a religious person to question the very roots of his faith. Habits are difficult to break. Paradigms set like concrete if you don't keep water on them. Meanwhile, God is always revealing Himself. At least He is as I understand Him. And yet I've not let God reveal anything new and endearing for a long time. My love for Him is stale. He doesn't seem like the grand mystery that He used to be. I feel a sense of excitement about starting over. Starting over always feels good.

Flagstaff is not as big as it looks from a distance. The main road breaks off into tributaries that climb the hillside; streets are lined with two-story brick offices, pubs, and retail shops. It is not as busy as I thought it might be. It is ten o'clock in the evening and the streets are vacant save the occasional cars and lone walkers. The air has cooled considerably. We've probably lost 30 degrees in two hours. All the way in, we were gaining altitude, so the coolness is due to elevation as well as evening. Trees are dense at this altitude. Pine and evergreen. Mountain air. This is how I imagine

Colorado or Montana, but not Arizona. I fancied Flagstaff as a desert town, but it isn't. There is shade and streams and small parks.

We round a bend and weave through town to find an exit road that cuts deep embankments in the side of the mountain. The road hugs the hill and we navigate tight curves banked by a wall of dirt on one side and pine on the other. Two lanes and no shoulder. Flagstaff fades and disappears into the trees and gets lost in the curves behind us. Patches of snow rest amidst pine needles. The temperature has actually cooled enough to allow snow to stick and stay. Our headlights sweep along the treeline as we round another curve. The lights peer deep into the forest and I can see the white-backed snow humps in with the brown and green. A very peaceful landscape.

"Are you seeing the snow, Paul?"

"Yeah."

"Cool," I say.

"Have you ever seen snow, Don?"

"A little. It snowed once in Houston but it wasn't cold enough to stick. It only snowed for a few minutes."

"Well, there's your snow." Paul says this with a smile.

"Yep, there it is. Stuck around just for me."

I've got my eyes looking for snow like a child would look for a deer after one had jumped across the road. I'm fixated by the idea of snow. People in Houston dream about it during winter. We celebrate Christmas with shorts on and get about five or six days a year that actually drop below freezing. Winter is just summer with an ice cube and a straw. As a kid I'd always dreamed about living in a place where it snowed. I picked Maine on a map because it was as far north as you could go and still run for president. To this day I carry a fond feeling for Maine. Someone says Maine and it has a soothing sensation. I picture Bob Newhart and Daryl and his other brother Daryl. I picture myself with a bed and breakfast, a cute little wife, and a typewriter in the attic where I write novels and poems about snow. You know, the kind of poem that people put on their kitchen walls like that "footprints" poem. My poem would be typeset over a snowy lake or something, not a beach like the footprints poem. I never liked the beach thing in the kitchen because mentally, sand and food don't go together. Snow is serene and peaceful and doesn't taste gritty in your ham sandwich. My snow poem will sell better than that "footprints" thing.

Flagstaff is behind us now. Every few curves we see a small house tucked into the woods. People living the simple life. They chop their own wood and grow their own carrots and beets and spend evening hours peering their beady eyes through Radio Shack telescopes, hoping to get a look at Luke Skywalker. This brings them fulfillment. As I said, it is the simple life.

Simplicity, as a Christian virtue, is important. Most Christians don't think much about simplicity, but I think Solomon understood. His understanding did not come from living the life of a minimalist, but rather through a process of elimination. He decided that owning an excess of things brought him no joy. The riches he inherited and accumulated were only clutter that kept him from understanding God. They didn't *have* to keep him from God, but they did. American Christians, for the most part, have embraced the idea of wealth. The American dream is a wonderful thing. It is as intoxicating as a speech by Zig Ziglar. We can work, own, work more, own more, work more, and own more. If we work hard enough, we will eventually work ourselves out of a job, and then think of all the time we will have to serve God. Blah, blah, blah. Don't get me wrong here. I love the American dream. I believe we are fools not to take advantage of the free enterprise system. Still, I am no fool. There is no joy in money. There is no joy in possessions. Christ did not chase coins or attempt to pitch His message from a pulpit of prestige. He was a carpenter. He had no home. He rode a donkey. His friends wore robes with blue collars. It was not necessary for Christ to be in circles of influence to be of influence. Wealth was not one of the tools He needed to complete His mission. Likewise, wealth is not one of the tools we need to complete our mission. Nor is it something we need in order to feel joy.

I am not old enough to be anchored by material possessions. I have a truck. That is about it. So I speak without the benefit of real knowledge. Had I a family, I might think differently. A home is an expensive thing. A family lifestyle is expensive. Vacations are expensive. I think that all of these things can be considered necessary. Still, every possession is an anchor. When we have too many of them, we move sluggishly. Soon, we have so many anchors, we simply don't move at all. I am not one to say that Christians shouldn't have nice cars or toasters. I will say, however, that a nice car and a toaster are not needed to do what God wants us to do. And, should we purchase these things, we musn't excuse ourselves by believing that God would want us to have them. I don't believe that God cares whether we have nice things. I believe He cares about whether we are obeying Him.

8. Canyon People

The area around the Grand Canyon is surprisingly flat. Dense with pine trees, the ground not taken by forest is brown with desert sand. A Disneyland atmosphere surrounds the place. Rangers and preservationists have tried to give the area a park feel (and it has some of that), but it is mostly a tourist trap and one more state decal stuck on the back of an old couple's retirement vehicle. There are lawn chairs and picnics and crying babies held by mothers who juggle diaper bags and strollers. Fathers have plaid shorts, white tennis shoes, and blue socks. They lead their families around the canyon edge like tour guides, explaining how many millions of years it took for the river to carve this hole in the earth.

Paul and I are set back $10 apiece at the entrance. We pay the sum in exchange for permission to enter the park. We decide not to pay the additional $30 required to camp. With the van, we agree that we can sleep anywhere and will head back into town if we need to. Our first stop within the gate is the canyon edge, where the aforementioned scene plays out before us. No amount of hype or brochure sales copy can prepare a person for the breathtaking depth of the canyon itself. From 20 feet away, we see an abrupt drop in the landscape. As we near the edge, the depth is all-consuming. There seems to be no bottom. No words are spoken here, and the sound of children fade to the background as a breeze whistles through sagebrush and a fiery red cliff drops under our feet. It is a top-of-the-roller-coaster feeling as I imagine myself plunging headlong over the rail. Enough emotion to take a step back and catch my breath. Regaining my senses, I lean over the edge and focus my eyes to find the bottom. Perhaps the Colorado river that Ben Bonham told us about will come to view. But it doesn't. What I see several miles down is a flat surface, a peninsula edged by another drop. A canyon inside of a canyon. We are not at the park's most popular overlook, but at a trailhead for those planning a hike all the way down.

"How many miles do you figure it is to the bottom?" I ask.

Paul looks down at a few hikers, looks again at the peninsula and shrugs his shoulders. "I guess we will know soon enough."

"Do you think we can start today?" I ask, half unsettled at the tremendous depth. I feel a weakness in my legs and am altogether unsure whether I have the stamina to find the bottom.

Paul notes the reservation in my voice.

"I don't know if we need a permit or anything. We can go to the information center and find out. We'll do fine, Don."

"I'm looking forward to it," I say with my most courageous face.

Paul turns and walks toward the van. A child licks his ice cream cone and an old couple passes binoculars back and forth. One is talking to the other about a certain shrub or tree that the other has spotted. "To the right," he says, as she swings the black tubes too far. "Not over there," he says, "here, honey." He points but she doesn't see, too busy fidgeting with the focus lever.

I near the trailhead and eye its steep switchbacks weave under each other. They are thin trails with no protective guardrails. One of the hikers gets caught by a gust of wind and leans back against the rock wall until it passes. One bad step could send her into a freefall that would last a minute or more. The trail becomes so thin to my eye that I lose it in the camouflage of red rock and sand.

Paul is more eager to hike the canyon than I am. He didn't look at it for more than a minute before turning away. The look on his face and the surety of his step tells me that, come rain or snow, we will hike to the bottom of this hole.

The information center is a cave of a structure. It is walled with river rock and has a wood porch like a cabin in the mountains. A big building with a big parking lot, RVs line the road for several hundred yards before we find the entrance. Paul and I drive into the lot hoping to find an open space. Families with matching sunburns stream in and out of the building. One family on the large porch gathers around their leader, who wrestles with the creases of the park map. It is all he can do to keep the map unfolded. It wraps around his arms like a fishing net.

Inside the information center, everything is dark. While not overly warm outside, the sky is bright and so our eyes adjust slowly to the brown decor of the large room fit with cement floors, ceiling fans, and brochure-lined walls.

Paul bypasses the brochures and the rock exhibit, making his way to the counter where a young girl in a brown uniform stands with a fake smile.

"Can I help you?"

"Yes. We were needing a trail map for the canyon."

"Are you going down?" she asks.

"Yes."

"Do you have your permit yet?"

"Well, I didn't know for sure if we needed one."

"You do," she says.

"We do."

"Yes," she says.

Paul turns and looks at me and then turns back. She's still got that same smile going and he's softly bouncing his fingers on the counter.

"Do you know if there is a cost for that?"

"The permit?" she clarifies.

"Yes." Paul answers.

"There's no cost. But you can't get a permit here. Permits are issued in the trailhead office."

"The trailhead office," Paul echoes.

"Yes."

I crack a smile as Paul walks the girl through every step of her job.

"Where is the trailhead office?" he asks.

The girl turns and grabs a three-ring notebook with a dozen or more pages, each page held in a protective glossy sheet. She flips slowly through them and sets her finger down firmly when she finds what she's looking for.

"Here it is," she says as she turns the notebook around so Paul can see. I walk over to get a look at the map.

"This X is the permit office?" Paul asks.

"That's the place."

"Now, where are we?"

"You...you...are here." And she places her finger only an inch from the permit office.

"So," Paul begins, "it looks like we should just go out the door and, well, it doesn't look like it's very far."

"Well," she says, "if you go out this door," she points, and look to the left, "it is right there. It's a brown trailer."

"It is right outside the door?" Paul asks in disbelief.

"Yes," she says and I audibly chuckle. She doesn't notice my laugh and then I see a sheepish look come over her face. She turns and points out the window. "Duh, I'm so silly. You can see it outside the window. That's it right there."

"Right there," Paul clarifies as he points to a brown trailer.

"That's it," she says and her smile turns big.

"Duh," I say with a gentle smile. Paul steps on my foot to get me to stop.

"I mean," I begin apologetically, "we should have known that."

"Oh no. It's my job," she clarifies.

"Duh," I mumble and Paul steps on my foot again and the girl smiles real big.

"Have fun in the canyon," she says with a huge smile.

"We will."

I let Paul go a few feet toward the door while I remain at the counter. "Paul," I shout. "Do you think we need a map to the door? It's awful dark in here." I turn back to the girl and she smiles and points to the door.

"Over there," she says.

"There," I clarify with a confused look and a point.

"He's got it," she says and looks at me like I'm stupid. "It's right there. He found it," she says.

"Thanks. Duh, I'm so silly sometimes."

"That's all right," she says, turning to the next person in line.

"I can't believe you did that." Paul holds the door open and greets me with a grin.

"She couldn't tell anything. I was just playing with her."

"Still, you could have hurt her feelings."

"No big deal," I say.

Paul eyes the brown trailer across the parking lot. "That's it. Let's go get the permit."

—···— —···— —···—

The interior of the trailer is wood paneling and brown trim. There is a tall man in a uniform behind a counter. Otherwise, the trailer is empty. Paul greets the uniformed man.

"Hello. We want to get a couple of permits for the canyon."

"You are in the right place," the man says. "Did you make a reservation?"

"No. We didn't know we needed one."

"Most people make reservations before they come. We can only have so many people in the canyon at a time."

"Do you have any openings?" Paul asks.

The man pulls out a three-ring notebook and files through pages. It is a thick book and filled line by line with signatures.

"I don't know if we can get you in any time soon," he responds.

"When's the soonest?" Paul asks.

The man looks back at his notebook, scanning down the page with his finger. He flips the page and scans down the backside. Paul sighs and gives me a hopeful look.

"I can get you in on Easter morning. You will have a permit to camp at the bottom that night. Indian Springs campground will have a space for you the next day."

"Indian Springs?" Paul questions.

"Indian Springs is the campground about halfway up. I can put you at the bottom on Sunday night. You will have to hike out the next day and come to Bright Angel. All I can give you is one day at Indian Springs. Then you'll have to come out."

Paul lifts his eyebrows and sighs. "If that's all we can get, we'll take it, I guess."

"That is all I can do for you."

Paul looks over and asks me what day it is. "Wednesday," I respond.

"You'll have to stick around for a few days," the uniformed man says, clarifying the importance of not breaking the rules.

"Fine with me." Paul glances my way.

"Yeah, that's fine," I shrug.

The man turns the notebook around and hands Paul a pencil. "You guys come back and check with me if you decide to leave. Plenty of people would like these permits."

He pulls out a pink piece of paper and hands it to me. It has a list of numbered guidelines. "Don't veer off the trail," he begins. "Pack out your trash, don't approach animals, carry plenty of water, don't wash your gear in the river, only make camp in a designated area, use no radios or other electronic devices that create an excess of noise."

The list goes on for a while and the man reads each rule carefully. He then hands us permits to sign.

"Keep your copy with you at all times," he says. "Do either of you have a heart condition?"

"Heart condition?" I ask, puzzled.

"A heart condition or any other medical problem that might get you into trouble."

"No," Paul says.

"No," I answer.

Looking directly at me, he begins his warning. "Last week a man had a heart attack about half way up from Bright Angel. There was nothing we could do for him. Rangers carried his body to the rim. If you get into trouble at the bottom, we will not send a helicopter down for you. There is no place for us to land. So, our policy is to float your dead body down the river and fish you out at Hoover Dam."

The man turns to Paul, straight faced and then gives a wink. "Just kidding," he says. "Still, a man did die last week. But if you get into trouble, we can bring you out on a donkey. But you have to be dead first. That's the only way you get a free ride out."

"Kidding?" I ask.

"I'm not joking this time. If you aren't sure that you can make it to the bottom and back, don't go. This is one of the most difficult hikes in the country. There is nothing easy about it. Nine miles in and ten miles out. An elevation loss and gain of over 5000 feet. Every year we have people die on those trails."

"We will be careful," Paul assures the man, folding his permit and putting it in his pocket.

We turn toward the door and my legs feel numb. I've got butterflies in my stomach. Houston is very, very flat. I've never been above 1000 feet before, much less from 5000 to zero and back. Or whatever the elevation is.

"You boys have a good hike."

"Well, bud, we're in." Paul raises his hand for a high five.

I meet his hand and give a good grin. "Can't believe it," I say. "We are actually going to do this."

"It is going to be great, Don. You are really going to love this hike. Your first big nature experience." He sees my grin turn down a little. "Think of it, the canyon walls, the red rock, the river flowing right by our camp, the stars from the bottom of the canyon."

The body floating down the river, I think to myself. The sound of the turbines at Hoover Dam, my crying mother, the bloated-blue figure that sickens the onlookers at my funeral.

"I'm pumped, Paul. This is going to be good."

"You bet it is," he says.

9. Dancing

I t is difficult to recall, much less recapture, the excitement of an adventure's beginning when one finds himself in the boring middle of it. Paul and I have been waiting for three days. Tomorrow morning we will hike into the canyon. My earlier reservations about the intensity of the hike have been allayed by a burning off of anxiety, accomplished by the twiddling of thumbs. But today we are off on short hikes to and from the day-use area and the canyon splendor has bewildered the depth of my imagination. We've seen every overlook the park allows. This gargantuan hole they call Grand has no less depth from any angle. To the human eye, it is bottomless.

The waiting has not been all bad. Paul, the cook, has been standing over an enormous pot of beans and rice for an hour and I have written postcards to family, friends, and Ben Bonham. The last of whom will receive a detailed description of the canyon edge, specifically worded to remind him and his wife of the beauty they twice knew.

A park ranger came through the day-use area and attempted conversations with several families. He spent a little time with us and answered questions about the route we've chosen to hike. Ours will be a loop down the Kaibab trail to where we will camp on the canyon floor. On Monday we will leave Kaibab and take the Bright Angel trail halfway up where there is a meadow and another camping area called Indian Springs. We will stay at Indian Springs two days and then finish the ascent on the third day. All in all, being only nineteen miles and over three-days' time, the hike doesn't intimidate the way it did a few days back. The ranger also told us about the sunrise service tomorrow morning. "Sunrise over the canyon is beautiful," he says. Apparently it is an Easter tradition and hundreds of people attend every year.

Our time in the day-use area has given me opportunity to reread Ecclesiastes again. On further consideration, Solomon does not seem the troubled soul I thought he was. The book is a memoir of sorts. He looks back through his life of accomplishment and asks the question, *What is this worth?* He may have experienced some trouble in his earthly pursuits, but this trouble is resolved when he finally agrees with God and claims, "The conclusion, when all has been heard, is: Fear God and keep His commandments, because this applies to every person."

It is hard to imagine that anyone could have made a more vigorous pursuit of meaning than Solomon. He did it all. It is widely believed that he was the wisest, richest, and most influential king in Israel's history. While most of us say, "If I only had such and such a thing, or such and such a job, or such and such a girl, I would certainly be happy," Solomon can say, "I had all things material, I had the greatest position in the country, I had all the women a man could desire, and none of it satisfied." He then did a humble thing. He agreed with God and submitted himself to Him. This alone gave him fulfillment.

I was raised to believe that the quality of a man's life would greatly increase, not with the gain of status or success, not by his heart's knowing romance or by prosperity in industry or academia, but by his nearness to God. It confuses me that Christian living is not more simple. The gospel, the very good news, is simple, but this is the gate; the trailhead. Ironing out faithless creases is toilsome labor. God bestows three blessings on man: to feed him like birds, dress him like flowers, and befriend him as a confidant. Too many take the first two and neglect the last. Most believers on the path have found that life is constructed specifically and brilliantly to squeeze a man into association with the owner of heaven. It is a struggle, with labor pains and thorny landscape, bloody hands and sweaty brow, head in hands, moments of severe loneliness and questioning, moments of ache and desire. All this leads to God. God is not merely the reason behind existence, nor the curer of ills and confusion. Matter and thought are a canvas on which God paints; a painting with tragedy and delivery, with sin and redemption. Life is a dance toward God. And the dance is not so graceful as we might think. For while we glide and swing our practiced sway, God crowds our feet, bumps our toes, and scuffs our shoes. He lowers His head, whispers soft and confident, "You will dance to the beat of 'Amazing Grace' or you will not dance at all." So we learn to dance with the One who made us. And it is a taxing dance to learn.

But once learned, don't we glide. And don't we sway. And don't we bury our head in His chest. And don't we love to dance.

If a man does not eat, he dies, so he must get food. Still, though eating and alive, another pain strikes us all. We are lonely. We desire friendship, we desire love. God has instilled in us certain needs and drives that create community. Had God not framed our biology with this need for each other, we might all be mountain men, independent and free of want. We would not have gardens or baseball. God's system is perfect in this way. It forces us to need and to desire and to interact and none of us are above it.

The chief commodity in life is not money; it is fellowship, the act of being known. By this I mean being considered, loved, and appreciated by our peers; to talk and have people listen. A man will give his fortune to gain this one fulfillment. We ache for the being known, the admiration, and the love. This, in itself, is not an evil thing. Without it we would be brutish. Having no need of it, we would not marry, raise children, or stop our cars at crosswalks. And, the ultimate tragedy, having no need of love, we would not love.

But gaining love does not satisfy us from hungering for more. The wealth does not quench, nor the garden feed. And all of our aching and all of our needing and all of our lonely are set in motion by God simply to near us to Him. For this is the reason we exist.

10. Easter Descent

Seven miles from Grand Canyon National Park there are sleeping pines that line the dark highway. They break their fences here and there to reveal stretches of moonlit desert that roll miles and miles back toward Flagstaff. On this particular stretch of road there is a hotel, where families sleep soundly in the early morning darkness. Behind this hotel there is a van, a Volkswagen with two tired, sleeping passengers. They cover their heads in blankets at first light and each think to themselves how they should wake the other up. But the lazy sun slowly climbs the lazy sky and the lazy passengers go back to sleep beneath the sleeping pines and care not about Easter sunrise service or about making memories or nearing God. And while Christ rises from the dead, the two lazy sleepers sleep.

On the road from the hotel to the canyon we are able to pick up a Flagstaff radio station. KTLY, an oldies station, plays the Beatles on Sunday morning. One of the first bands to utilize stereo technology, the Beatles often produced their early records so that the lead vocals are committed to one speaker and the music and back-up vocals are given to the other. Short one speaker, we have a built-in karaoke machine. Paul and I are unsure in our singing. Is it *Help me if you can I'm feeling down, and I do appreciate you being round*, or is it *Help me if you can I'm feeling down, and I do appreciate you coming round?* My money is on *coming round*. Regardless, the words *Won't you please, please help me* come in clear from the driver's side.

The disc jockey has a middle-aged voice. He's one of those guys who tries to act cool around the younger generation. "This is Geoffrey Clark and you're listening to All Beatles Sunday on KTLY Radio, 102 FM Flagstaff, Grand Canyon. That was 'Please, Please, Help Me,' and now, one of my personal favorites, a really groovy tune called 'Paperback Writer.' "

We picked up some resealable bags from the National Park grocery store a couple days back and Paul is filling a few with day-old beans and rice. We've got bananas and apples and several tea bags and hot apple cider mix.

"You probably want to put that in the top of your pack," Paul says after handing me a bag of brown, mushy beans.

"Do you think we've got enough water?" I ask.

"Four canteens should get us to the bottom. There will be fresh water there and I've got purification tablets if there's not."

I place one change of underwear, two pair of socks, and a T-shirt into my bag. Pushing them deep, I make room for my Bible and Emily Dickinson book. My sleeping bag is not one of those fancy, light ones that campers have nowadays. It's cotton and wool and doubles the weight of the pack when I fasten it to the frame. I tie my metal cup to one of the side straps and my toothbrush and toothpaste fit neatly in a side pocket.

"Do you have toilet paper?" I ask.

Paul doesn't look up but pats a side pocket on his pack. "Yeah, I've got some in here." He is pulling on a strap, tightening his sleeping bag to the top of his pack.

"Do you have any to spare?"

"Got plenty."

A couple of hikers lift their packs, tighten their straps around their waists and stroll past us. I watch them out of the corner of my eye as they disappear behind a boulder and then appear again a good fifty feet down. They round a corner and disappear again.

"How are we going to get back to the van when we come out?" I ask.

"Well, we will just hike back to this trailhead when we come up from Bright Angel. We can probably hitch a ride if we want."

"Yeah, that sounds good," I say.

Paul opens the big sliding door on the van and rummages around.

"What are you looking for?" I ask.

"Just looking. Want to make sure I got everything."

I bought a Swiss Army knife for the trip. It has a fork, a knife, a toothpick, and a corkscrew. They had one with a spoon but it was twenty dollars more. I put my knife in the backpack but then decide I want to carry it in my pocket.

"Is this your hat?" Paul asks. He's holding a Panama-style *Maxfli* hat.

"Yeah, that's my golf hat."

"You play golf?" he asks.

"A little. Hand it here, I may as well wear it down."

I pull the hat firmly over my head. It has a tight, elastic band so it fits nice and comfortable. I lift my pack by the frame and swing it around to my back. Feels like lead. It's so heavy, with the water and books, I stagger a little.

"Looks like you've got a heavy load there, Don."

"No doubt," I say.

Taking the pack off, I remove my Emily Dickinson book and my Bible. I grab my little travel Bible out of the glove box and place it in the pack instead. I also remove an apple or two thinking that I will just make do with the food that I've got. The food is making the pack heavy. I have five meals with snacks and reduce this to four and no snacks, save two apples. It is not wise to hike so long without enough food, but the beans and rice are potent enough to fuel a race horse, so I use that excuse to put one of the bags back into the van.

Paul slides the door closed and rounds the van to lock the doors.

"I guess we're ready," he says as he lifts his pack over his shoulders.

"We really are a couple of characters, aren't we?" I suggest, looking at our reflection in the window of the van. Paul has an old army pack that he picked up at a surplus store on Galveston Island, and I've got this old pack from the '70s that is bright orange. Like a vest on a road worker, the pack is so bright it might very well glow in the dark.

"I don't think I'll be losing you in the canyon," Paul says with a laugh.

We round the boulder and stand side by side at the edge of the trail. There are clouds building in the distance, but the sky around them is deep and blue. It climbs as endlessly as the canyon descends and we experience one last bit of awe before we depart.

"All this beauty makes a person realize how insignificant they are," Paul says.

"How insignificant I am. You're the insignificant one."

He grins real big as he realizes how his words sounded. "I didn't mean it like that," he chuckles.

"No, I know what you meant, bud. I was just thinking kind of the same thing. I was looking at all this depth and it came to me how very shallow you are."

"Ha, ha," Paul chortles. He takes a few steps down the trail and then turns. "You know, Don, I was just looking at this little flowery cactus here and thinking how nice it looks and it made me realize how ugly you are."

"Is that right," I say. "Well, I was just considering how smart these rocks look and it made me realize how dumb you are." With that I give him a little kick in the backside.

"How smart these rocks are?" he heckles. "Well, I was just looking at that cloud up there, reflecting on its beauty and stuff, and it hit me how much you smell."

"Is that right?" I say. "The cloud made you realize that, huh?"

Paul distances himself a little and keeps turning to see if I am going to kick him again. He's got this grin going like he got the last laugh.

"You know, Paul, I was just looking at this pebble and it made me realize that I'm going to tackle you and throw you off the ledge."

"I see. That's real deep, Don. The pebble. You got that from a pebble."

With that I give chase, and Paul, with his quickness, gets away. He turns and takes a little rock and throws it down on the trail. "Try getting around that," he says.

I jump over the rock with an exaggerated, Superman, slow-motion step and he sighs and covers his mouth.

"Oh, no," he says. "Please don't hurt me, mister."

Our fun turns to work as we wind down the switchbacks. Some descend 30 and 40 feet in only a few paces but the canyon offers splendor at every turn. It is a wonder that they carved a trail into the canyon at all. It is onerously steep. At times the trail thins to three or four feet, with nothing but drop as a border. The mind gets used to the danger so that a hiker can set his stride only inches from the cliff, making pace, caring not about his fall. It gives me a sense of pride as I narrowly navigate the trail and keep steady with Paul.

There are numerous spiritual analogies about climbing mountains. We call our times with God *mountaintop experiences*. It is unfair that mountains get all the respect and canyons are thought of so negatively. After all, it is no less a miracle that there is a towering pile of dirt and rock than an absence of it. And who cares that there is no view from the bottom? Half the time you can't see anything from the top of a mountain anyway and they are terribly difficult to climb. In terms of analogies, canyons are sorely neglected. A canyon can be used to describe hell or sin or confusion or all sorts of important spiritual realities. Without canyons, mountains would have no point of reference. A canyon is, after all, an upside-down mountain. Except they most often have rivers at the bottom, and mountains have no rivers on top. Just snow and little flags that represent different hikers from different countries, and little frozen bodies clinging to frozen flags and that sort of thing.

The Grand Canyon, as Paul tells me, is not the deepest canyon in the United States. I didn't know that. The deepest canyon is on the Oregon-Idaho border. It is Hells Canyon, and drops more than 6000 feet from rim to river. Paul tells me that it is a gradual slope with a road that goes to the bottom so it doesn't have the dangerous view that this canyon has, and that is why nobody recognizes it as spectacular. I cannot imagine anything more deep than this.

The trail does not give in its slope. My toes are sliding into the front of my boots and my heel has not felt shoe in an hour. Looking up, the canyon rim does not seem so far. We've hiked a mile or more and still the bottom of the canyon is not in view. We only see the first ledge which hides the river. And there is no telling how far the river is from the first ledge. Still, it doesn't seem like we've made progress at all.

"Doesn't seem like we've gotten anywhere does it?" Paul says as he looks up at the rim.

"I was thinking the same thing. This may take a while."

As we hike, Paul gets ahead of me by a switchback and then another. I'm growing tired and my toes are really getting to me. My right big toe rubs against the side of my boot. I can feel the skin getting tender so it slows my pace and Paul gets a little further ahead. His pace is slowing too, but he still gets away. He's four switchbacks down and I can see him when I come to the edge and look directly down. I walk through the pain, quicker and quicker, just trying to ignore it. I grimace as I step and there is a rocking in my stride. Coming within one switchback of Paul, I see he has a drag in his step. No smile. No grimace, but no smile. He's not having it as tough as I am, but it sets me at ease to know I am not a complete wimp. This hike is actually difficult, even for Paul. He rounds the switchback and I notice he gives a nod to someone underneath my trail. He engages in a conversation and I wind down the corner to see two hikers sitting in the mouth of a shallow cave. One is dipping his Swiss Army knife into a jar of peanut butter. He has a piece of bread on his knee. The other hiker is leaning against the rock and looks exhausted. His legs are stretched out over the boulder in front of him.

"How long have you guys been hiking?" the one without the knife asks.

Paul looks over and shrugs his shoulder. He turns back. "About two hours. Probably two hours. How about you guys?"

The guy with the peanut butter handles his bread and doesn't look up. "We left the bottom about four hours ago. Maybe more."

"Four hours," I clarify.

The one on the right rubs his leg. "Don't worry, it takes a lot longer coming up than going down. You guys should be there in three hours."

"You said that right," the other adds. "Coming up is a bear."

As we leave, the guy with the peanut butter pulls his knife from the jar. He has the knife that includes the spoon. It has a bigger blade too and it makes me wish I had paid the twenty extra bucks to get that one. Peanut butter, however, doesn't sound very good. Too thirsty.

"How are your feet?" I ask as Paul drags his steps in front of me.

"They're getting to me a little. How about yours?"

"Mine feel fine. Feel like a million bucks."

"Is that right?" Paul inquires.

"Sure. Feel like I could run a marathon." My smile gives away my lie.

"Is that why you were making that grunt noise back there?" he asks.

"What grunt noise?"

"Back there when you leaned against the rock and started crying for your mommy."

With that, I give him a good kick in the backside. He jumps a few steps and kicks a little dirt back on me.

"We'll see who's crying mommy," I say.

Paul gains a few paces and then turns, looking at my feet.

"Seriously," he asks. "How are you holding up?"

"My toes are killing me, and I've got a blister starting on my right foot."

"I've got duct tape if you need it," he says.

"Duct tape?"

"Yeah, it's great. Put duct tape over your blisters and it's like having second skin. Feels good."

"Just one more use for duct tape," I add.

"The stuff is great, isn't it?"

"Sure is, I used to fix all the vapor hoses on my Datsun with...whoa...hey now." A gust of wind catches my pack and I lose my footing. Coming to my knee only an inch from the cliff, my body and most of my weight look over to see a few pebbles bounce down the rock face. They move in slow motion and twist and turn and catch ledges all the way down. At least a thousand feet. Paul grabs my pack and pulls me onto the trail.

"You alright?"

"I'm good," I say, and get back to my feet, being careful to stay away from the edge. "The wind caught me like a sail."

"It almost had me, too," he says. "We've got to watch these corners."

"No doubt." My heart is racing. I can still see the pebbles falling through the air. I shake it off and begin again, slowly and cautiously. Step by step.

I can feel the dirt on my knee drying up and it is tight, like a bandage wrapped over a scar. The wind continues to threaten and every few switchbacks it presses against me and rocks me a little. Paul is having trouble too, but manages it well and walks through the wind with a determined look. He gains a switchback and then I lose him around the corner. Too tired to catch up, I move slowly and can really feel the pain now. The blister on my toe is screaming, and my knees and shins are beginning to get tight. I thought that hiking down would be easier than up, but it occurs to me I am using muscles I've never used before. My legs are having to stop my weight from falling and they are weak and can't take much more. Rounding the corner, Paul is a good distance ahead. A couple hundred feet down maybe. He shows no sign of stopping for a break, so I try to pick up my pace. It is no use. Moving slow helps the pain. I grimace with every short step and begin to count the hours since we left. It must be three hours now. We left at around ten and it has to be one or two o'clock. I left my watch in the van thinking I wouldn't need it, so I'm not sure of the exact time. Still, the canyon looks deep and judging up from down, we are only about halfway. This is going to be a tougher hike than I imagined.

We are probably moving at three miles per hour, and it is a nine-mile hike. That means three hours to the bottom. We can't be moving that quick or we'd be there. We must be moving at two miles per hour, that would mean a little over four hours. Maybe the canyon is deceiving and we are almost to the bottom. No, no way. There's a long way to go. I still haven't seen the river.

We've been at it for four hours now. Paul is a good 300 feet down. He's slowed his pace, but is still increasing the distance from me. Every step sends a jolt through my legs. I can feel the raw flesh on my toe. The skin folds up and then down every time I take a step. It is a terrible pain. My knees feel arthritic and my mouth is cotton dry. I'm too weak to get water and there is too far to go to stop and take a break. Besides, if I stop, I won't get going again. This isn't a pain that is eased by resting. My pack is heavy and bends my back straight. It rubs weight against me and I feel it slide left and right as I rock my body down the path. Who cares about the ledge? Who cares about the cliff? Quicker to the bottom, that's what I say. Quicker to the bottom. Could slide right off and beat Paul to the campground. Just lie there and wait for him and when he comes walking up, say, "Hey, what took you so long?" "Don, what happened to you?" he'll ask. "You're as flat as a pancake." That would be funny. Man, this hurts. This hurts bad. This is torture-sort of pain. This is worse than the torture they do to fighter pilots when they get shot down. *I will not tell you any secrets. I am a good soldier. A good soldier. Ouch, okay, okay, we have missiles aimed at your cities. We're going to fire them tomorrow after the president eats his breakfast. There, leave me alone.*

Four and a half hours, I've lost Paul but I have seen the river. Back a few switchbacks, I got my first glimpse of it and it looked like heaven. Except it looked like hell too, as it was so far away. I must be inside the second canyon. The one that isn't visible from the top. There is some grass down here and the path is wider. It has cooled off significantly and the air feels good. There is a thundercloud building overhead and it gives welcome shade. No rain, but good, fresh shade. I plod the trail, keeping my head down and eyes fixed on the dusty, cursed path. My mouth is still cotton dry and I can't gather enough spittle to moisten my tongue. Everything is aching. I've reduced my pace to that of a turtle. I'm depleted, almost completely out of energy.

The path takes a bend and becomes a narrow ledge that overlooks a small, green valley. The rocks are no longer brown, they are gray. I follow the brown trail down the gray rocks as it makes a wide, deep loop and ends up below and opposite me. There is a narrow creek, a little stream that feeds some plant life, giving the valley color. My eye is so pleased at this sight, this very different sight, that I am energized and lift my feet a little above a drag as I take in the view. I haven't seen green in five hours. And water. Look at it. Listen to it lightly tap against the rocks. Following the stream with my eye, I see the trail where it meets the creek and there sits my old friend Paul. He has his pack off and is eating an apple and wearing a smile with bright eyes.

I really pick up my pace here, showing off for Paul. Making out like I'd not had such a rough go of it.

"We made it, bud," he greets me as I come toward him on the lower part of the trail.

"This is it?"

He holds up a finger, "Only one more mile. And it's an easy one."

"How do you know?"

"A ranger told me."

"Where is he?"

"He went back to the campground."

The stream gurgles next to us and the air lifts off it, cool and moist.

"How long have you been here?" I ask.

"About twenty minutes." Paul throws his apple core into the grass on the other side of the stream. "How are you feeling?"

"Like a million bucks," I say. "How about you?"

"I'm thinking about going for a little jog later."

"A jog, huh?"

"Yep," he says.

"Well, I suppose we should crank out this last mile. If I stop, I'm not going to get started again."

"Yeah, I'm game for that," Paul says as he lifts his pack. "You want water first?" He's got a canteen open and he hands it to me. Without answering I take about five swigs. Big swigs that fills my belly and suddenly it feels like I've eaten Thanksgiving dinner. I'm full and feeling a little queasy.

"You sure you don't want to stop and rest?" he asks.

"I'm fine."

The texture of the trail has changed. It is more sand than dirt. White sand and at places it becomes thick. My feet drag into it and sink an inch or so. Paul has these red tennis shoes on and when he steps the sand goes over his heels and spills down into his shoe. When he lifts up his foot, I can see that he has covered a blister with duct tape.

"How's that duct tape working?"

"Hurts like crazy," he says. "You got blisters?"

"Big as Texas," I say.

We both drag and rock and sway with grimacing expressions. The trail swings away from the stream and, once again, begins descending.

"It's a lot cooler down here," I say. "I wonder if it is because we are close to the river?"

"I don't think so. I mean, we are close to the river, but it feels to me like a cold front moved in while we were hiking. That cloud up there. I bet you it's got cold weather in it."

"You think?" I ask, making conversation with short breaths, holding back the pain in my legs.

"I think so," he begins. "We dropped a lot of altitude today. It should actually be warmer down here than it is up there. And instead it's gotten cooler. I think it is a cold front."

"Makes sense, I guess."

Just as the pain is about to do me in, the trail offers a view of the broad, milky brown Colorado River. It has no beach, only canyon walls. This is it. The bottom of the Grand Canyon. Only a few hundred feet down. The river snakes its dark, flat belly around a bend and it is something to see. Dirt-brown water with white-foamy ripples on the banks. It is slapping its sides against the canyon wall like a dragon caught in a fishing net. Really powerful looking. The trail bottoms out where the stream that we were near empties out into the canyon. We follow the trail as it begins to climb, up to a ridge where an enormous, steel-cabled bridge crosses the river. It's only as wide as a sidewalk, but sturdy as a bridge can be. They must have built it to withstand a flood. It is a good fifty feet off the water and they have burrowed a hole through the rock to get to it. Paul leads through the dark opening and rounds the corner where we are met by a grated walkway that is walled by tight-cable handles. Stepping out on the bridge, the Colorado is visible directly below us. We make our way to the middle and stop to take in the view. Below the bridge, to the right, there is a little beach where another stream empties into the river from the north side. This must be Phantom Ranch, the campground we are staying at tonight. A few white-water rafts are pulled onto the beach. Enormous rafts they are, with built-in coolers in the middle. They look like they could seat twenty people or more. The bridge sways and the river blows air through the grate like a fan.

"I think we made it," I say.

"Looks like we did." Paul turns and takes tired steps down the other side of the bridge where the trail drops immediately onto the beach. The tall, narrow gateway that is the river basin lifts hundreds of feet above me.

I make my way behind Paul and the pain darts through the tendons in my legs. All I am thinking about is getting to our camping space and sitting down. The pain increases with every step. A ranger stands at a wooden gate down near the beach. He welcomes us and points us toward Phantom Ranch which is another hundred feet up in a little side canyon.

—— —— ——

The camping space is small and marked with little rocks that separate us from our neighbors. It slopes toward the creek and there is a big rock right down on our very own beach. The water rushes over it and makes a soothing sound. I drop my pack to the ground and have a seat on the picnic table. Then I lie down. My muscles tighten and throb. They relax, then they tighten and throb again. My head is spinning and my belly is still filled with sloshing water. Even though I am still, I can feel it sloshing. My body rocks the way a body rocks when you've been in the ocean all day, and you still feel the waves lifting you long after you are on dry land. I can feel the blood running through my veins. I feel it pulsing in my legs and in my feet. I feel it in the arteries around my sore heels and around my toenails that for more than five hours were pressed forcefully against the front of my boot.

Paul sets his pack down on the ground and rests his back against it. Then he slides down and uses it as a pillow. As he takes off his shoes, I can see he's got a little blood coming from his heel. It makes me wonder what my heels looks like. I don't have the energy to take off my boots. Just want to lie here and watch that thunderhead roll over. It rolls soft and slow. Deep and dark. The cottonwoods frame it nicely and the river plays gently with the rocks and I ache and rock and sway and the blood runs through my veins.

11. Phantom Ranch

There is a buzz, or rather a moan, about Phantom Ranch. Hikers are in pain to the right and the left. In the site next to ours there is a girl with an enormous backpack. She has taken off her boot and is now peeling her sock from her foot like a second skin. Her foot is poultry-white and swollen. She massages it with her hand and grimaces. She's a small girl and I feel for her. Her pack is twice the size of mine. She unstraps her sleeping bag, pushes the backpack off the table and unrolls her bag to slowly lay on top. One booted foot and one bare foot hang off the table and she rests on her stomach and uses her arms as a pillow. She makes me think I've not got it that bad.

Paul is doing what he can to make camp. He finds a soft piece of ground and unrolls his sleeping bag. He takes his little stove out and fiddles with the propane knob. Getting it right, he strikes a match and the blue flame shuffles through the black burner.

"You want some cider?" He asks.

"Not right now."

There are a couple of pros in the site behind us. They've carried a big tent and are efficiently putting it together. They are wearing all the right clothes and have expensive shoes. Their packs are large frame-packs and they've brought the gear necessary for a long stay. Their stove makes Paul's look tiny. It has four burners and a large propane tank fastened to the side.

Across the creek is the trail we hiked in on. Five or six campers are making their way up the trail. They must have come in on rafts because they show no sign of being weary. They are laughing and getting along.

"You hungry at all?" Paul asks.

"Yeah. A little. Haven't eaten since this morning."

"Do you want to warm your beans on the stove?"

Paul and the stove are ten feet away. Much too far to walk. And in order to get over there, I'd have to come down off this table. I'm not sure I can do that.

"Nah. I'll just eat it cold," I say.

"A real man," Paul says.

Leaning my pack against the table, I can see down into the pouch where my clothes and Bible are. I am thankful for having left Emily and my heavier Bible in the van. The added weight might have done me in. I pull the beans out of the side pocket and grab a spoon from the same pouch.

"You want Tabasco sauce?" Paul has a little bottle of Tabasco and he throws it over. "The stuff is potent," he warns.

I pour about half of the little bottle into the bag.

"Don, I'm telling you, it's hot."

"I know what I'm doing."

"That's right. You're a Texan."

"Let me show you how it's done," I say.

Paul is right. The stuff is hot. This isn't pecante sauce. This is flaming hot. I try not to let on, but Paul has a good laugh as he watches me suck air.

"No problem," I say and then cough. "Whoa. This is good stuff."

"I think your tongue is on fire, Don."

I reach down for my canteen and drink it to the bottom. The water offers no relief.

"You want some more water?" He holds up his canteen and I go over to get it. He holds it so I can't get to it and I'm coughing something terrible.

" 'I know what I'm doing,' " he mocks.

"I'm fine. Just thirsty." I pin him down with my knee and grab the canteen. Doubled over, I cough and my eyes are watering. I take the water and hold it in my mouth, in my cheeks and run it over my tongue.

"Texas boy had some trouble with that," Paul chuckles.

"No. No, it just went down the wrong tube."

Paul gives a good laugh and slaps my back. I return to my bag of beans and dip my fork ever-lightly into the food like a chip in a bowl of hot sauce. Twice shy.

Having eased my hunger pains, I lay myself down on my bag next to Paul. We talk about the day, about the hike, and about tomorrow's departure. We will leave just after sunrise. We'll get a jump on it, we say. Leaving early will have us at Indian Springs campground just after noon or so and so we may get in a day hike before sundown. I'm not solid in my thinking about this. I imagine I will be in great pain tomorrow morning, and another hike once we arrive at Indian Springs, right now, seems out of the question. But tomorrow is tomorrow and tonight all I can do is rest.

A ranger comes around and tells us there is a gathering up near the cabins. A little show that the rangers put on. Paul looks over and raises his eye. I shake my head that I am not interested and he seems to lose interest with me.

"I don't think I will be going anywhere till tomorrow morning," I say.

"I'm all for that."

"You know, I'm really not looking forward to tomorrow's hike. I'm in a lot of pain. It's going to be tough."

"We'll go slow," Paul says. "We've got all day so we can take our time."

The sun is under the canyon rim and what is left of light is shaded by the thunderhead. It rolls over, thick and gray, threatening rain. Visible from Phantom Ranch is just a sliver of heaven. The cloud breaks here and there and reveals a little blue. It is a deep blue, an evening blue with the showing of a few stars that struggle against the lingering sunlight. From our camp we can see where the gathering is going to be and the rangers have a fire glowing. I can't make out the flames, but the canyon wall is dancing with shadows and light.

The rafters go merrily from their camps to the gathering. They laugh and make conversation and walk with a certain skip in their steps. They get along pretty well. One tells a joke and they laugh and another adds to it and they laugh again. They go on like that all the way up the trail and over the little crest to where the shadows are dancing on the wall. What is joy? I ask myself. Why are these people happy? Is it the beauty that surrounds them? Is it the company they keep? Are they consumed by the adventure they are on? Don't they know that there are bills piling up in their mailboxes? Don't they know that they have to return to the work that pays their bills, to the tension that exists in at least some of the relationships they left behind? Don't they know that their joy is balanced on the pinhead of ignorance, and that any second the whole thing will come crashing down? When they look into the eyes of their lovers, how can they look past the inevitable separation that will come with death? Why aren't they clinging to each other in fear?

To understand this, I must rely again on my theory of dual joys: ignorance-based joy and truth-based joy. Some find joy in the lack of knowledge. They have blinders on, so to speak. I'm beginning to believe that the only real joy is in Christ.

Though I have been a Christian for many years, I have never given myself completely to God. I have never allowed myself to belong to Him. The body of Christ, to me, is simply an association of the like-minded. I am a Christian as I am a Republican, or a businessman, or a member of a certain club, or a fan of the Houston Astros. It is a part of my identity but it does not encompass me.

The crux of my situation is that, while I understand and accept the Christian message, I often do not view my life through this paradigm. I am a Christian, but do not see the world as a Christian should see the world. Case in point: A person who has a Christian perspective will turn the other cheek, knowing that it is more important to win his foe with love than seek revenge. This same Christian will give his money cheerfully, knowing that it will go to strengthen the gospel message. He will ache with the lonely and the hungry. He will be aware that many around him are spiritually lost and take steps to introduce them to Christ. He believes the Scriptures. He knows joy because he knows he is a child of God, that he is forgiven and can trust God to care for his needs. He praises and worships, he reads books about the God he has come to love. Life is good for him; the air is crisp and the weather is beautiful and his wife and children are a gift he feels he does not deserve. God is always giving him little things and they have a special, personal understanding of each other. He has a Christian perspective, you see.

But let's say this good man does not go all the way in his belief. Let's say he attends church, reads Scripture here and there, but goes no further. His demeanor may turn sour. His wife may lose her charm and he may feel like God gave him this terrible woman to live with. He doesn't like to give his money because he thinks the pastor lives in a house which is too big. Bigger than his, anyway. And this isn't fair to him.

He has a Christian understanding of life, but still subscribes to the world's way of looking at things. He is miserable and his self-pity is all centered around his lowly life. How could God do this to him? Why has God made him to be so miserable?

To explain my current state, I must tell you that I am somewhere in the middle of these two paradigms. I am not miserable. My introspection is not fueled by depression. But neither am I satisfied. If God has more for me to enjoy, more for me to understand, more of a communion to be given, I want it. What fool wouldn't?

Tomorrow, when I am not so tired, I will make a little check list of errors in my thinking; bitterness, sloth, and that sort of thing. Perhaps I should really break this list down and get specific. I have a sharp tongue, for instance. But tonight I am too tired. I'll do it tomorrow.

The sun has set in the canyon. Outside this hole there are probably purple clouds on the horizon. But we are in darkness now. The cloud overhead has blended with the black and there is little light around Phantom Ranch. The flames flicker against the rock but the distant laughter has silenced and the campers are probably gathered around a ranger who explains away the canyon in Darwinian terms. And the campers "ooh" and "ahh" like children following the pied piper.

Paul pushes his pack back a little and takes a restful position, and finally, after a short battle of will, he closes his eyes. I take the same position but the tiredness doesn't lure me. I am thinking about tomorrow's hike and the many miles to the rim of the canyon. What pain I experienced today might double tomorrow. "It is harder going up than coming down," the hikers we met had said. If Bright Angel trail is as steep as Kaibab, I am in for a good bit of discomfort.

Lord God, I made it to the bottom of the canyon. I'm not being completely honest with Paul about my fear. I don't know if I can make it out of here. It's a long way to the top.

I guess I'm asking for some confidence. Maybe some relief from the pain in my feet and legs. I'm worried, Lord.

The campsite is still. There is a light, moist breeze that carries the scent of cool weather. The cloud is getting thin in places and moonlight shines through in a withdrawn glow. It comes down in the cottonwoods and falls peacefully on the creek. The fire that flickered on the canyon wall is extinguished and I am left with soft, faded moonlight from a quarter-moon now visible in the silver fringes of the cloud. Stars number endlessly, shallow and deep, all sizes fixed in clusters. A few share no stage. They are solo and bright and enjoy an inch of deep blackness on all sides. I remember Abraham and how God said his descendants would number as the stars. One of these is me and one of them is Paul. My mother is one and my sister and all the folks back home. If they could only see me now. Stuck in a hole so deep it invites tourists from around the world. My friends look down and smile and twinkle and it makes me miss them. This one, to the right and deep, is Mom. She's got all sorts of little ones around her and she's teaching them a Bible story. And that one is Fred. He's twinkling and competing for attention with neighboring stars. He's always got a show going on.

If You could make a little of the pain go away tomorrow, I'd be much appreciative. It would help a great deal.

That star there, that is Kristin. I miss her. She is bright but fades quickly. Beautiful and shy, just like Kristin.

Lord God, I lift up Kristin. Kristin and Mom and Fred and all the guys back home. Be with them, Lord. Show Yourself to them like You are showing Yourself to me and Paul. Help me out of the canyon, Lord, I'm going to need Your help out of the canyon.

12. Bright Angel

Paul is out of his bag and so are most of the other campers. The early bird catches the worm. But I have never been one for worms. I am not sure what the late bird catches but I will feast with him today. Probably porridge.

By the time Paul returns from brushing his teeth, I have two pair of socks on each foot and am dealing with my boots and their tightness over the two socks.

"Little nippy this morning," Paul remarks. "Did you get cold last night?"

"Didn't notice till I got up."

"Cold front must have moved in," he reports.

We make talk about the weather for a while and then Paul gets serious about hitting the trail. He's moving with a weariness but has determination in his motion like he's working through the pain.

"If we get moving we'll warm up," he counsels.

"Yeah." Under my breath.

My ankles are weak and my knees are stiff. Not as bad as I thought they would be, but stiff nonetheless. I bend my knees and walk around camp, rolling my bag and tying my gear on my pack. Paul hands me a banana and I peel it slow, taking my time. We sit on the picnic table and take one last look at Phantom Ranch.

"How do you suppose they got the wood down here to build those cabins?" Paul wonders.

"Helicopter?" I offer.

Paul looks down the creek toward the Colorado. "I bet you they brought the wood in on the river."

"There's white water on that river, isn't there?" I ask.

Paul looks up and studies the canyon walls. "It's too narrow here for a helicopter. They had to use the river. I bet they used the river."

"Helicopter," I say, studying the walls. "Do you think we could catch a ride? There's probably another supply coming in soon. We could make like construction workers and hitch a ride."

Paul sticks his thumb out like a hitchhiker and looks up at the sky. I do the same. We look and look but no helicopter. I lift my thumb way up in the sky and make a pouty face. "Hello, helicopter," I say. We have a good laugh as two hikers come up the trail and make strange, subtle glances at us.

"You feeling okay?" Paul asks, breaking the joking mood.

"Better than I thought I would."

"That's good."

"Yep."

"You ready to get going?" He asks.

"Yep."

"Why do you suppose they call it Bright Angel trail?" Paul asks. "Do you think it's an Indian thing?"

"I don't think so," I say. "In fact, I know that's not why. You see, Paul, there was this traveling fellow named Bright Angel, that was his name, and he discovered this path down the canyon. So they named it after him. He was good friends with Henry Grand, who discovered the canyon initially."

"Is that right?" Paul says. And I knew he would say that.

"Sure is."

"You know, Don," Paul begins. "I've taken for granted how smart you are."

"I've been meaning to talk to you about that," I smirk.

I've embraced Paul's mentality about working through the pain. My weak ankles strengthen and I find my stride to keep pace with him as we begin the ascent. Within minutes my breathing is full. My lungs are at capacity. He isn't moving so quick and part of me believes he is going slow to be considerate. No matter, this is fast for me. At least this first hour.

This trail is different than Kaibab in texture and color. The rock is gray here, where Kaibab showed red and brown for the entire descent. The cliff on the right side of the trail is not so steep. As we climb, we go deep into the canyon wall. We are following a flood course of some sort. I imagine this little gorge as an enormous creek bed that empties into the Colorado. It carries nothing but rock, now, but there are grasses and shrubs deep in the crevasse. There is a little water in there somewhere. There must be a small trickle.

I think to myself about the weight in my pack. Last night Paul and I talked a bit about the passage in Hebrews that says, "Lay aside every encumbrance, and the weight which so easily entangles." We said that sin-habits were unneeded weight and that carrying them was like taking a refrigerator with you into the canyon. Paul went on about it and it really began to sink in for him. He talked about how silly it would be to take heavy things on a trip like this. And he said that God has a plan for everybody and when we sin, we carry the unnecessary baggage. When we try to carry the baggage for a worldly life on the difficult incline of the Christian life, we lose heart. That's how he put it. Meanwhile, I was thinking, why is it that Christians have to make analogies out of everything? I once heard a sermon where a fellow explained away the power of the Holy Spirit by comparing it to the miracle of airplane flight. He said that God had made certain laws and when we are in sync with the Holy Spirit, it is like an airplane being in sync with the sky. If we do things right, the Spirit of God will lift us up. Silly.

Jesus used parables. This is the party line for every preacher, every Sunday school teacher, every Christian writer who uses too many stories to illustrate a point. The point usually gets lost in the story anyway. Besides, Jesus was always having to explain His parables. The disciples never got it. Theologians still have to explain those parables. Could it be that Christ was speaking to the spirit of man, not the sleepy-headed pilgrim who is looking for sheep to count? Too much chicken soup for the soul is not a good thing. Working men eat meat and potatoes.

Paul's analogy isn't so bad, though. The Christian life doesn't involve much except studying the Bible and living by faith. And this verse in Hebrews really helps out. Sin is like a brick in your pack, Paul said. We wouldn't want to hike the canyon with a pack full of bricks, would we? He had a good long thought about that. I didn't dare say anything about the contemporary Christian abuse of analogies. This just wasn't the moment. And like I said, he had a good one. And I suppose I thought about it a little myself. As long as I am making a list of those issues where my view of life does not match the Christian view of life, I might as well make a list of sin habits too. Bricks in my pack, to follow Paul's analogy.

So two lists are in order. When I get to Indian Springs, I will take a sheet of notebook paper and create two columns. In one column I will write my view on a certain issue, and on the other I will write the way God would want me to think about the issue. Money, for instance, is an issue, or a category that I could list. Sex is another. Art and entertainment could be one. On art and entertainment I would put "pleasure" on my view of it and "edification" on God's side. This to say that I view art and entertainment as a way to please myself, and God views it, or gives it to us, as a tool to edify each other and return praise to Him. So my view on art and entertainment is off by a mile. I imagine my view on money and sex are going to be off as well.

Coming down the trail is a family with nice clothes, nice shoes, and fresh, store-bought backpacks. I give trail and they thank us as they amble by. One of them, the lady, asks us if we're heading all the way to the top or just to Indian Springs. Indian Springs, I tell her. Not much further. Just around the bend. They move on and I look back at Paul as if something isn't right. We've been hiking for three hours. We couldn't be there already.

Paul steps out in front. "Didn't take long."

"Not at all. I thought it was halfway."

"Thought so too."

"Seems like we just got started."

"We did. It's still morning." Paul looks up at the sky, finds the sun, and makes a shadow on his eye with his hand. "It's about 11:00."

"Really?" Eleven o'clock, Paul?"

He takes his hand down and grabs at the straps under his arms. "Yes. Eleven o'clock."

I look up with my hand making a shadow on my eyes. "About 11:17. Right about 11:17 if you ask me."

—ᵛᵛ— —ᵛᵛ— —ᵛᵛ—

I'm worried about not splitting the hike evenly. If we've only done three miles today, tomorrow will have six for us. And if we've only risen a couple thousand feet then we have the other thousands for tomorrow. That's a long walk. I'm about tuckered out now, and today was an easy day. I don't let the fear get in my eyes, though. Not for Paul to see. We're having a good time all around. Even with the toughness of the climb.

I follow him around the bend to see green and trees. Indian Springs. I don't know what I imagined, nothing really. I never pictured it, but certainly didn't expect this. Patches of grass, shrubs, a big rest room area, and picnic tables with concrete covers. It's a Texas roadside park right here in the canyon. They brought it in on helicopters, no doubt.

We come into the campground from the rear. There is a well, with a bucket on a rope, built from river rock with a stream running beside it. Willows line the stream and tall grasses stand in bunches. A broad space built in a valley, the National Park Service has lined the trails with rock and the stubble grass grows in with cactus in the places they don't let hikers walk. There must be 30 or more campsites, each with a picnic table and a cement structure slanted above it. There are no cabins. Only one building and it's a large outhouse with a girl door and a boy door. Paul chooses a picnic table furthest from the trail.

"This alright with you?"

"Fine."

Eat, drink, and be merry. Whoever said that had more than beans and rice, that's for sure. Eat what, beans and rice? Whoever had a good time eating beans and rice? Look, off in the distance, the prodigal son! Cook up the best beans and boil some rice. Get out the canteens and pour water in everybody's cup until they run over. We're gonna party. Let the water flow. Bring out the Tabasco sauce. The prodigal son is coming up the bayou, yonder, and we're gonna cook beans and rice for sure.

What is it they eat in Arizona anyway? In Texas we eat bar-b-que and it's good. Restaurants such as Luthers and Central Texas Bar-b-que. They cook their meat in huge, black, greasy pits made from old barrels. Two-hundred gallon barrels. In Louisiana they eat crawfish and boudan. They have those deep-fried donuts in the French Quarter and drink coffee and listen to poor men with worn shoes play "When the Saints Go Marching In." But what about Arizona? Mexican food, I guess. Southwest cuisine. My mouth is watering even now. Scrambled eggs on flour tortillas. Pecante sauce with fried onions on a big, thick ceramic plate that screeches when you run your fork across it. I'd love a plate of that right now.

Paul shifts his weight and notices the ache on my face. "You thinking deep?"

"Deep?"

"You've got a deep look on your face," he says.

"No."

"No what?"

"Not thinking deep."

"What are you thinking about?"

"Food."

Paul sits up. He lets out a gasp, a sharp gasp like he's got an empty stomach too. "We've got beans and rice. A banana?"

"Later. I'm daydreaming about real food right now. You know, real food. Truck stop food or Mexican food."

Paul lifts his tired body out of the dirt and wipes the dust from his shorts as he sits beside me on the table. "If you could have any food right now, what would it be?"

"You're not helping. I'm really hungry."

"Think about it. What food would you want?"

"Chicken fried steak," I say. "But I don't know."

"Sounds good. That's one thing I'm going to miss about the South, Don. The food. There isn't any food in the world like Texas food."

"You can say that again. I've never been much outside of Texas, but I can tell you that there is no food anywhere like we've got it...anywhere."

"Any food, Don. What would you have?"

"You listen to Lyle Lovett much?"

Paul shrugs his shoulders. "What does Lyle Lovett have to do with anything?"

"I'm getting there. He sings this song called "Nobody Knows Me Like My Baby." You ever heard it?"

Paul shrugs his shoulders again. He doesn't answer but looks out at the field of grass and sand and lets his eye climb the tall wall of rock where he finds a skeletal tree frozen against the sky. His eye stops on the tree and I can tell by his look that he's calculating the distance to the top.

"It's a good song," I say.

"What does it have to do with food?"

"You'd have to hear it to understand."

"You're gonna tell?"

"Well...it goes...and I don't remember the words exactly, but it goes *I like to sleep late on Sunday, I like cream in my coffee, I like my eggs over easy, with them flour tortillas.* He says *them* flour tortillas. He doesn't say just flour tortillas but he says *them* flour tortillas, you know. With that Texas dialect."

"He's a Texan?"

"Yes, from Houston. Went to Texas A&M and his roommate was Robert Earl Keen Jr."

"Who's that?"

"Doesn't matter. Listen to how the song goes..."

"He sings a song about food." Paul looks frustrated as he ponders the distance to the tree in the sky.

"No, it's not about food. It's a love song," I say.

"A love song about sleeping late and eating eggs. Your kind of love song, Don."

"Listen to how it goes. He sings, and it's real slow, by the way. Just him and this real slow guitar part and he goes *I like to sleep late on Sunday, I like cream in my coffee, I like my eggs over easy, with them flour tortillas. And nobody knows me like my baby.*"

Paul rests easy and lets his eyes come off the tree in the sky. He puts his eyes on the field of grass and sand and thinks to himself.

"See how the song is?" I begin. "It's about this girl. His wife maybe, I don't know. But she knows everything about him. About how he likes to sleep late on Sunday and have breakfast with flour tortillas and about how she's the only one who makes his coffee right. It's a love song like that."

"Sounds like you're hungry for more than food, Don." He says this with a laugh. A narrow laugh.

"I don't know, but for about an hour I've had that song on my mind. Maybe because it's the only song I know that has food in it."

"You miss Kris?" Everyone back home called Kristin "Kris." Paul is referring to the girlfriend I broke up with.

"A little. Last night I missed her a little."

Paul gets a sly look on his face. A to-the-point, sly look. "She ever make you breakfast like that? Like that song?" He knocks my leg with his fist.

"Kristin?"

"Yeah. She ever make you breakfast?"

"No. And I know what you're getting at."

"Just asking."

"She's not like that. I hope I'm not either. But she's pretty strong. We did all right."

"Didn't mean to pry."

"Don't worry about it. You weren't prying. But she isn't like that. She's a pretty good girl."

"You think she's the one, Don?"

"You mean *the* one? The one and only?"

"Yeah," he confirms.

"No."

"I guess that's why you broke up with her."

"Yeah. I guess." The sweat on my legs and arms is beginning to chill. I'm wishing for a jacket or a sweatshirt. "You know, Paul," I start, "I think she was going to break up with me anyway."

"What makes you say that?"

"Little things. She would say little things. Do little things. I don't think she was really into it."

"How long did you two date?"

"Not long."

"How long?"

"About six months or so."

"That's pretty long. Some folks figure it all out in that amount of time."

"I really liked her, Paul. She just wasn't in it. I think I dropped the bomb first. But she was about to do it anyway." That last sentence is said with tenderness. As if to release some small ache. Paul's expression gives sympathy. But he doesn't know it is more the pain in my legs than the pain in my chest that is causing this melancholy. Kristin is Kristin. A beautiful girl. My first girlfriend and I miss her. But she and I were never meant to be. She was in between boyfriends and was too pretty to go without. I was there like a number in a bakery. She pulled the ticket, glanced at it, and waited to exchange me for some loaf of bread or cake or pie or feeling that she was beautiful. I'm just a sap who adored her and wanted to hold her hand or sit close or look into her eyes. But I gave her the slip. Came right out of her hands before she could claim her prize and I bet you, I bet you a million dollars she doesn't even remember that number. She'll just pull another ticket, glance at it, and wait for them to call her out. She won't remember the things I said and won't realize I had never said them to another girl. She'd heard them before and it all ran together like bad poetry. You could see it in her eyes when I talked to her. You could hear it in the way she said *thank you* when I complimented her dress or the color of her eyes. And I suppose if I'm honest with myself, if I'm truly honest, I'd have to say I loved her. I do love her and want to cling to the thought that maybe she wouldn't have ended it. Maybe we would have made a couple like we talked about. And maybe it isn't the pain in my legs or the empty in my stomach that is making me mellow. Maybe it's this canyon, and the feeling that I'm in so deep I will never get out. And maybe I'm carrying a pack so heavy, so filled with bricks that it won't so much as move. And I'm too stupid to leave it where it is.

"You know what I'd want? If I could eat anything right now?" Paul licks his lips. "I'd like a big bowl of Raisin Bran. With big, plump raisins and cold milk."

"That does sound good, Paul. Raisin Bran."

"You never answered my question, Don."

"What was that? What meal would I want?"

"A meal. Any meal. What would it be?"

I rest back and look up at the tree in the sky. "I'd like eggs over easy. With them flour tortillas."

13. Reward

My feet are frozen. I roll myself over to my back-pack and pull out every article of clothing. I shove the underwear and T-shirts to the bottom of my sleeping bag and wrap my toes in the fabric. But nothing helps. This is an Antarctic cold. A cold that has gone from blue to black. There is no light on the horizon. The sky is so heavy it drips dense shadows down the canyon walls. I look over at Paul and he's deep into his sleep. He is zipped up and snoring and though his breathing is not loud, or even both-ersome, it irritates because he is doing it and I am not. He told me I'd be cold tonight. He said my bag was a "fair-weather" bag and the temperature would likely fall below freezing. He was right. The bag serves no purpose.

The cold didn't come gradually. It woke me about an hour ago and I've been in pain ever since. I won't be falling asleep again. A fetal position helps my hands and when I raise my shoulders over my neck I can feel some warmth. But I am shaking now. My teeth are chattering like a Dickens' character; an orphan on the streets of old London. Gaslit brick streets with blue tints and iced-over potholes.

I read somewhere that the Earth is perfectly situated. Far enough from the sun that we don't burn up, close enough to keep us from freezing. But we are too far away tonight. The astronomers are awake and at their telescopes and calling each other to confirm that we have slipped out of our orbit. We are spiraling headlong toward the edge of the universe where it is very cold. Or am I just dreaming? Perhaps I am only dreaming.

"Paul," I shake his sleeping bag. "Paul."

He rolls over and runs his hands up the inside of his bag to find the zipper.

"What is it?"

"I'm freezing out here."

Paul opens and closes his eyes slowly. He checks the sky and looks around camp in a daze. "You're cold?" he questions.

"Freezing."

"I'm sorry."

"That's okay. But I need you to do something."

"What's that?"

"Sleep on my feet."

"What?"

I press my feet under his bag. "You have to sleep on my feet. They feel like they're on fire."

He checks the seriousness in my eyes and says nothing. Just lays himself over my feet. I go back into my bag without humiliation or embarrassment. This is beyond anything social. I have to get warm.

Before we left on this trip, my mind's eye had me on mountains, writing poetry in coffee shops, and talking with various proponents of differing worldviews. I had myself in the embrace of beauty, of waterfalls and colorful meadows. I had imagined a pilgrimage. Two sports looking for joy within the truth we knew. And yet here I am, tired, weak, miserably cold.

When James asks us to "Consider it all joy, my brethren when you encounter various trials," is he speaking of tonight? Of the cold and the misery? Is this the joy we are looking for? If so, then I am weak. Most certainly.

The canyon wall carries the sun's shadow like a sundial. I chart its progress, knowing that it will shed warmth on my bag. But it is slow, slow, slow; moving with all the speed of syrup. I set my head deep into the bag and hold my arms around myself to find warmth. Paul has moved off my feet, but I don't wake him because he was no help.

I figure I slept about an hour. Maybe two. Every minute was counted with a thousand clicks of my teeth. The sleepless night has set a sting in my dry eyes. My nose is dry too. The wind rolls through the canyon and it feels like I have no sleeping bag at all. I move my fingers to check the fabric for fear that the whole thing has blown away. I pull my head from my bag to check the progress of the sun; an inch or two. And a mile to go.

I ease my aching body from my sleeping bag and stretch my legs before me. I reach for the sky and yawn. Rolling over, I set my hands against the ground and stand. I feel the bones in my back and my ribs separate from the cartilage. My legs are stiff and my feet are laden with sharp points of pain. My belly is empty.

I had agreed to make my chart when I arrived at Indian Springs. Didn't do it. If I remember correctly, I was going to draw a line down a piece of paper and write "God's Perspective" atop one side and "My Perspective" atop the other. Then I was going to find several areas where my paradigm is out of kilter. Money, Power, Sex, Romance, Church, and so on and so on. Maybe I should begin my task before we leave. I wonder if Paul would be up to sticking around for a while.

"You were right about the cereal, Paul."

"What's that?"

"The cereal. Being the best thing to eat right now. I could go for a big bowl of cereal and cold milk. I might even take that over the eggs and tortillas."

"Now you're coming around. You can't beat cereal. What kind would you want? I'd want Raisin Bran. That's the best."

"Raisin Bran. I'd want Raisin Bran too."

"You know," Paul begins. "It's funny. Two weeks ago when we talked about things we wanted or our aspirations, we would have talked about houses or boats or fast cars. Now that we've been on the road for a while, everything is reduced to a bowl of cereal." Paul develops a smile. "Isn't that just beautiful? Cereal. There are people in this world who are killing themselves because they want more and more of nothing. And the only thing you and I want in this world is a bowl of cereal."

"And a boat," I say.

"What's that?"

"I wouldn't mind a boat. A nice, big sailing boat with a wooden hull. I'd like to eat my cereal on my boat."

"You ruin everything, you know that," he says.

Paul has his bag rolled up and is fastening it to his pack. "We should get going. It's getting late."

I break my blank stare and realize that I am not packed. Paul looks eager to hit the trail. "How are we going to get the van?" I ask.

"We will hitchhike to the other trailhead."

"That's right."

"You ready?"

"I need to pack and stuff. I will be ready in a minute."

"I am going to go brush my teeth in the stream. Want to come?" Paul pulls his toothbrush from his pack.

"I think I am going to get some journaling done. Would you mind if I took some time to do that?"

"Are you going to write for a while?"

"I don't know. I want to get a few thoughts down before I forget them. It may take awhile, but I can probably do it tonight, once we get back to the van and all."

"No, don't worry about it. If you want, I can start and you can follow a little later."

"You mean on the trail? You want to go separately?"

"Whatever you want. If you want to write, I could get started." Paul shrugs his shoulders. "Whatever you want, Don."

"Yeah, I might as well do this now. I'll meet you at the top."

"Cool." Paul takes off with his toothbrush and I go over to my pack and pull out my pen and notebook. While rummaging around, I try to remember exactly what it is I am trying to get down. A grid of some sort that shows my perspective on things versus God's perspective. Or maybe how I currently think about things and then how God would want me think about them. Two columns is all I need.

I sit down at the picnic table and draw a big "T" on the page. Over one column I put "me" and over the other I write "God." Then I go down the far left side of the page and begin writing the different aspects of life that I want to apply to the grid. Sex is the first. Being a guy, this is always first. Then money and possessions, then church, and then friendships. I can't think of anything else right now. Paul comes back up the trail and puts his toothbrush in his pack. I add "hygiene" to my list just for fun.

"I will probably go ahead and get the van. Is that cool?" Paul asks.

"Sure. I shouldn't be far behind you."

"You're just going to stay here and write?"

"I can do this later, Paul. I figure you are going to want to hike faster anyway though, so I thought this would be cool."

"Nothing's wrong?" he asks.

"Dude, no. No way." I get up from the table and go over by Paul. I feel uncomfortable, as it is obvious he thought I was shrugging him off.

"No," I say. "I just wanted to get some stuff written down. Besides, I'm not looking forward to being the slow boat up that hill, you know. You are going to be a mile in front of me before you reach the top anyway. I'm saving myself some face by sticking around."

"Cool," Paul says.

"It's cool" I confirm.

"It's cool, Don. But you haven't eaten or slept and this is the worst part of the hike. You are going to have a tough time. I'm just telling you."

"I hear you. I'm going to get out of this canyon. Stop trying to be my big brother. I'm older than you, remember?"

Paul gives me a grin and a pat on the shoulder. He ambles down the trail with a jug of water sloshing, dangling off the center of his pack. I follow him with my eye as he disappears behind a rock and then appears again. He isn't wearing shoes. He doesn't have any shoes on!

"Paul!"

"Yeah."

"Your shoes?"

"My feet are bleeding. No shoes today."

"You aren't going to wear shoes?"

"No shoes. See you at the top."

He turns and continues, hitting the first switchback in a brisk stride. He rises like a man on an escalator and turns in fluid motions to the up and the up of each switchback. In no less than a few minutes, he is a hundred or more feet in the air and he won't be slowing down for some time. Probably won't even stop for water. Paul is just about the coolest guy I know. That's for sure.

Back at the table I've got my "T" drawn and my "aspects of life" identified. I begin to jot my perspective on these things and then God's perspective in the other column. It goes slow at first, and it is difficult not to lie to myself and to God.

I know about canyons now. I know their depth and their length. I'm half out of this one and I feel as though I've been through a war. My mind is in a canyon too. All of our minds are. We are miles deep in the garbage we were taught in school, in life. The stuff about how we don't matter and how we were accidents. I would have told a person, had they asked me a month ago, that I was no accident; that God had made me and planned me out deliberately that I might have air in my lungs and feeling in my chest, but I don't think I would have believed it. Deep down anyway. Nobody really believes they were put here on purpose, do they? Does anyone believe that anymore? I write down a fifth "aspect of life" on my page. I put "self." And under my column I write ACCIDENT and under God's column I write ON PURPOSE.

Hiking through all this beauty helps me realize that life is like a canyon. We begin at the bottom of something and we spend our lives coming to the top of it. When we begin we don't know anything and we learn and we learn and, well, okay, life isn't really like a canyon at all. Life isn't really like much of anything except life itself.

Life is too complicated to use analogies to describe it. I am but one person and there are billions of other people and each of us have a different understanding of what life is and is about. I am not one of the Christians who believes he has a corner on truth. I believe that Christ has a corner on truth. I actually have the audacity to believe that He was truth. But I am often weak in understanding the truth.

I love books and I wouldn't want to be without them, but we don't learn so much about God from books as we do from day-to-day life. I have a friend who reads two books per day. He is brilliant. But he spends so much of his time in study that he has forgotten what the sun looks like. I have another friend that reads romance novels end to end and yet is scared of boys. She fulfills her fantasies in the stories of others. So it is with the Bible. We read about God's propitiation with the sacrifice given on the cross, yet we do not really accept the forgiveness for ourselves. We really don't believe we've been forgiven, do we? And then there is all this about being altruistic and caring about others. We read that we are supposed to visit orphans and widows, but we don't. It's nice to read about these things, but living them out is another issue. We are no better than the woman who escapes through reading romance novels. We read about our religion, but it is all just theory.

Christianity is a belief system that makes sense and I can call my own. But it should be more to me than something I can believe in, like a fan who roots for a football team.

There was a girl I once knew for several years. She went to my school. A friend, she sat by me in a few classes and we would often study together after school. One day she walked into the library and sat down across the table from me. I cracked a joke and she laughed. She sat back in her chair and smiled and told me I was funny. I looked down and then looked up again. She smiled and I got butterflies. Suddenly, after knowing this girl for years, I developed a crush. She hadn't changed at all. Same girl, same great smile, same warm personality. But this time, and I don't know why, she gave me butterflies.

I say this to illustrate the recent development in my faith. It's not that I have a crush on Christ. The analogy breaks down in that respect. I only mean that I have heard countless sermons about Christ and grown up in a culture that extols Him as God, but it is only recently I have understood this idea on a personal level. And I must say it feels good. He is not only the God of the Southern Baptist Convention, He is my God too. He made me to know Him. He wants me to follow Him. He has gone to prepare a place for me. It is a personal relationship.

I have always tended to associate my spiritual life with church only. But I rarely brought Christ home with me (I say this figuratively). I rarely included Him in my decision-making, in my thoughts about money, socialization, politics, or romance. I treated church like a coach's talk before a big game. I would sit and listen to the game plan outlined and memorize my assignment. Then when game time came I was nowhere near the field.

I literally feel like I am starting over with all of this. I am showing up for the game, helmet on, bright lights overhead, and a cheering cloud of witnesses bellowing their reinforcement from the heavens, from the living text of the Bible itself. And I am making headway. I'm climbing out of my old thinking. I have packed my gear, strapped on my pack, and am leaving the immature paradigm of youth and climbing headlong into a personal relationship with God. So life is like a canyon after all. I was right! I knew that this canyon analogy would come in handy. *Okay, God. I've learned my lesson. You can send the helicopter now.*

There is an exhaustion that strikes deeper than muscle and flesh. It is a bone-deep exhaustion and is all new to me. They talk of a runner's high. I have spent no time running today, but did feel a bit of energy seep from my chemical brain an hour or so ago. It is gone now. The trail continues remarkably steep, but there is traffic on the footpath. Lively children walk briskly with their parents in tow. I sit down on a rock in a crag and look down over the canyon, marveling at the beauty of God's creation.

I have taken more rests without Paul. He would have trudged quickly. Without his quick step to keep me accountable, I struggle. My water is more than half gone. It sloshes in my stomach like a bag of fish. I could throw it up if I wanted. My face must be blue or green. Women have pity in their aspects and men walk by quickly with eyes averted.

Amazingly, I was passed awhile back by a fellow I met years ago in Tennessee. I recognized him coming, but didn't have the breath to address him. He literally grazed my shoulder. I turned, but he was gone before I could process that it was him. He did not recognize me and I can't say I was eager to make contact at this point.

Strapping my canteen to my pack, I shoulder my load and step back onto the trail. My feet drag and slide. My footprints must be long but I am too tired to look and see. The traffic gets heavier with each switchback and the Disneyland atmosphere that surrounded me a couple days ago is coming back to mind. So many happy families on their vacations. Fathers and mothers and grandparents. The presence of older people tells me that I am nearing the rim. A group of elderly folk come down the trail in leisurely strides. The women wear big hats and guard the sun from their eyes with cupped hands. The men grab at their women's elbows when I near, carefully protecting them from a dangerous fall.

I am utterly exhausted and ashamed at my inability to conquer this canyon with dignity. I am passed by nuns, who offer water. One tells me that I am almost there. I nod. Almost there. If only there were here. If only I could drag the rim to me, rather than me to the rim. I am not beneath crawling the last quarter mile.

Finally I see the trailhead. It is close. I stop and lean against the canyon wall to eye my heaven. The trail rises before me and beyond it is the sky. Thirty more steps will have me out of this hole. I make like a good scout and walk the last switchback with no drag in my step, the noblest behavior I can muster. And coming over the ridge I see the Grand Canyon Hotel big and brown across a lawn. One hundred or more tourists are taking pictures. And there is Paul. He has a grin across his face like a man whose wife has delivered a baby. He sits on the beam of a wooden fence and greets me. I walk the last few steps and shake his hand. My good friend Paul. I lean against the fence and look out over the Grand Canyon. A canyon I now know intimately. Paul sets his hand on my shoulder and tells me that I've done it. I hiked the Grand Canyon. None of that matters to me now. Perhaps it will tomorrow or the next day. I am only glad to be done with it.

"I got the van," Paul says.

I acknowledge him with a grunt.

"Had time to stop at the store."

"Is that right?" I whisper.

"Got you a little something while I was there."

I hadn't noticed that Paul was holding anything, but he sets it in my hands. I look down into the tin cup and eye the golden flakes of rapture. Paul reaches into a grocery sack and pulls out a small carton of milk. I hold the tin cup like a beggar and watch the milk flow around the flakes. The raisins lift and swirl. The flakes float to the top and he drops a spoon into the cup. Paul smiles and tells me this is my reward.

14. Miracles

As far as I know, Hoover Dam was engineered by a guy who later made vacuum cleaners. After that he ran for president and had the carpet in the White House clean and fresh for foreign dignitaries. He no doubt felt sorry for the people of Nevada. They live in so much brown. He surveyed the land and decided on a spot to dam the Colorado and give the people of Vegas a place to swim. Lake Mead is big and blue and holds up large party boats with striped canopies and bar-b-que grills that make the boats look like they are on fire when the smoke billows out from under the canopies and lifts gray signals into the desert sky.

I've been driving for a while. Neither of us tired, Paul has been telling me how it goes with a rattlesnake bite. We may do some hiking, he says, and one of us could get bitten. It's a good thing to go over it. He tells me I have to take a razor blade and cut all around the bite, taking a good quarter inch of flesh in the operation. Then the cut has to bleed. It isn't always necessary to suck the blood out, he tells me. I can just let it bleed if I get a good, deep cut going. Most of the poison will bleed out, and while I will feel like I'm dying for a few hours, there is a good chance I will live through it.

All of this is very comforting.

I've been doing some thinking, trying to get my mind off performing surgery on my snake-bit legs. I've been thinking about the little chart I made in the canyon. It all seems idealistic to me. Looking back, I realize I created it when I was tired and my thinking wasn't very clear. I wonder if it is possible for me to think the way God wants me to think. Doesn't seem too easy. Does God really expect me to think as though my mind were a Bible? But this is a silly question. Of course He does. How else would He want me to think?

I do not believe that I have a thinking problem as much as a feeling problem. What I mean is, I know the Christian answer to most questions but I do not always live accordingly. I am no pagan. But my "goodness" is the product of moral upbringing, not of a coherent biblical worldview. I tend to do and think as I feel like doing and thinking. There is rarely an exception. I am guided by Pavlovian instincts. Church culture has a vocabulary, and I have learned it well. There is a dress code too, and my clothes are well within the acceptable parameters. I wear Dockers and plaid shirts, as is silently required of twenty-something Christians. I only vote Republican, which is also silently required.

But I do all of this, not because I want to live scripturally, but because church culture has a certain rhythm. And when you have marched to this beat since infancy, it is difficult to break free from.

But what if my thinking is more controlled by the culture in which I was reared than it is by Scripture? What then? How does a person separate true, personal religion from a religion of conformity? Christianity is not really as white and wealthy and judgmental as we might want it to be.

And perhaps Jesus is not our next candidate for president. Maybe government is government and religion is religion.

But I do not want to be a clone of church culture. Nor do I want to offend it just to demonstrate my individuality. I want to be what God wants me to be. So I must think scripturally about things. Which brings me right back to where I started, like Pooh and Piglet following their own tracks in the snow, searching for the heffalump. So what does godliness look like? How does it sound and what does it wear? Does a good Christian girl want a man who is godly, or does she just want a man who wears Dockers and plaid shirts and gets along well with the pastor, good golf game and all?

I am asking the wrong question. I am smart enough to realize that. When I begin by asking what godliness looks like, I have the wrong end in mind. It is the *process* that is godliness, not so much the end result. A godly man will involve himself in the *process* of being godly. For godliness is not so much a place we are going as it is the going itself.

I do not view my feelings as an accurate measure of truth. They cannot tell me whether I am living a godly life. James Dobson wrote a book called *Emotions: Can You Trust Them?* I didn't read the book, but I know the answer: yes and no. You can trust them if they are right and you can't trust them if they are wrong. Pretty profound, huh? There are passages in the Psalms where David asks God why He has forgotten about him. Did God actually forget about David? Of course not. It is not possible for God to forget about anyone. We are His children and He has numbered the hairs on our heads. David is speaking from his emotions. He's downright depressed, if you ask me. But then, in each of these Psalms, David reflects on where God has brought him and concludes that God never forgot him at all. David does a very interesting thing in Psalm 16. He tells his emotions how to feel. He talks to his soul and tells it to get in line. David is not so foolish as to allow his emotional state to dictate truth.

I have a difficult task ahead of me. This chart I have made tells me where I need to go in my thinking. And I have identified that my emotions do not follow suit. That is, I do not always feel like living my life God's way, or thinking about life God's way. But if this is where God wants me to go, then go I must. Go must we all.

"Water moccasins are a completely different story."

"What's that?" I ask.

"Water moccasins. They are completely different. You can't just cut and get the poison out. It's not that easy."

"I see."

Paul goes on a bit about the variety of snakes in this region compared to the South and the Northwest. He says that there are no water moccasins in Nevada because there is no water. There are rattlers out here, however, he reminds me. We are bound to see one pretty soon, he says. I just drive and watch the road. He has his feet up against the glove box. Red tennis shoes with white stripes. Canvas Adidas. He has an elbow out the window and the warm, midday air swirls in around his ears and lifts his hair to tickle his forehead. He keeps wiping a hand across his face to soothe the itch, all the while talking about snakes.

The road we've chosen is bare. We are coming up from below Vegas. We chose this route because it looked scenic on the map. We thought we might camp out here and hike off into some valley. But so far, the terrain looks rugged and the only good cut through these hills and canyons is the road we're on. The hills are not tall, but steep, so I have to downshift as low as second as we climb. Then back to fourth. Then second again. As we crest a hill, I push the stick out of second and find no resistance in the transmission. I slide over to fourth to drop it in, but the stick is loose. It doesn't go. The van whines in a high rev and races as I press the gas. I pull the stick hard to jam it into fourth but it won't go. It feels like the transmission has dropped out.

"Paul."

"Yeah."

"We've got trouble."

"What is it?"

"No gears. No fourth gear."

"Try third."

"No third. No gears at all."

I spot a small pull-out at the bottom of the hill and navigate the van over the shoulder and down a small dirt inset that parallels the road. Coming to a stop, clouds of dust roll over from the back of the van and down the windshield before dissipating. Again, I try the gears. Nothing.

"Is it the clutch?" Paul reaches over and feels the stick.

"No. The clutch is fine. There wasn't any grind to it at all. I just lost it completely. It can't be the clutch. It's the tranny. Something broke."

"Dog," Paul says. He slaps his hand against the dash. "Dog, dog, dog."

"Dog?" I question.

"Shut up," he says.

I kill the engine and open my door. Nevada is quiet as though it is hiding something. The wind whispers a suspicious sigh. Stepping out of the van, the aches in my knees and muscles flare for a bit. But I can pace it out in a few steps. Paul, without saying a word, gets out of the van and rounds to the driver's side. He presses the clutch and motions the stick to first, second, and all through the gears.

"There's too much play," he says.

"There are no train tracks out here," I announce.

Paul rests his weight and drops his limbs like he's frustrated. "This is crazy. Did you feel it going out?"

"Didn't feel anything. I went to downshift and it wasn't there."

"That's not possible, Don."

"That's what happened." I lean against the van with one hand and hold a thumb out for a ride. No cars are on this back road. We haven't seen one in about twenty minutes. Paul has a frustrated look, both arms laid across the curvature of the steering wheel. He's shaking his head at me now. Thinks I'm acting silly in a serious moment. I point my thumb up a little higher.

"I'm gonna get us out of this jam," I reassure him. "There's no reason to panic."

"I'm not panicking." Paul shakes his head.

He has really had it with this van. It won't surprise me if he burns it. Right here in Nevada. Burns it to the ground. He's got that look going now. Like he lost everything on a bad bet. This is no time to make jokes. I come around the front of the van and stride up to the driver's window. He doesn't follow me with his eyes. He keeps them fixed as if there were some speck of dust on the windshield that had, in the smallest possible print, a word which, if spoken aloud, would solve all the world's problems.

"Frustrated?" I don't look at him. Don't really expect him to answer.

"What do you think?"

"Things could be worse."

"I don't want to hear it, Don."

"You know, Paul, when I was in the orphanage...did I tell you I was in an orphanage?"

Paul shakes his head. There is a beginning of a grin on his lips but he looks away and holds his frown and then looks back at the window.

"When I was in the orphanage, me and the gals used to sing this little song. Paul, I'd like to sing it to you. Maybe you'd like to sing it with me. You'd like that wouldn't you, Paul? Wouldn't you?"

"I don't want to hurt you, Don. I really don't."

I burst into a high-decibel rendition of "Tomorrow," from the Broadway musical *Annie*.

I stop singing because I have forgotten the words. Paul is looking at me without a smile. No frown, but no smile. He reaches over and pats my head. I grin like a dog. Then he grabs the back of my hair and attempts to pull me into the van through the windshield. He's rubbing his hard knuckles against my head. He's singing my little song too.

"Paul, I knew you'd come around. I knew you'd sing with me, bud. Hey, Paul. This kind of hurts a little. I don't like this kind of playing. The girls in the orphanage never did this. They never did me like this."

I stand up to break my mood. I kick a few pebbles across the road. Dust stirs and blows across Paul's lap.

"Sorry," I say. He doesn't move.

Anxious for a change of scenery, I cross the street, set my foot on the bumper of the van and climb up the windshield, careful not to break the wipers with my boot. From the top of the van I can see a bit further. There is nobody out here. Nobody at all.

"Don," Paul yells. He's looking up at me.

"Yeah."

"I'm seriously discouraged."

I look down at Paul. He raises his legs and folds his arms around his knees.

"I don't know what to say, Paul. I can't think of a way out of this mess. We may be here for a while."

"Yeah."

"A car will come. Surely a car will come."

"It's been half an hour."

"Did you ever see that movie 'Trapper John, M.D.'?"

"What?"

"That movie on television: 'Trapper John, M.D.' "

Paul looks up with his hands cupped over his eyes. "It wasn't a movie. It was a television series."

"But you saw it, right?"

"A few times." There is a long silence. "Why do you want to know whether I saw that television show?"

"I feel like Trapper John, M.D."

Paul shakes his head. "Why? Why do you feel like Trapper John and why does it matter?"

"He had an RV and he used to go out in the parking lot and sit on top of his RV and bake in the sun."

"Yeah. So what?"

"I feel like that. Up on the van and all. Makes me feel like Trapper John."

"That's great. But for your information, it wasn't Trapper John who had the motor home. It was the other guy. The guy with the curly hair. The younger guy."

"I thought it was Trapper John."

"Nope."

"Are you sure?"

"Yep," Paul sighs. "What does this have to do with anything, Don?"

I look down at my miserable friend. For a second, I think I'm the crazy one. There is no reason for me to be fooling around. We have no water, so we need a ride. And there have been no cars for the better part of an hour. The sun is in midsky, so even if we get a ride, where do we go? And how do we fix this thing? We don't have money for a transmission and there's no telling what is eaten up under the van. It is basically useless. We will probably have to hitch the rest of the way. Neither of us are going to call home for help. I know that without asking. It is not an option.

Paul looks up and meets my eye. "Do you want to pray?"

Of course. How could I have forgotten about prayer? Leave it to Paul to strike right at the heart of a problem. "Yes. I do."

Paul lowers his head and rests his chin on his knee. He closes his eyes like a schoolboy. His words are soft and low. *"Lord, we are stuck in the desert and the van doesn't work. We don't know what to do. We don't know whether to leave it or what to do. I guess we need a ride or something."* I'm looking out over the hills, watching time dance with the earth. You can almost feel time getting angry. It's getting angry because we didn't ask it to solve our problem. We went outside of time, to a being, a deity, a person who exists outside of time. Paul continues, *"I guess we just need a ride and we'll be fine..."* I interrupt Paul in something like a loud voice. *"We need a mechanic, Lord. That's what we need. If You could send us someone to get us on our way, to help us with this transmission, that would be great."* Paul looks up at me in disbelief. His expression reads: How could you have made such a request? *"Amen,"* I say. Paul stands up and wipes his pants. I'm watching him and feeling stupid because I made such a request. He crosses over in a leisurely stride. I can tell that he is still praying. He wipes his forehead with his hand then pulls his hair back. He paces slow down the shoulder, his back to me.

"Paul." He hears me but he does not turn.

"Paul!"

He turns and responds with a whisper, "Yeah?"

"Look." I point over the horizon. He can't see it yet, but there is a car coming.

"Is it a car?"

"Yes."

He walks quickly to the other side of the road and stands gazing. He's half in the road.

"Be careful," I tell him. He steps back onto the shoulder.

Over the hill comes a station wagon. Brown in color, it matches the landscape. The wagon slows a little as it nears, but speeds up again as the driver realizes it is not a wreck or anything worth looking at. He drives by at about 30 or 40 miles-per-hour and hardly looks our way. There's a man at the wheel, and a woman in the passenger's seat with a few kids in the back. As he passes, the children turn to look at us through the back window. His brake lights flash and then come on solid.

"He's stopping," Paul says.

I slide down the windshield and catch the bumper with my boot. The reverse lights on the wagon come on and the man backs up onto the shoulder. Dust kicks out on either side as the station wagon weaves backward. It's a brown wagon with brown wood-panel trim. A real gas guzzler.

He is a bearded man with a red baseball cap. His beard is untrimmed and his wife looks troubled that he decided to stop. The children are quiet in the back seat. One looks over at me without any expression, then turns back to face forward. The other two do not look. They do not even look at Paul who has begun a conversation with the man. Paul steps away from the door as the man reaches through the open window to pull the outside handle. A closer look at the car reveals it to be quite the jalopy. A rope fastens the hood to the bumper and another of the same sort fastens a suitcase to the roof.

The man steps out of his car and pulls up his sagging pants. Running his hand across the front of his shirt, he tucks it in. He has a tattoo on his forearm of a woman without clothes. She probably had a good figure at one time, but she looks faded, oblong, and tired of being attached to her present company. The man is talking to Paul about the van. He's asking what Paul thinks is wrong with it. Paul tells him it's the transmission and the bearded man just shakes his head and looks out in the desert and shakes his head again. "Sounds really bad," he says.

"Well, you boys are in luck. Probably haven't seen many cars out here, have you?"

Paul confirms that we haven't.

"Not many people get out this way. You could have been here for hours if it weren't for me stopping to help. Not a lot of people would have stopped, you know."

"Thanks," Paul says.

"Don't mention it." The man removes his cap and runs his hand across his thick hair and puts his cap back on. "I'm a mechanic," he says.

"You are? I mean, huh, is that right?" Paul leans against the van and looks away.

"Can you help us?" I ask, trying to get the man to get to the point and ask for the money which is probably the only reason he stopped in the first place.

"Well, I've got business in Las Vegas, and it really does set me back to stop here. I've got an appointment and all, you know."

"I see," I say. "Well, you better get going, then. We wouldn't want you to miss your appointment." Paul looks over at me with a cold look, telling me with his eyes to keep quiet.

"Well, now, wouldn't want to leave you boys stranded. Like I said, there's nobody going to stop for you out here. You were lucky I stopped. Certainly didn't have to."

"Like I said before, we don't want to keep you. We'll figure something out. You can go on."

"I can take a look at it real quick, if you want. I normally don't do this for free, but I can help you out I guess." The bearded man, I don't care to know his name, stands there with his hands in his pockets and rocks back and forth on his heels.

Paul looks at me questioning whether we offer him money. If we do, I think to myself, we will really be running short of cash. Simply can't do it. I don't even think the thing can be fixed anyway. The last thing I want to do is give the man twenty dollars to tell us there is nothing he can do and then tell us he can't give us a ride because his wagon is full. So I tell him we don't have any money. I clarify and tell him we can't spare any money and then I ask him if he is still willing to look at it. Feeling guilty, he kneels down, lies on his back and slides under the van. I shake my head and Paul gives me a little punch. We both get down on our backs and slide under the van with the man. Plenty of room under this piece of garbage, that's for sure.

The mechanic asks again about the problem and Paul says it won't go into gear. "Not even first gear?" the man questions. And Paul says we have no gears at all. "Happened all of a sudden," the man mutters and Paul confirms that is the way it happened. The bearded man runs his finger up along the underside of the tranny, looks down the long side of the underneath, and squints his eyes to see to the front. He moans a moan which means he sees something and then slides his short frame a few feet toward the front, about three or four feet from the transmission itself. He slides his fingers along a rod that runs the length of the van. He pinches the rod and pulls it up and back. It slides easy. He has found the problem. It isn't the transmission, he tells us. It's the shifter rod. There's a little plastic or aluminum piece that fits right here and it's gone.

"See here. These two rods snap together right here and that piece fell off. It has four teeth. Two on each side. Two fasten toward the front and two toward the back. You are getting all the play in the stick because it's not connected to the tranny. This is definitely your problem."

"Can it be fixed?" Paul asks.

"Yes."

"We need the part?" Paul asks.

"Yes."

"Where can we get the part?"

"Junkyard. That's the only place."

"There's no junkyard anywhere near here, is there?"

"No." The mechanic continues to study the problem. "Do you have a clothes hanger?" he asks.

Without answering, I slide out from under the van and open the big door. I begin to sort through some of Paul's stuff when he surfaces and tells me he doesn't have a clothes hanger so don't bother looking. A voice from under the van tells us to ask his wife, so Paul goes over and asks her. She gets out of the wagon and opens the back to remove a clothes hanger from a stack of clothes that rest on an ice chest with "Miller High Life" printed on the side. Without so much as looking at Paul or saying anything, she hands him the clothes hanger and closes the back of the wagon. She returns to her seat.

Our mechanic unwinds the clothes hanger and threads it through the fittings on both rods. He pulls it tight and then threads it through again. I am watching him on bended knee with my head ducked low. He looks over and tells me to pull the stick down into second gear and leave it there. I do as he says, and he shouts from below to pull it harder. I press down with all my wrist and forearm and hold it with my other hand. I can feel him jerking against the stick, trying to pull it out of gear. Hold it, he shouts. I pull it back even harder. As he threads the wire through the fittings, the stick jerks up and back a few inches. Finally, the motion subsides and he slides out from under the van. I let go of the stick.

"You will have to keep it in second gear. That will allow you to get going, but you will have to drive to Vegas pretty slow."

"Better than nothing," I say.

Paul shakes the man's hand and thanks him. He straightens his cap and tells him it was nothing. I thank him too and he tips his head at me.

"You boys have a good day," he says.

15. Vegas

Nevada has no ocean. You come over dune and dune and dune and no water washes up on no shore. Las Vegas is an island of lights and smells, and the desert laps against it on four sides. Trucks are ships and trailers are sails. Desert winds wash them upon casino shores to import hot dogs and poker chips, scantily dressed women and magicians, showmen who can't sell albums anymore, and memories of Elvis and Neil Diamond. It is an oasis for hard-luck cases who spend small fortunes on a shortcut to the American dream. Vegas feeds itself on the pocketbook of the poor and the naive. P.T. Barnum eat your heart out. This is a circus too heavy to travel. The show doesn't come to the people, the people come to the show.

We have come one hundred miles and both the tortoise and the hare have passed us laughing.

A junkyard is the only place in Vegas we are dressed for. I step to the counter and ask the man if he has a Volkswagen van. He tells me he has two but they have been gutted. There's nothing on them, he says. But then he tells me it's a dollar to go in the yard and see for myself. I look at Paul and he pulls a dollar from his wallet. We walk with heavy heads down a ramp on the backside of the trailer which fronts as an office. We look out on a sea of cars on concrete blocks and wheel rims. There are Toyotas and BMWs and all sorts of disasters and tragedies that are kept for their little jewels: bumpers, rotors, and hubcaps. Another man points us toward the Volkswagen section, so we wander in and out of Buicks, through Ford and Chevy to the endless line of Volkswagen Beetles. They are like snails lined up for a race. Red ones and blue ones and yellow ones with patches of rust. Behind the first line of Beetles are two vans. They are ghosts of what they were. They are nothing but shells. No doors, no windows, no camper tops, or headlights. A gentle wind blows through them.

"Unbelievable," Paul says.

"Not much there," I add.

"Nothing," he confirms. Paul stands silent and puts his hands in his pockets. He turns to go.

"You don't want to take a look?"

Paul weaves through the Beetles before he turns. "What for? There's nothing there. Let's go."

"Come back, Paul. Let's have a look. You never know."

Paul comes back over. He is only pacifying me.

"You want me to look or do you want to look?" I ask.

"I'll look," he says, and drops to a knee. He lays himself on his back and slides under. I go to the other van and do the same. Underneath, the van is gray and empty. There are no brake lines, no muffler, no gas lines, no nothing. Just the bottom of a shell. I could set my fists against the bottom and bench press the thing off its cinder blocks. But then I see the shifter linkage, and a sense of hope stirs: a butterfly circus in my stomach. I follow the linkage with my hand and eye and there it is. "Paul!" I shout. He doesn't answer. I turn over with a giant grin. "Bud, you won't believe it." Paul is lying beneath the other van with both his hands clasped and resting on his belly. He's wearing a smile like mine. "Paul!" He doesn't answer. Then he laughs. "No way," I say.

"Yes, sir. It's here," he says under his breath.

"There's two of them." I say, half in disbelief.

Paul, still wearing a smile, closes his eyes. It is obvious he is praying. He's thanking God.

I give him a few seconds. "Hey, bud."

"I'm praying," he says.

"This is cool, huh?"

"I'm praying, Don."

"Sorry. It's cool though, huh?"

"Yes, it is."

"Are you through praying?"

"No."

"Are you going to pray for a long time?"

"Yes."

"Are you happy?"

"Yes."

"Very cool, huh?"

"Yes, Don. Very cool."

I let Paul go on with his praying. I think about praying also but there is too much energy going through me right now. It's all too amazing for me to consider. Paul rolls himself over on his back. He rests his head in his hands and wears that same big grin.

"Don."

"Yeah."

"Why don't people believe?"

"Why don't they believe what?"

"In God."

"I don't know. Not everyone has a Volkswagen."

16. California

We easily replace the spiderweb of hanger wire with the neat, plastic piece from the junkyard. Paul tests the linkage by testing the gears. Everything works the way the Germans intended. Funny when you think about it. We've got cars now that you have to hook to a computer to fix. They may get better mileage and run more quickly, but in terms of ease and dependability, these vans have to beat all. Perhaps the complexity of the modern engine is just a parts racket. They make more gadgets so more gadgets will break. Gadget makers laugh all the way to the bank.

Paul kills the engine and says he's hungry. I agree, but hadn't thought about food until he brought up the idea. He says that we've got beans and rice and we could warm the pot up and eat that. I cringe. He says it doesn't sound all that good to him either.

"How much money do we have?" I ask.

"Not enough to justify anything lavish."

"Maybe we could go to a grocery store. We could make sandwiches or something."

"We really don't have enough money for that," he says.

"For sandwiches?"

"We can only spend about $5 per day."

"Five dollars each?"

"No."

"Five dollars total?"

"That's about it," he confirms.

I recommend that we hit a grocery store anyway. Some stores have day-old bread and maybe we can stir up enough for some meat or lettuce or anything that isn't beans and rice. He agrees and we are off. Puttering through the streets of Vegas, we salivate and drool on our shirts. Paul starts talking again about the perfect meal. He has changed from Raisin Bran to pancakes and sausage. Though it is dinner time, pancakes and sausage sounds perfect. A meal like that would really hit the spot. Paul spots a Safeway and steers the van into the parking lot. Five dollars, he says. All we can spend is $5. I confirm that I agree, but my mind entertains visions of stacks of pancakes with butter and syrup and hash browns.

We walk into the store and are embraced by an air-conditioned breeze. It's cold in here, Paul says. The aisles are filled with old people who are squeezing melons and testing grapefruit. I feel like a kid in a toy store. The only real food I've eaten in two weeks was a small cup of cereal and four bowls of the same cereal about an hour after the cup. The only thing Paul has eaten is a cup of cereal. He watched me eat the four bowls of cereal but that hardly counts for eating any of it. I made sure to tell him it was good.

I grab a shopping cart and lean my weight over the handrail. I push it along like a little kid. As we go through the chips and salsa aisle, I toss two bags of Doritos in the cart. Paul laughs. I grab a set of Tupperware dishes from the housewares aisle and also one of those little dishwashing tools with the spongy head. When we get to the bread, Paul begins comparing prices. I run my arm along the shelf and dump eight loaves into the cart. Paul only gives me half notice, peering at me over his meager loaf. He picks one out and heads toward the back of the store where they keep the meat. Along the way, I make sure to stock up on toilet paper and the current issue of *People* magazine. I also grab three cans of Alpo dog food, as Safeway is running a special. As I round the back of the aisle, Paul is standing in front of the meat.

"Lunch meat is too expensive," he says.

"How much?"

"Too much. We can get a jar of peanut butter for the same price. Peanut butter will last a whole loaf of bread and meat will only get us about two sandwiches."

"Well, let's get peanut butter then."

"Alright." Paul turns his back to the meat and wanders lazily, with a defeated posture, along the back of the store. I follow him, after grabbing two cans of Spam and a no-stick frying pan. Paul doesn't notice the endcap of bleach as he turns down the peanut butter aisle. I mumble under my breath something about what a great deal this is. I grab three gallons and set them in the child's seat so they don't squash the eight loaves of bread. As I draw closer to Paul, he eyes my cart.

"We don't have a dog, Don."

"What do you mean?"

"You got a few cans of dog food there. Don't you think that's a bit much?"

"*You* have to eat something, Paul. I don't want you getting hungry on me or anything."

"I see. Thanks for thinking of me."

"Don't mention it."

Paul reads the label on the peanut butter. He places it back on the shelf and side steps toward a cheaper brand. The one with the bland label. He asks me if I want chunky or smooth and I ask him if they make a brand with chunks of steak. He shakes his head and asks again about chunky or smooth. Chunky, I say. He grabs the chunky jar.

"What about jelly," I ask.

Paul turns and walks down a few feet to the jelly. "Whoa," he says. "This stuff is expensive. The peanut butter was three dollars and it's another three for the jelly. With the bread, we are over budget by two dollars." He puts the jelly back.

"We can't have peanut butter without jelly," I tell him.

"We can't afford it, Don."

"Two dollars?"

"What happens when we run out of gas?"

"The dude gave us the Volkswagen part for free," I remind him.

"The part was never in the budget in the first place," he reminds me. "We should only be spending four dollars because we spent a dollar at the junkyard."

"I've never gotten a look at this budget you keep talking about."

Paul points his finger at his head. He says it's all in his mind and it's very clear.

"I see," I tell him. "I've got a budget too, you know."

Paul looks down at my cart. "I see your budget."

"I'll put the dog food back."

"What about the frying pan?"

"It's a keeper." I place my arms over the contents of the basket so he can't take anything out.

"Well, we can't afford peanut butter and jelly. Something has to go. Will it be the peanut butter or the jelly?"

"We can't refrigerate the jelly, so let's keep the peanut butter."

"My thoughts exactly," he says.

Paul heads toward the checkout counter with just a loaf of bread and a jar of peanut butter.

"Wait!" I exclaim.

"What?"

"We can't just eat bread with peanut butter," I tell him.

"We'll warm up the beans and rice. We'll have peanut butter and beans and rice." He begins walking toward the checkout again. I follow him with my cart, adding a jar of jelly and a can opener and a potato chip clip that looks like a giant clothespin.

"How much money is the bread and peanut butter going to cost us?" I ask.

Paul is searching for the shortest line. "The bread is $1 and the peanut butter is $2.50."

"That leaves us $1.50."

"Yeah."

"What can we get with that?"

"We can save it for tomorrow. We will have $6.50 tomorrow. Just think, if we do this every day, we may be able to afford a watermelon or something big."

Paul finds a short line at the nine-items-or-less counter. I stand behind him with my cart. He looks it over again and asks how I'm going to pay for all of it. I tell him I have a coupon. The lady checking out customers tells me that this is a "nine-items" or "$20" counter. Paul tells her that I have a coupon and I smile. She says unless it's less than $20, I need to go to another line.

"Sorry, bud," Paul says.

I ask the lady if I can get any nine items in the store for $20. She looks confused. I clarify:

"Ma'am, this sign says nine items or less or $20 or less, cash. Does this mean that I can chose any nine items and only pay $20 for the whole batch?"

Paul looks over at the lady and the lady looks at Paul in an attempt to find someone exhibiting sanity. Paul lets her down by telling her that the sign does in fact say what I said it said. She explains the details of the rules and clarifies that the items have to add up to less than $20 or there has to be less than nine total items.

"You can understand my confusion," I tell her.

"Not really," she says.

Paul tells me that I had better put the stuff back, so I head off with my cart in tow behind me. I disappear behind an aisle and reappear, stopping at an endcap for a bottle of ketchup.

"You put all those groceries away that quickly?" Paul questions.

"They are in a better place now."

"What are you talking about?"

"It's taken care of," I clarify, giving my friend an understanding look.

"What's this?" He's looking at my bottle of ketchup.

"Ketchup."

"What for?"

"The beans."

"Beans."

"Yes. I don't mean to offend you and your cooking, but they lack flavor."

"We have several bottles of Tabasco, Don."

I give Paul a desperate look. "Give me this," I say.

――― ――― ―――

Paul opens the sliding door and pulls the pot of beans from under the sink. He sets the bread down on the floor and takes a spoon and stirs the thick gravy so it breaks off into chunks and then becomes slightly fluid. I look down into the pot and think to myself about pancakes and biscuits and gravy. I take a slice of bread and spread peanut butter over the top with my Swiss Army knife. One piece, folded over and thick with peanut butter is enough to cover the roof of my mouth and the back of my teeth. Paul does the same, leaving the rice and beans to sit and age. We have two peanut butter tacos and then Paul gets the idea to add ketchup to his third sandwich. I watch him, not in disbelief, but in wonder. The two, in my mind, have never gone together. He takes a bite and rolls it around in his mouth. He lifts his eyebrows and nods, handing me the bottle of ketchup. I spread peanut butter over another slice of bread and then squeeze a dab of ketchup along the crease. I fold the bread over and ketchup bleeds through the side and out the top. I eat it the way a boy at camp might eat a bug. It's not all bad. The texture is the redeeming quality. Ketchup is light and peanut butter is heavy, so they go together like that. I consider the depth to which we've plummeted. Peanut butter and ketchup sandwiches. The depravity of it all.

I forced Paul to stop at a casino as I had never seen one from the inside. He reluctantly pulled over at the last one on the edge of town. Inside, we found scores of old people sitting around green felt tables and tossing chips into different squares, throwing dice, and laying down cards. There was lust in every eye and sweat on every brow. Very few smiles or grins. Even the winners kept straight faces.

We only stayed an hour or so. I could tell that Paul wasn't really comfortable with all the buzzers and lights. He's more the outdoorsy guy than I am. I keep forgetting that he has no tolerance for city stuff. I rather enjoy all the noise and sounds, though. It doesn't get to me. Not that I could settle down in Vegas. Too much glitz and glamour covering too much murk and mire. Nothing really makes sense in Vegas. I don't know what Jerry Tarkanian ever saw in the place.

Once on the highway again, Paul perked up and wanted to talk. He went on about how God had taken care of us with the mechanic and all. He was really feeling spiritual. This is another difference between Paul and me. We feel our religion differently. Nothing much surprises me anymore. I grew up in a Baptist church that was always looking for and receiving signs from God. They played everything up quite a bit. It was better then the circus at times. A great place for a kid. But older now, nothing much moves me. But the mechanic thing is really getting to Paul. He really feels like God is taking us somewhere. He feels like we're supposed to be on this trip and he's trying to piece it all together. The way I figure, if God is taking us somewhere, we'll get there. If we try to pin it down, we may get it wrong in our imagination and then we'll be upset and let down if the thing we think is going to happen doesn't. I knew this girl once who really liked a friend of mine. She told me that God was telling her they were going to be married some day. Having the inside track, I didn't have the heart to tell her that God wasn't telling him anything like the same. She just went on and on dreaming about the guy until she had her heart broken when he began dating someone else. The thing is, she didn't settle it well in her mind. She blamed it all on God. She couldn't figure out why God wouldn't just piece everything together for her. He was going to be a doctor and she wanted to be a nurse. They both wanted three kids and they liked Volvos.

He ended up marrying another girl who works at an art gallery and she is working so he can pay for medical school. The funny thing is that my friend, the one with the broken heart, would have never worked so someone else could go to school. So in my mind, God did a good thing with the art gallery girl. They are pretty happy together.

I learned a great deal from this strange love triangle. I learned that coincidence is coincidence and providence is something entirely different. I learned that providence usually looks like coincidence, but that I shouldn't get too worked up trying to differentiate them. Best I can calculate, a Christian has plenty to do just obeying all the precepts in the New Testament. Why try to use God like a palm reader or a fortune-teller? We're just begging for confusion when we get into all that stuff.

I'm not accusing Paul of being foolish. He has a legitimate reason to be excited. There's no doubt in my mind that God answered our prayer with the arrival of the mechanic. It was the hand of providence, without a doubt. But these are small blessings: The more important thing is the big picture.

———— ———— ————

Leaving Las Vegas, the van treads a long highway that climbs steeply up the side of a mountain. There are no curves in the road, just a straight line up the saddle of a mesa. Paul has the pedal flat against the floorboard. Trucks are grinding slowly around us. Everyone has their engines racing and we can smell brakes. Though our pace is not fast, the van has a healthy whine about it.

We pass a road sign which announces California 11 miles ahead. I never realized how big those signs are. The sign must be half the size of a billboard and the letters are made of hand-sized reflective pieces of plastic. They glimmer as we near and pass. My notions of California are not entirely good. I understand they have a great deal of crime on the West coast. They have earthquakes too.

Having passed so many miles through the desert, the road seems to exhale as it hands us to its western neighbor. There is an official border post in California. Like no other state, California stops cars and pays frumpy men to peer through windows. The crossing is wide, allowing three cars through three booths. Light traffic has us one car back and the guard is asking questions to the woman in the car before us. We are on a mountain pass, and the van is heaving heated pistons and ticking. We climbed five steep miles to the border and the van had a rough go of it. The car in front of us pulls ahead and the border guard motions us forward. Paul pulls the van to the lowered railing and the uniformed man leans into the driver's window. He speaks as he looks around and he asks if we are carrying any fruit or vegetables. Paul tells him that we aren't. He asks our reasons for coming to California and Paul tells him we are traveling around the country. The man nods and tells us to enjoy our time on the West coast. He hits a button and raises the gate and we pass into the golden hills of California, which, at least at the border, don't look any different than the golden hills of Nevada.

Immediately, it seems, other drivers become reckless. They weave in and out of lanes and come close to our rear bumper before passing. Drivers pass, and for a moment I imagine the driver in the car next to us pulling out a gun. But it wasn't a gun, it was a burrito.

—w— —w— —w—

Inside the van, hot air riffles the pages of a book on the back bench. The pages are open and are folding into each other and slapping around, ruining the binding. I step back to close the book and set some weight on it, when I first catch the scent of gasoline. Gasoline like a gas station, really strong. I close the book, set a blanket over it, and return to the passenger's seat. Looking over at Paul, he has his hand on his mouth and a finger resting along the bottom of his nose. It occurs to me that he had already noticed the gas smell. He looks over but doesn't say anything. I place my hand outside the window and cup the air, guiding it in through the window. While an engine light is a problem you can ignore, the smell of gas is not. We could explode or something.

"You think that's us?" I ask

"What?"

"The smell. Smells like gas."

"I smell it."

"So you noticed it too."

"Yeah, a ways back," Paul says.

"Do you think it's coming from the van?" I ask.

"Yes."

"You do."

"Yes."

"How do you know?" I ask.

"Because we've been losing gas on the gas gauge."

"I see." I say.

Just when you feel like you're getting to know someone, they do something that you can't explain. I knew this girl once who dressed like Holly Hobbie. She was real cute and soft-spoken. She carried a Bible with her at all times and always talked about what God was doing in her life. Anyway, a bunch of us went out to eat after church one Sunday. She had this sun-dress on and was sitting next to me She leans over and says, really quietly, to look over at her shoulder and she moved her strap over. Right there in black letters was tattooed the word "Toyota." She said that she had just got a little sports car. Her first car. She was excited about it because it was so fast. So she went to a place in

Houston called Dragon Mike's and got a tattoo that said "Toyota." Dragon Mike was a real nice fellow, she said, and she was able to share the gospel with him. But he wasn't interested. He liked to drink beer and ride his Harley Davidson and didn't want to get involved in religion at the moment. My homeschooled friend said she understood and didn't want to push or anything. All the while, Dragon Mike is tattooing the word "Toyota" on her shoulder. Like I said, you get to feeling that you know all about someone and then they reveal something that lets you into a room of their life where you just don't feel like you needed to go.

Why Paul would drive for several miles knowing the van smells like gas, I have no idea. I wonder if he realizes there are two of us on this trip. I just sit and be quiet and pray we don't burn up.

Paul eyes a gas station and steers down the off-ramp, stops at a stop sign, and crosses the street to the station. He pulls alongside the pump and kills the engine. Through the dusty windshield, I squint and see a line of liquid that trails all the way down the off-ramp, makes a small puddle at the stop sign and wraps around to the back of the van. We are literally dripping a stream of gasoline. Unbelievable. I point it out to Paul and he just shakes his head. Unbelievable.

We get out and Paul opens the engine compartment. The van is hot and ticking. The metal is cooling and making tired noises. The back of the van smells like grease and gas and if anyone within ten feet were to light a match, we would surely explode, sending a line of fire all the way back to the border.

"We might as well pull it off to the side and try to fix it before we put any gas in it."

"Yeah," I agree.

The sun is setting in the west. It's down on the other side of the gas station now and the tall overhang above the pumps stretches its shadow across the gravel parking lot of a neighboring restaurant.

Paul starts the van with a cringe on his face. He's worried about igniting all that gas. He quickly throws it into first and crosses the street to park alongside the restaurant. Paul goes around back and opens the engine compartment and I open the sliding door and grab the toolbox. Paul uncovers both carbs and sets the lids on the ground with the appropriate nuts stored in the bowl of the lids. I tinker around with some wire, stretching and pulling levers, looking for a place where gas could be leaking. Paul lies down on his back and slides underneath. He runs his fingers along the bottom, searching for a hole.

"It's dark under here. Can't see anything."

"Pretty dark up here too," I say.

Paul keeps running his finger along the bottom of the engine.

"I smell it but I can't see it," he says.

"We may have to wait until morning."

"Sleep here?" he questions.

"Any other ideas?"

"No."

Paul stands up and stretches his back. He takes a look around the place, at the mountains in the distance and the sun setting behind the gas station. Trucks buzz by and the place has a lonely ear to it.

17. Milkshakes and Pie

Tossing and turning, both of us are restless. Were we not leaking gas, we'd be driving. I have learned to sleep inside the shake and rattle of the van. But this is a quiet town. Only a few cars have pulled into the parking lot and even the highway in the distance seems to have gone to sleep a bit early.

Paul has his hands under his head and he's staring at the ceiling. He's thinking about the gas leak, wondering where the problem lies. He turns on his side and faces the opposite window, then he shifts back over, sets his hands under his head and stares at the ceiling again.

I break the silence. "What are you thinking about?"

"Nothing much. Just the van."

"You getting pretty frustrated with it?"

"Getting frustrated?" he questions.

Paul kicks his blanket off of him and sets his feet on the back of the driver's seat. He takes his feet down and rolls over to his side, sits halfway up and rests some of his weight on his elbow.

"I can't figure out why the carburetor would start leaking gas for no reason. It doesn't make sense," he says.

"Something probably rattled loose. We just need to find it and fix it. I'm sure it will be obvious to us in the morning."

"Hopefully you are right."

Paul's face catches the passing glow of a headlight that sweeps through the van. The light is accompanied by the low growl of a motorcycle. Without looking I can tell that it is a Harley Davidson. I stretch my neck to peer out the window and sure enough, a Harley has pulled up to the front door. A large man dressed in black dismounts and stretches. He releases a yawn, bends over to stretch his back, then leisurely walks into the restaurant.

"You sleepy?" I ask.

"Nope."

"You want to get some coffee or something? Maybe decaf so it won't keep us up all night."

"Well, I've got some change in the ashtray. We could use that."

"I'm perfectly willing to dip into my sock of money for this one," I proclaim.

"Sounds good."

——— ——— ———

A cowbell mounted atop the swinging glass door sounds as we enter the restaurant. Decked out in pink, the place was obviously decorated by a woman. Pink walls and pink curtains. There is a long bar with swivel padded-top stools and a step up to sit on them. It's like walking onto the set of Mel's Diner.

Paul and I stroll up to the bar and rest our elbows on the counter. An older lady with an apron and a funny, lacy thing on her head comes over with a pad and pencil in her hand. She sets the pad and pencil down and hands us menus. She doesn't say anything, just smiles. Her nails are painted deep brown and she wears a large wedding ring. Her hair is blonde but should probably be gray, judging from the lines on her face. Her look is somewhere between Vegas and California. She's probably one of the ones who heads into town on weekends and gambles away her tips.

She rounds the counter and heads over to the man who came in on the Harley. He mumbles his order and she scratches it on her pad.

Paul searches through the menu for the coffee prices, but his eye comes to rest on the milkshake column. He can't get away from it. He sets the menu down and pulls a handful of change from his pocket. Counting it aloud, and shifting the coins from one pile to another, he finds $2 with 27¢ to spare.

"I'm not getting coffee, dude."

"You're getting a milkshake, aren't you."

"Maybe."

"You wouldn't let me have jelly and you are getting a milkshake."

Paul rotates a little metal holder on the bar and pulls several little containers of jelly out of the center compartment. He sets them on the counter and slides them my way.

"Jelly!" he says.

I give him a smile of approval and place two of the containers in my shirt pocket.

"Let's get milkshakes, Don. We deserve it."

"I want coffee."

"You sure?"

"Yeah. I've got a hankering for coffee. I'll be fine with just coffee."

"Do as you wish."

The waitress comes back over and asks for our order.

"What's your special today, ma'am?"

"Ma'am?" she questions.

"Yes, ma'am. Ma'am."

"Well, if you are going to be such a gentleman, I figure I can knock fifty cents off the chicken fried steak." She says this with an endearing grin, which stays as she waits for my response.

"Now, do you make that steak yourself, or some fellow in the back makes it."

"A fellow in the back."

"Well, then I'm just not interested. I'd like to eat some of your food. You look like a woman who can cook."

"Well, I don't do the cooking here, honey."

"You don't cook anything at all?"

"I cook, but not here."

"I see." I ponder a bit. "Do you make the coffee?"

"I sure do."

"Well, then I'll just take a cup of coffee. That will be fine."

"I'll make you a fresh pot. How's that?"

"Perfect. Decaf if I could."

"I suppose." The lady looks over at Paul.

"Chocolate milkshake, please."

"Now, I don't make the milkshakes. Are you okay with that?"

"I'll take my chances," Paul laughs.

"Thank you, boys." She takes the menus and sets them in a slot between the countertop and the cash register. She speaks clearly through an opening in the back counter where the dishes are stacked. "Chocolate milkshake, Bob." Bob, a black-haired man with a white cooking apron nods to confirm the order. The waitress clips the other fellow's order to a spinning contraption and turns it so the cook can see it. He wipes his hands on his apron and grabs the order, squinting and holding it away at arm's length.

"Where you boys from?"

"Texas," I answer.

"Texas? What are you doing way out here?"

"We want to be in movies," I say.

The waitress laughs and leans over the counter, resting her elbows on the bar and holding her head in her hands.

"You tired?" Paul asks.

"Been here all day," she says.

"Long day. Must be tough."

"It's not all that bad. I'm used to it. Been doing this for 15 years."

"You've been here for 15 years?" I question.

"Fifteen years," she confirms.

"That's a long time to work in one place."

She stands up and rests her weight against the counter. She smiles and says that we are certainly young. Used to be people would get a job and wouldn't leave. Today's kids, she says, can never stay in one place. We're always looking to get ahead and move up. Paul nods in agreement and the waitress turns around to start the coffee brewing. As she works, Paul eyes the pies in the pie case that separates the backside of the bar from the shelves where the dishes are stacked. He nudges at my elbow and points to the pies. He licks his lips. I look over to see a lemon meringue with a slice cut out and a pecan pie too. The pecan looks rich and brown. I can taste the pie on my tongue, and the thick, cool texture of the filling, and the light, fluffy brown of the crust. It's enough to make me want to jump through the glass.

The waitress turns around to see us staring at the pies.

"They look good, don't they?"

"Yes, ma'am, they do."

Bob, in the back, tells her her order is up and she turns to lower a bowl of soup and corn bread onto her tray. She rounds the bar and sets the bowl on the motorcyclist's table. Bob takes a metal cup and holds it upside down over a large glass mug. Paul's chocolate milkshake comes out thick and slides down into the mug. The waitress comes over and sets both the shake and the metal container on the counter in front of Paul. He kindly hands me the metal container and drops a spoon into the cup with a clink. There's a good inch of milkshake at the bottom and I gather it into the spoon and tip it upside down over my mouth. In one gulp, the milkshake is gone.

"That's good stuff," I say.

"Best milkshakes this side of the Mississippi," the waitress tells us.

"Best milkshakes anywhere!" Bob corrects her from behind the dishes.

The waitress lifts her eyebrows and shakes her head. "Bob owns the place. He's a bit partial. But the milkshakes are good. He knows how to make them."

"Sure does." Paul says, sucking the thick shake through a straw.

The waitress turns my cup over and pours my coffee.

"What's your name?" I ask.

"Betty," she answers with a smile.

"Nice to meet you, Betty. I'm Don." Paul lifts his head and wipes his mouth with his sleeve. "I'm Paul," he says, then returns to the milkshake and the straw.

"So you want to be in pictures, huh?"

"Yes, ma'am. Come out here so they could put my mug on the silver screen. Big as day. Just like James Dean."

Betty's eyes tell me she liked James Dean. "He was something else. You've got dimples, you just might make it."

Paul lifts his head up from his milkshake. "Don't feed his ego, Betty. I've got to travel with him."

"You hear that, Paul. James Dean. She thinks I look like James Dean."

"You look like my big toe," Paul says with a laugh.

Betty smiles and shakes her head. She turns and opens the pie case. She lifts a slice of lemon pie and sets it on a plate. Then she slices the pecan pie, lifts a piece and sets it on the plate. She turns and sets the lemon pie before me and the pecan pie in front of Paul.

"What's this?" I ask.

"Pie. Don't worry. It's on the house."

Bob peers through the opening and eyes the pie. He gives Betty a look and shakes his head. "You're gonna put me out of business with all that charity, Betty!"

"Mind your own business, Bob. These boys look hungry. Besides, they're going to be famous someday. They're gonna be in pictures."

Bob smiles and moans as he cuts into an onion.

"Thanks Bob," Paul yells.

Bob moans again and keeps cutting his onion.

Just before Paul slices into the pecan pie, I snatch it out from under him and slide the lemon pie along the bar. He doesn't hesitate, he just lowers his fork right into the white foam and yellow cream. I could have set a shoe in front of him and he'd have stuck a fork in it.

18. Breakfast

Inside, the restaurant has a different feel than it did last night. There are only a few open booths as most of the tables and chairs are empty. Paul and I settle in at a booth along the back wall, closest to the rest rooms. A waitress comes over and turns our coffee cups over, filling both of them. She asks about cream and I nod my head yes. She sets two menus down and I read through mine as if it was poetry.

Last night we were given a little business card on which Bob wrote "free breakfast" and signed his name. Real nice gesture. Little did he know we would eat him out of profit.

Paul closes his menu and sets it on the table. He takes a little packet of cream, opens it and pours it into his coffee. He opens a packet of sugar and pours it in and stirs his coffee with a sigh. He slides back in his seat and asks what I'm going to order. The Mexican, I tell him. The Mexican? he questions. Yeah, the omelet. The Mexican omelet. I'm getting the combination plate with two of everything, he says. Then he adds that he's getting a side of hash browns. You're ordering a side item also, I question. Yes, he tells me.

I hadn't thought about adding something extra. It would be entirely unfair for Paul to get a bigger meal, so I search through the side items. The waitress comes over and asks if we are ready. Paul looks over at me and tells her that it looks like we need more time. No, I shout. I'm ready. I want the Mexican omelet with a side order of biscuits and gravy. That's it. That's what I want. Paul tells the waitress that he wants the number two combo plate with a side of hash-browns. The waitress writes it all down, collects the menus, and heads back to the kitchen.

A restaurant like this is where you find the heart of America. Nobody makes reservations or combs their hair to eat in a place like this. There are no false faces. There are no trite conversations. A person comes here to eat and sort out their boredom.

"Where are we going, Don?"

"Pardon."

"Where are we going? Are we going to hang out in California or what?"

"I don't know. What were you thinking?"

"Doesn't matter to me. But we are running low on money, you know. We may need to get to Oregon pretty soon."

"How long have we been on the road?" I question.

"About three weeks. Maybe more."

"That long?"

"It's been a while," he says.

The waitress comes toward us balancing plates in her hands. Passing us, she sets the plates down on the table behind me.

"Smells good," Paul says.

"You can say that again."

"Smells good," Paul says again. I crack a smile.

"You know, I've got this friend in Visalia, California. Is that near here?" I ask.

"Visalia. It's between Bakersfield and Fresno. Who's your friend?"

"His name is Mike Tucker. Real cool guy."

"How do you know Mike?" Paul asks.

"We met in Colorado at camp. We hit it off and he came out to Texas to visit me last year. It might be nice to swing by and see him. If we have time."

"Sounds good," Paul confirms. "Do you think he will mind?"

"Not Mike. He's great. He'll be glad to see me."

"Maybe you should give him a call. See if he would care if we stopped in."

"Yeah. I'll do that. I think I have his number somewhere in my stuff."

Our waitress comes along with our food in her palms. There are also plates running up her arms. She sets a Mexican omelet before me and slides Paul's plate toward him. She carefully maneuvers the side dishes of hash browns and biscuits and gravy off her arms. She's a real pro.

"You boys look hungry," she says.

"Yes, ma'am," one of us answers.

"You call on me if you need anything."

"Yes, ma'am."

She steps away and straightens her apron, checking the table for condiments. Paul asks for Tabasco sauce and she turns to another table and lifts a bottle, setting it on our table with a smile.

"Thank you," he tells her.

Paul eyes his food and I eye his food. He eyes mine and I eye mine. He shakes his head and says let's pray about this. I agree, but tell him he needs to make it fast or I'll steal his hash browns while he has his eyes closed. Paul bows his head to offer a blessing. I can tell that it's hitting us both. Answered prayers and all. First it was the van, now it's food. God is here around us, it seems. Feels like church. Paul says amen and I pick up my fork and dive into the yellow omelet. There are bell peppers and cheese and onions. The omelet has a layer of salsa over it and all of it bleeds and runs together as I slice it with my fork. Man, it tastes good. Tastes like Texas. Tastes like early morning breakfast when me and my buddies would stay up all night talking, then hit IHOP first thing to cap off the night with pancakes and conversation.

There is no talking now. We focus on our breakfast like math homework. We slurp coffee between bites, unaware of the outside world. I half finish my omelet before slicing into the biscuits and gravy. The white, fluffy cloud of bread, covered in gravy with chunks of ham and bacon, settles deep into my stomach. It must have been something like this with the loaves and fishes. All those families settling down to picnic and having everything provided by a bunch of bleary-eyed disciples. And Jesus busy like a chef, splitting fish and bread, wiping his wet hands against his clothes.

After eating, Paul rests back and holds his stomach. I do the same. We look at each other, completely satisfied, sipping coffee and making comments about the meal. Good stuff, I say. Great, Paul says. Hit the spot. No doubt about it.

Neither of us want to face the broken van this morning, so we sit and talk. We talk about California and about John Steinbeck and Hollywood. I ask Paul if he's ever been through an earthquake and we make small talk about the comfortable weather in Los Angeles. Paul says he could never live in a city with that much smog. We both agree that we will steer away from L.A. on our trip. After Visalia, we'll head up to Oregon.

"Do you think you will ever go home again, Don?"

"What do you mean?"

"Do you think you will go back to Texas?"

"Where else am I going to go?" I ask.

"Anywhere. You can live anywhere. It's a free country."

"I don't know. Haven't seen anything that hits me yet."

"Could you leave Texas?" he asks.

"Maybe. It would be tough to leave my family and all. But I suppose I could if I found a nice place."

"You will like Oregon," he says.

"Yeah?"

"Yeah."

"Why is that?" I question.

"You've never seen true beauty, have you?"

"What do you mean?"

"Mountains and all. Streams and waterfalls. Forest."

"Sure I have, Paul. I've not been hiding in my room all these years."

"Where? Where did you see mountains?"

"Colorado. I spent a few summers at the Summit. It's this Christian leadership camp in Colorado Springs where they teach apologetics, politics, and all that. They teach you to defend your faith at college. It's a great deal they've got going."

"Is that where you met this guy Mike?"

"Yes. Mike and a few others of us really hit it off. We were inseparable that summer. Mike is crazy. He drives around in this old Toyota Landcruiser."

"He has a cruiser!" Paul expresses with enthusiasm.

"Yeah, man. It's a great truck. So tough."

"Dude, *I* have a cruiser."

"You do. Where?"

"In Oregon. I have one back in Oregon."

"Where?"

"In the woods."

"Pardon?"

"Yeah, it's out off this forest service road where nobody will find it. When I bought the van, I hid it so I could go on the trip."

"You hid a car in the woods?"

"A cruiser. Not a car. A cruiser. Yes, I hid it deep in the woods and buried it in brush. Nobody will find it out there."

"You know, Paul, sometimes you seem like a bottomless pit of interesting stories."

"What do you mean?"

"You hid a Toyota Landcruiser in the woods, bought a Volkswagen, and headed to Houston."

"Yeah, so what."

"That doesn't strike you as odd?"

"Why should it? I had to hide it so nobody would vandalize it. Actually, it's in pretty rough shape, so I don't think vandalism would have made a difference. But still, I don't like the idea of kids climbing around in it and that sort of thing."

"I see." I shake my head. Can't believe this guy.

"So," Paul begins to change the subject, "do you know anybody from Oregon? Did you meet anyone from the Northwest at this camp in Colorado?"

"Why do you ask, Paul?"

Paul cracks a smile. "Free food, man. A place to stay when we get there."

"I see how you are."

"What, dude? We are going to run out of money when we get there. You know that, don't you?"

"It crossed my mind," I say.

"Well, do you know anybody?"

"You are the one who lived there, Paul. Don't you know anyone?"

"That's different. It's home to me. I can't just go barging in on people I already know. They will think I am irresponsible or something."

"I see. So it's okay for me to look irresponsible but it's not okay for you to look bad. Is that it?"

"Exactly!"

"Very funny. But, no. I can't think of anyone in Oregon. I have a good friend named Julie in Seattle. But not Oregon."

"Seattle is too far north," Paul says. "We wouldn't go that far."

"Sorry to disappoint you, Paul."

"Don't worry, buddy." He says this with a sarcastic smile.

"You know," I begin, "I do have another friend in Washington. She's in Ridgefield. Very cool girl. You would like her, actually. She's a granola like you."

"What is that supposed to mean?"

"Nothing, just that she likes nature and stuff."

"Is that right?" he questions with a curious face. "Where in Washington?"

"Ridgefield," I say.

"Ridgefield. Ridgefield is just north of Portland. It's practically Oregon."

"Portland is that close to Washington state?"

"Yes. It's near the Columbia River and Washington is on the other side of the Columbia. Ridgefield is just up Interstate 5."

"Well, then maybe we can go see Danielle."

"Yes." After a few moments, "So..."

"So what?"

"So, is she, you know, good-looking?"

"Danielle?"

"Yes. What is this 'granola' like?" He pronounces the word granola as if I had been speaking of some kind of disease.

"If you must know, it so happens that she is good-looking. Like I said, she's a lot like you, Paul. You might like her."

"Well, let's go then. I've got this girl to meet. This granola friend of yours."

I try to settle Paul down a little. "Hold on, here. I'm not a matchmaker or anything. You never bothered to ask if I was interested in Danielle. You just automatically claimed her for yourself."

"You said she liked nature, dude. What are you going to do with a woman like that?"

"I happen to like nature too. I'm not all city."

"Let me get this straight, Don. You want to get involved with this nature girl, Danielle, and then marry her and take her to Houston?"

"What's the problem with that?"

Paul eases way back in the booth. He looks at me like I just told him the moon is made of cheese.

"I don't mean any disrespect. I truly don't. But Texas isn't nature. Texas is city and smog and humidity and heat. Texas is not for a girl like Danielle."

"You don't even know her. How do you know what she is like?"

"You said she is a granola. A grapenut."

"I never called her a grapenut. I just said she likes the outdoors."

"Like me." Paul is really going here. "You said she's like me."

"Yeah. She is, but that doesn't mean anything."

The waitress comes over with the bill. Paul interrupts his interrogation to hand her the little business card with Bob's message about our free breakfast.

"You know Bob?" she questions.

"Met him last night. Here at the diner."

"Well, he must have taken a liking to you. He doesn't give free meals very often."

"Yes, ma'am." I say. "Give him our thanks, will you?"

The waitress flips the card around in her hand and slides it into the pouch in her apron. "I will do that. By the way fellas..."

"Yes?"

"Bob's free meal doesn't include the tip."

"Oh," Paul begins. "We were going to leave you a big tip. My friend Don here is going to take care of it."

"Good thing," she says.

I smile. Paul smiles. I dig into my pocket and pull out a few dollars and lay them on the table. They are all crumbled up like child's money. The waitress looks with a grimace. I pull out another dollar and she nods and walks away.

"Thanks, Paul."

"Don't mention it."

"You ready to get out of here?"

"No. You haven't told me yet."

"Told you what?"

"Danielle. Are you interested? Is there anything there?"

"Let's go."

"No. Tell me."

"She's a close friend. A pen pal. But, if you must know, no. There is nothing there."

"She's not your type, huh?"

"I didn't say that. She's great. A great girl. Just not my type."

"She's not as pretty as you said, is she?"

"She is, Paul. This girl is beautiful."

"What does she look like?"

"I'm not going there."

"Why not?"

"Let's go," I say.

"Why not? Tell me."

"Well, not that she'd ever be interested in you. But she's got brown hair and brown eyes. She's athletic."

"...like me."

"Whatever. She's very intelligent. She doesn't read Louis L'Amour books, that's for sure."

"She's smart?" Paul frowns.

"She is. Very smart. A literature major. Very intelligent. Good conversationalist. Her letters are like poetry."

"Are you serious? You're just pulling my leg."

"No, I'm not. That is how she is. She writes and reads poetry. *Like you.*"

"I hate poetry," Paul grumbles. I shake my head.

"Don't tell her that."

"What do you mean?"

"Better freshen up on your Byron."

"Who's Byron?" Paul asks.

"Lord Byron, Paul. The poet."

"Is he a friend of yours?"

"He's dead."

"Oh, sorry to hear it. Did you know him?"

"Yes. He was my uncle."

"Oh, and Danielle liked his poetry, huh?"

"You aren't on this planet, are you, Paul?"

"What planet?"

"Let's go," I say, standing. Paul sits thinking about my Uncle Byron while I walk out the door.

Paul walks lazily around behind the van. He picks at his teeth as he watches me tinker with pulleys, levers, nuts, and bolts. I look back to see his expression of confusion at my work. I grab a screwdriver and tighten this, grab a wrench and tighten that. I make little noises like I'm figuring it all out. Paul's expression is the same, and we banter back and forth with groans and sighs. I pull a hammer from the tool box and begin to tap against the frame. Paul's eyebrows lift at this and he grunts as if to say he hadn't thought of that. I bang a little harder, and he clears his throat. The joke isn't that funny anymore.

"You got that thing figured out yet, Don?"

"Sure do. I see the problem."

"What is it?"

"It seems to be the flux capacitor."

"The flux capacitor?"

"Yes."

"What's that?" he asks, still picking at his teeth.

"It's much too complicated to explain. You just stand there and look pretty. I'll take care of this."

He kicks me on my backside and I rock my weight into the engine compartment. Acting like I'm stuck, I make Paul laugh.

"Sorry about that, dude. Didn't mean to put so much weight into that one."

"Don't mention it," I say, pretending to struggle inside the engine compartment with my arms and one of my feet. Inside, I notice a small hole in the top of the casing. And, believe it or not, there is a bolt sitting in a gully on the frame. It couldn't be this easy. No way.

"Hey, Paul."

"Yeah."

"Look at this."

"I thought you just wanted me to look pretty."

"I'm serious."

Paul leans in and I shift a little so some sun shines on the hole. "You see this?"

"Yeah," he says.

"And this bolt?"

"Yeah."

"Do you think it goes in this hole?"

"Couldn't hurt to try."

I set the threads into the hole and screw it in. The hole smells like gasoline. This must be the top of the fuel filter. Just like a lawn mower. Doesn't surprise me at all. Paul goes around to the front and starts the van. I keep my head down to look for a leak, and nothing comes. I can't believe it was that easy. I close the engine compartment and take my place in the passenger's seat.

"How long did we work on that thing last night?" Paul asks.

"About half an hour. Maybe more."

"How come we didn't see that hole?"

"It was dark."

"No."

"It was dark."

"I know," Paul begins, "but there is no way we could have missed it. And the bolt being right there and all. No way."

"What are you saying?" I ask.

"Think about it, Don."

"Think about what?"

"A meal. God wanted us here to meet Bob and Betty. He wanted us here to feed us a meal."

"I never thought of it like that. Do you really believe that's true?"

Paul lets silence come up around our ears. He sits and looks at the windshield and picks at his teeth with his toothpick. "I'm starting to, you know. I'm starting to think this is God working with us. Helping us along and all."

"Could be," I tell him.

"Could be?" he questions. "Is."

19. Night Golf

We have come through one dusty range and then through another. In the Mojave Desert, the van heated like an oven. Paul kept calling me Hansel and wanted me to call him Gretel. Joshua Tree National Park was on our left for miles. The van rattled and hummed. We picked up a hitchiker named Tom Joad, who was heading to Salinas to do farm work for the summer. We dropped him off in the foothills of the Sierra Nevadas and he said he'd hitch a ride west because we were going north through Bakersfield and then into Visalia. But we're not to Visalia yet, and California has taken me by surprise. The Sierra Nevadas have towering peaks just like the mountains in Colorado. We find green pastures just an hour from the Mojave, sloping meadows with creeks running through them.

——— ——— ———

The interstate runs just west of Visalia, so we exit and head east through a pasture and come into the part of town where they have a ballpark. Apparently a double-A baseball team plays here. Probably a farm team for the Dodgers or the Giants. Paul pulls the van over and I use a payphone to call Mike. His mom answers and I tell her that we are swinging through on our way to Oregon and could Mike come out and play?

"Who are you?" she asks.

"A friend from Summit. Mike and I met in Colorado."

"I see. Well, he is at work," she tells me. "He will be home in half an hour or so. Would you like to come to the house? Would you like lemonade?"

"Yes. Lemonade sounds good. We went through the desert and I dreamt about lemonade."

"Well come on," she says. "It will be ready when you get here."

We drive slow and look around at neighborhood after neighborhood. They are mostly the same. The town is as flat as Texas. We came all the way through rolling hills and ended up in the Texas part of California. Could have stayed home for this. Could have just driven around the block and camped in the driveway. But then there is Mike. I haven't seen him in a year or more.

We arrive at Mike's place and Mrs. Tucker makes us lemonade. She's such a nice lady and I can see Mike in her face and her gestures.

"Mike will be home any minute," she says.

"I noticed his cruiser in the driveway, Mrs. Tucker. Is he on foot?" I ask.

"No. Not really. He's on skates."

"Skates?"

"Well, what are those things? They aren't skates. They call them something different." Mrs. Tucker scratches her head and looks at the ceiling.

"Roller blades?" Paul asks.

"That's it. He's on roller blades. He only works a few blocks away."

"What does he do?" Paul asks.

"He's a waiter. He's been a waiter for years now. He was doing fine dining for a while, but now he's at this little breakfast place. He likes it better because there isn't as much pressure. At the fine dining place, he actually had a dessert that he had to set on fire in order to serve it. Mike was always afraid he was going to set a customer's tie on fire. He hated it when people ordered that dessert. If you ask me, I think the flaming dessert, or whatever it was called, is the reason he left. Hated setting that thing on fire." She pauses. "Are you boys staying here tonight?"

"I don't think so, Mrs. Tucker. We don't want to put you out or anything."

"No, sir. You are not putting me out at all. People are always staying here. One of Mike's friends, Keith, slept on our couch for several months. We didn't hardly notice him. Don't worry about it."

"You had a fellow living in your front room?" Paul questions.

"Yes. He was living in his car for a while and Mike asked if he could stay here. Mike knew him from the local community college. A real smart kid, he lived out the rest of the term right here."

"I see," I say.

Mrs. Tucker puts the Tupperware pitcher of lemonade back into the fridge and steps in front of the sink, in front of the kitchen window.

"There he is," she says, spotting him. "He's coming up the road."

Paul and I step outside and walk down the short driveway behind Mike's Landcruiser. Paul checks out the cruiser up close and I walk down to the street to meet Mike.

He's coming up slow, tall and skinny with bright red hair. Mike is another good-looking fellow like Paul. He's always got some gal writing him or calling him, I figure. He's wearing baggy khaki shorts and a T-shirt. He has a backpack on and he's sliding like a fellow on ice skates. His weight slides left, then right, and he rocks his arms at his sides as he propels forward. About a hundred yards away, he comes to a stop, sets his hands on his hips. I stand at the end of the driveway with a grin. He gets a big grin on his face and laughs.

"I don't believe it. You're home from the war!" he says.

"What's up?" I say.

"What's up? You're up. What are you doing here, old friend?" Mike skates up to me and gives me a bear hug. He wraps his long arms around me and pats my back like I was choking on something. "Man, Don. It's good to see you. What are you doing here?"

"Passing through. Had to stop and see you."

"You better have, man. I didn't know you were going to be in town!"

"I should have called. We were just driving, you know and, well..."

"You don't have to explain it to me," he says.

That evening, we drive north of Visalia a little and Mike parks the cruiser in a parking lot across from a golf course. I'm in the back seat and Mike turns to tell me there are several golf clubs back behind me. He tells me to grab the nine iron for him and to pick one out for myself and one for Paul. I do as he says, handing Paul the seven and keeping the eight for myself. Mike hands Paul an empty plastic grocery sack from the glove box. He keeps one and hands one to me. Paul asks what we're doing and Mike tells him it's called night golf. I don't ask any questions.

It's just past midnight and Visalia is asleep. We sit in a parking lot and across the street is a fence that protects a golf course. Mike points out a spot along the fence that is hidden in the shade of a tree. Street lights illumine most of the fencing, but that one spot is hidden in shadows.

"That is where we need to jump the fence," Mike announces.

"I see." Paul eyes the fence.

Without speaking, Mike jumps from the truck and runs across the street. He throws his body over the fence and sprints into the darkness. Paul and I sit in silence, looking deep into the shadows across the street. We sit a little more and then a little more. Paul has his golf club at his side, he looks it over and fidgets with the handle.

"I think he wants us to go and jump the fence, Paul."

"I thought you met this guy at a Christian leadership camp."

"I did."

"We're jumping a fence with golf clubs, Don."

"I know."

"So?"

"Well," I say. "I think we should follow him."

"That wouldn't be right, Don."

"It's golf, Paul. We're not robbing a bank."

"I know. It doesn't seem right, though. We didn't pay or anything. We're running when nobody is driving by and then we are jumping a fence. It isn't right."

"It's no big deal, Paul. It's going to be fun. Don't be such a..."

Paul jumps out of the truck and runs in a zigzag across the street. He's playing the part of a bank robber. All his motions are exaggerated. He pretends to see a car and lies down on the road. Then he gets up, freezes and puts his arms out, pretending to be a tree. He throws his club over the fence, puts his plastic bag in his pocket, and scrambles over the chain-link wall. I can see his shadow as he picks up his club and runs deep into the darkness. I study the thrill of it, sit a while as a car is passing, and then join the fun. My pants snag at the top of the fence and I am suspended by my beltloop, which breaks and drops me hard to the ground. I gather my club and bag and run fast. I run with no context. I cannot see my hand before my eyes, it is simply that dark. I see the tops of trees so I guess where their bottoms are and I don't go near them. I feel the eyes of a thousand police officers on my back. Images of the television show "COPS" flash through my mind and give speed to my steps. I run straight and long, away from the fence. The ground beneath my feet gives way to mud in a step and then another step has me knee deep into water. My foot anchors into the mud and I splash face first into a pond.

I decide to wait for Paul and Mike to find me, rather than looking for them. Besides, in an hour or two I may be able to dry out and save myself the humiliation of admitting I ran into a pond. They'd get a good laugh at my expense, but it wouldn't bother me. The uncomfortable moments in a person's life make great stories down the road. Life would be boring without moments like this.

The night sky has a quality that makes a person feel small. Yet my worldview has me believing that, somehow, I, among the billions of people who live on the planet, and the billions of people who preceded these people, am something of significance to God. To be honest, I am not exactly certain why I believe this. Something inside me compels me to believe. Life is, without a doubt, complex and confusing. My faith is my sanity. There are people who choose to live on the surface of things. I have yet to find the surface. And, with all the beauty in the underneath, I am not certain I want to live on the surface should I find it. I stopped looking a long time ago.

God has me on this journey. I am sure of that. I can look back on my life and see God placing me with certain people or in a certain setting or wrestling with a certain scripture; all to bring about the experience of change. The more I ponder God's way, the more I believe He changes a person, or molds a person, through enlightenment. He changes a person's mind. When people walked with Christ, I mean actually walked with Christ the way it is presented in the Gospels, He changed their minds. He was a teacher. When we ask ourselves if we are walking with Christ, I believe we need to ask ourselves this question: Has Christ changed the way I view the world lately? Am I more compassionate? Do I appreciate and understand the character of God with a greater significance than I did yesterday? Do I have a stronger belief in Him? This is what walking with Christ looks like. It is, and has always been, difficult for me to admit that I am wrong. I do not like to be wrong. And this is a direct hindrance to my walk with the Lord. Earlier, in the canyon, I made a chart of how I feel and think about certain issues, and contrast them with how God thinks about the same issues. But I am weak. I do not have the strength to let go of all my erroneous thinking and exchange it for God's truth all at once. I tend to hold onto my own way, even when it lands me in one of life's muddy ponds. But at least I have identified the path. This is a step. I know what it is that I need to do.

I had a friend who told me of a childhood perception she had that was quite innocent and beautiful. She said that she thought stars were simply holes in the sky, and through these holes we could see the brilliance of God.

Through dark trees and moonlight, I hear my two friends laughing. They cannot be far off. I gather my senses, lift my wet body, stand to my feet, and shake like a dog. I feel like I have fallen into a bowl of soup. There is mud on my back and my shoes swish, swish, swish with every step. I walk in the direction of the voices and there I find Paul.

"Psst. Don, is that you?"

"Yeah."

"Where have you been?"

"I don't know. Back there somewhere."

"What took you so long?"

"I didn't know where you guys were. Where is Mike?"

"He's over there." Paul points but I can hardly make out his hand. My eyes have adjusted slightly, but it is still too dark to navigate.

"What's he doing?" I ask.

"Same as me. He's picking up golf balls and putting them into his bag."

"Why?"

"He hasn't said why. But this is night golf and this is how it works."

"I see," I say. "So what am I supposed to do?"

"Pick up golf balls."

"Where are they?" I ask.

"They are everywhere."

"Everywhere?"

"Yes. We're in the middle of a driving range."

"Oh. I get it. But what are we going to do with the golf balls?"

"Hit them," Mike says. His voice seems to come from out of nowhere.

"Hit them where, Mike?" I ask.

"At each other."

"Pardon?" Paul questions.

"Yeah," Mike begins, "We get at opposite sides of the driving range, and we try to hit each other."

I cannot make out Mike's expression, but the tone in his voice tells me he is serious. And the idea itself is not bad. Mike disappears into the darkness. I realize the importance of the moment and drop to my knees, scurrying for golf balls. My sack at my side, I scoop and fill, scoop and fill. The rush of adrenaline aids my speed. From a distance, and through the dark night, we hear Mike yell incoming. Paul dumps his bag on the ground and takes stance. I take my half-filled bag and run off into a dark corner of the range. I can hear Mike's club hit the ball. The pop splits the air like a gun shot and then, about 50 yards away, I hear Paul yap, giggle, and take a swing back at Mike. I devise a strategy to never hit from the same spot. The only way we can identify each other is from the sound of the club hitting the ball. If I stay on the move, there is no way they can figure out where I am. So, I drop a ball to the ground, and hit it toward Mike. I hear the ball land and hear Mike laugh. I got close, I know that much. Rather than dumping the balls on the ground, I take my club and run 50 yards further. I hear Paul hit another ball and it flies past me. The whistle of it tells me it's moving quick. That would have been a painful blow. So I drop another ball to the ground and take aim at Paul. I'm about 75 yards or so away, so I loft the ball so as to land on his head. No sound from the enemy, I missed. And I move another 25 yards down the length of the driving range. As I am running, I hear Paul give a serious yap and moan. He's hit. He's laughing. Probably on the ground rubbing the knot on his head. I drop another ball and hit it toward Mike. Another miss. Mike hits one toward me and it lands just in front of me so I have to jump out of the way. The balls are not visible until they are right upon you. My eyes are able to focus a little better through the darkness and I can see the reflection of Mike's club as he swings. He's aiming at Paul again.

It occurs to me that Paul and I are under an unfair advantage. Mike knows the range, and he's played the game before. I run back over toward Paul. As I near, he takes a swing and lands the ball into my side. I fall down in a moan and a groan and roll over saying I'm hit, I'm hit. Both Mike and Paul have a good laugh at that.

"Paul. Psst, Paul."

"What?"

"Let's work together."

"What do you mean?"

"Mike is better at this. Let's gang up on him."

"How?"

"Let's run around behind him and take swings."

"Where is he?"

"He's over there, come on."

Paul gathers some balls into his bag and we run the length of the range, outside the boundaries behind trees. We hear Mike take another swing. He laughs as the ball leaves the ground. His club glistens for a second in the moonlight and I stop Paul from running, draw him near, and point toward the place I saw Mike. We are even with him, but he is a good 50 yards out, and he's still facing the place where Paul was standing.

"Lose the clubs," Paul comments.

"Why?"

"Let's get up close and pelt him."

"Just throw them?" I question.

"Yes."

"Good idea."

Paul grabs a handful of balls from his sack, sticks them in his pocket and does it again with his other pocket. Pretty soon we are both loaded with ammunition.

"Paul, you go around back and I will get him from the side. Don't throw unless you get a good view of him."

"You got it," he says, and with that, Paul runs around to the back of the range. I wait to hear him charge, and then run toward Mike. Paul hits him and Mike goes down. Paul pummels him from the rear as I hurl golf balls from the side. He yells uncle but we do not let up. Mike gathers his senses, stands, and begins to grab at golf balls. He throws one toward Paul and as he releases I can see the complete outline of his body. I take aim and fire, hitting him on a bounce. He goes down again and gathers a few more balls. He throws one toward me and hits me squarely on the shin. That stings.

Paul yells charge and we move in close and fast. Soon enough, we are on top of my old friend and are pelting him good. Mike can't stop laughing. He's rolling around on the ground so I jump on him and give him a good licking. Paul, however, sees us wrestling in the grass and begins to pelt both of us with golf balls. Mike and I stand and return fire. This goes on for about half an hour, when Paul finally calls a truce.

20. The Oregon Trail

We were out till 4:00 A.M. last night but we are up by 6:00. Mike has to work the breakfast shift. He tells us to come in for breakfast, but Paul and I have already eaten well. Mike fed us before we went to bed and we are both full. We tell him we need to hit the road and Mike seems let down.

"I can't thank you enough for letting us stay, Mike."

"Dude, stick around," he says. "You've got nowhere to go."

"We're trying to get to Oregon. We should probably hit the road."

"Oregon is only about eight hours away. Leave tomorrow."

I look over at Paul and he shrugs his shoulders. We are at the kitchen table and Mike's mom has made us coffee. Mike refills my cup.

"You're not putting me out, dude. You always feel like that and it's not the case. What's the rush with Oregon anyway?"

"No rush, really. I've just wanted to see it and that's where we're heading, you know."

"Go if you want," Mike shrugs.

"I've got a better idea," I say. "Join us, Mike. Come with us."

"Yeah!" Paul says.

"I can't," Mike sighs.

"Why?" I ask.

"Work."

Paul chimes in again. "Come with us Mike. Have you ever been to Oregon?"

"Never been," he says.

"You'll love it. It's awesome."

"Mike," I begin, "we're going up to Ridgefield to see Danielle."

"From Summit?"

"Yes," I tell him.

"The girl in the red dress?"

"Yes."

"What red dress?" Paul asks.

"Go take a cold shower, Paul," I tell him.

"Dude, that's tempting. She's a babe."

"I knew it," Paul says. "Tell me about her, Mike."

"Look at this guy," Mike says. "Acts like he's got a shot."

"She's that pretty, huh?"

"She's a great girl. Strong faith, you know."

"Yeah, yeah, tell me more."

"You want some ice water, Paul?" I ask him.

Mike begins to encourage Paul. "She's great. She would actually like you. She's earthy, you know."

"I told him," I say.

"Tell me more."

"Don knows her better than I do. Do you still write her, Don?"

"We keep in touch."

Mike starts explaining to Paul how we met Danielle. He tells him how smart she is and that she's a great soccer player. We were all really close at the Summit, he says. We were inseparable. We'd climb Red Mountain for sunrise. Real nice view from there.

"I've got to meet this girl," Paul exclaims. "Let's get out of here. Mike, come with us."

"Can't," he says. "I have to work. You guys have a good time. Don't forget me."

"Never," I tell him. Mike meets my eye and holds a fist over the table. I tap his fist with mine and he calls for his mom. She comes in the room and Mike tells his mom we're gonna pray and see these guys off.

Mike stands and puts his arms around his mom. Paul and I stand and Mike starts praying, "Give them wisdom, Lord. Show them beauty and keep them safe. Calm Paul down about Danielle (Paul laughs). But, Lord, show them Yourself in everything they see. Let them know You better when they reach Oregon than they know You now."

———— ———— ————

With Paul at the wheel, we drive west to Interstate 5 which will take us through Oregon to Portland.

Neither of us in the mood to talk, I begin to ponder what Mike said about finding God in everything we see. I suppose that is how it should be. God made the planet and He made us, leaving telltale signs of Himself everywhere. He made the orange trees that border the interstate, and the earth that grows the orange trees. He made the animals and humans who feed from the orange trees, and He gave humans a mind to ask about who made the oranges, and who made them.

I started this trip in search of joy, in search of fulfillment. And now I wonder if my aim was sufficient. To know God, and get to know Him better and better, surely involves some effort. It is not all joy and fun and games. It is serious business.

I guess I've always hoped that earnestly seeking God would bring joy. And I still believe it does. But it also brings sorrow and anger and hardship. This seems to be part of how God works with people. Even among the saints you see the full gamut of emotion. We learn from the pain of life as well as the pleasure. Perhaps we even learn more from the pain.

———

The van enjoys the absence of slope. The road is flat. We found our pace 100 miles ago and the van has not wavered, choked, or coughed in complaint since then. We are sailing through the dry bottomland of America's golden state.

Paul tells me we should make Oregon by sunset, and then Portland before midnight, or shortly thereafter. I ask him if we intend to drive the night, and he shakes his head, saying he doesn't know if he can make it.

"Is this a pilgrimage?" I ask my friend.

"A pilgrimage?"

"Yes."

"What do you mean?" he inquires.

"Are we on a spiritual pilgrimage?"

"Well, we said we wanted to deepen our knowledge of God. We said that when we left, remember?"

"Yes."

"So, I guess we are on a spiritual pilgrimage. If that is what we are doing."

"Is that what we are doing?" I ask, with a puzzled voice.

"We have both spent a lot of time in the Word. You have read Ecclesiastes about 50 times, Don."

"I know. I just thought it would feel different."

"What do you mean, feel different?"

"I read about Muhammed, you know. Or the Muslims going to Mecca. And it sounds so romantic. Spiritually romantic. And then there is the Indian who goes on a vision quest. What we are doing doesn't feel like that."

"But we are not Muslim or Indian. We are Christians," he says.

"I know. I just wondered if we were making progress."

"Do you think we are making progress?"

"Yes. Something like progress. So I do believe God is working, taking us to some place. I was just thinking it would feel different."

"I think that is a big problem with a lot of Christians, myself included," Paul begins. "We want it to *feel* special. And there are times when it does, you know. But not all the time. Sometimes life just feels like life. We have to put our faith in God."

Despite my understanding that emotion is emotion and faith is faith, I am still waiting for some feeling that God is working in my life. Some sign that He is taking me someplace.

A person's life has ups and downs. Much of the emotion felt has more to do with what he ate for breakfast than with what God is doing in his life. There are times, and maybe this is one of them, when my emotions feel distant, but truth tells me that God is not far off and that He is still looking after me.

"It's just that everybody wants God to move now," Paul continues. "They want to know who their wife is going to be and where they are supposed to go to school and whether they are supposed to be missionaries or whatever. But I don't think that God usually works like that. I think He leads us in and through situations. We are guided, not just told what to do."

"I get it," I confirm. "I see what you are saying. We may not know what this trip, this pilgrimage is all about for years. Later we'll look back on it and see it as God leading us. But in the here and now, we simply have to focus on God and let Him do His work."

"Something like that, yes. Does that answer your question?"

"It wasn't really a question. More of an unsettled feeling."

"I see," Paul says. He leans his head forward and turns his neck a little. He's stretching his legs as he drives.

"You tired?" I ask.

"Very tired. We didn't get much sleep last night."

"I know. I'm feeling it a little, too."

"You think you could drive?" Paul asks.

"How far is Oregon?"

"About three more hours. We should hit mountains pretty soon. They aren't too big, but we should start seeing them."

"I can drive," I tell him.

Paul pulls the van to the shoulder. He gets out and stretches, bending over and arching his back. He sets his hands against his sides and leans backward. I slide over into the driver's seat as Paul gets in on the passenger's side.

Steering the van back to the road, we rock and sway, bumping over the edge of the shoulder. I look over at Paul and only a mile down the road he is sleeping. I speak his name and get no answer. His head is against the window and he's out.

Fifty more miles has us in hill country and approaching mountains. We've been out of Visalia for six hours now. If Mike was right, we should hit Oregon pretty soon. These hills are thick with evergreen. Redwoods line the road. The trees are enormous at their base and extremely tall. This is what I'd always imagined Narnia to be like.

Another two hours down the road and Paul is still asleep. The interstate has woven through redwoods this way and that. The mountains have given to subtler slopes, but we go up and down all the same. Gradual climbs and quick descents. My eyes are heavy and thick. Dark lays itself over the landscape. There is light in the sky, but no sun. I find myself justifying a quick closing of the eyes, catch myself thinking about my eyes being shut, then open them quickly, and shake my head to wake myself up. But it's no use. I'm fading.

For a change I weave between lanes, running my tires over the divider reflectors. The thump, thump, thump offers a change in sound and that helps. I roll down the window and stick my head out like a dog. I sing to myself. I talk to Paul, who is asleep. I take both hands off the wheel and say look, Mom, no hands. I honk the horn. I talk to the trees. I sing again and talk to Paul again. But something ahead catches my eye. I slow, pull the van to the shoulder, and park it like a car at a drive-in movie. Before me is the screen and in giant, reflective letters it reads: Welcome to Oregon.

21. Sinatra

I never bothered to move the van from the shoulder last night. A police officer wakes Paul up as he is still in the passenger's seat. I crawled into the back and buried myself in blankets. I hear the officer tap on the passenger's door. Paul wakes up frightened, and wipes the drool from his chin. He rolls down the window and the officer asks him what he's doing. "Sleeping, officer." "Here?" The officer asks all sorts of questions. We are parked in the grass, directly between the two posts that hold up the "Welcome to Oregon" sign. I figured if they meant it, they wouldn't mind us sleeping beneath it. I don't think the officer agreed.

Paul stretches after the officer leaves. He grabs my foot and I kick him, moaning and covering up again with blankets. I hear the engine start and the van jar through the ruts in the grass and onto the road. Oregon. We're in Oregon, I think to myself. I was too tired to get a good look at the place last night, so I uncover my head from the blankets and peer through the side windows. Not much different than northern California really. Same trees and same road. I get up from my bed and take my spot in the passenger's seat.

I had imagined Oregon to be greener. Not that it's not lush, it is. I guess I imagined a rain forest. Paul tells me Oregon can be divided into three major sections. There is the valley, which we are in; the mountains to our right, not visible through the thick trees; and the desert on the other side of the mountains.

"Like the Mojave desert?" I ask.

"No," he answers. "More like high desert. There are canyons and rolling hills. Juniper trees and sagebrush."

"Do you think we will get over there?" I ask.

"Sure," he says. "We may have to head that way."

"Why would we have to?"

"To get jobs. We are going to run out of money sometime soon. I don't know whether you noticed that."

"I thought about it. But I knew you had a plan."

"I see," he says.

"So?"

"So what?"

"What is your plan, Paul?"

"For jobs?"

"Yes."

"Well, for the past three summers I've worked at Black Butte Ranch. It's outside of Sisters in the Cascades."

"Sisters is a town, right?"

"Yeah. I told you about it. It's a great place except for the cone lickers."

"Cone lickers?" I question.

"Yeah. Tourists, you know. They come in droves and walk down the streets licking ice-cream cones."

"I get it. Cone lickers."

Looking at the map, there seem to be only two major interstates through Oregon. Interstate 5, which we are on, heads north and south. It comes up from California and passes through Eugene, Salem, and Portland before heading into Washington State and through Seattle into Canada.

Then there is Interstate 84 which heads east and west along the northern border of Oregon. There don't seem to be very many towns on 84. It goes all the way through Idaho to Salt Lake City, Utah.

Oregonians are all by themselves up here. I am used to Texas, where there are a dozen major highways that head to half-a-dozen towns with more than a million people. I feel like I'm traveling into the deepest remote parts of Alaska or the northern territory. There is a spot on the map, in eastern Oregon, where I can place my entire hand and not lay it over a town. There are only a few minor roads that head out that way and they all seem to dwindle off like weak creeks and streams. We're in the outback.

Paul rolls down his window and breathes the air. It's fresh air. Mountain air. Smells clean and thin. You can smell nearby rivers and green, green growth.

"Tell me about Black Butte. What will we do there?"

"I will work as a lifeguard. I've done it for years. About three summers."

"What about me?"

"Janitor."

"Are you serious?"

"Yeah. Janitor. It's good work, Don. They pay well."

"Whatever," I tell him. "How much money do we have?"

"Not much. About $100. That will get us to Ridgefield, maybe Seattle if we want, then back to Black Butte. No more than that."

"I have about $50," I say. "That will get us a little further."

"Food," Paul starts. "Don't forget about food. We have to eat. The fifty will pay for food."

"I forgot about that. Danielle will feed us. I'm sure of that."

"Did you ever call her?" Paul asks.

"I didn't. I meant to call her from Mike's but we left in a rush and I was tired. I didn't think about it."

"Maybe you should call her. We don't just want to drop in."

———   ———   ———

Paul exits the interstate and drives a few blocks into the city. I notice a coffee shop and think a cup of coffee sounds good. But then I see another. Two coffee shops on one street. We don't even have two coffee shops in all of Houston, much less two on one street. When we stop for gas, I wander over to a phone booth and call Danielle. It's long distance, so it costs me a dollar in quarters.

"Hello, is this Danielle?"

"No," a tender voice answers.

"Did I reach the Bjur's?"

"This is the Bjur's. This is Shirley Bjur."

"Are you Danielle's sister?"

"I'm her mom. Thanks for the compliment!"

"Hello Mrs. Bjur. This is Donald Miller. I met Danielle at Summit. We keep in touch through letter."

"I know about you, Don. It's good to talk to you. Do you want me to get Danielle?"

"If that is okay. It was nice to talk to you."

"Nice to talk to you, too," she says, and then sets the phone down. I hear her call for Danielle and hear Danielle answer and talk to her mom as she comes to the phone.

"Hello," Danielle says.

"Hey there."

"Hi." Pause. "Who is this? I'm sorry." She sounds confused.

"Don Miller."

"Donald!"

"Yeah."

"It's so great to hear your voice. Did you get my letters?"

"Which ones?"

"From Costa Rica!"

"Costa Rica?"

"You didn't get them?" She sounds upset.

"No. Were you in Costa Rica?"

"Yeah. I got back this morning."

"No way. I can't believe that. I almost missed you," I tell her.

"What do you mean?" she asks.

"I'm here. I mean not here, but close."

"Close to where? Here?"

"Yes. I'm in Oregon!"

"No way!" she screams. "Where in Oregon?"

"A town called Eugene."

"Don, Eugene is just down Interstate 5. You're pretty close. Are you coming up here? You'd better."

"Yeah, we're heading to Seattle maybe. I don't know exactly where we are going, but I'd like to come up and see you."

"Please do, Don, please come here. What in the world are you doing here?"

"A friend and I are traveling around in this Volkswagen van, we're seeing the country and..."

"Like hippies!"

"Yeah. Only not like hippies, but yeah. We're living like people in the 60s and all."

"You have to come here, Don. Are you coming?"

"Yeah. If that's an invitation, we're coming."

"It's an invitation! Come!" She is jumping up and down at this point. Her mom is in the background asking what is going on. Danielle is trying to explain.

"Well, tell me how to get there!"

I hang up the phone and walk toward Paul with a smile on. He has the van started and asks how it went. He asks if I told her about him and I tell him that I forgot.

"You forgot?" he says.

"How far is Ridgefield?" I ask him.

"About three hours or so," he tells me.

"I told her we'd be there before sunset."

"We'll be there before that, dude."

"Well, we can hang out in Portland or something. You should get a shower if you are going to impress this girl. You're smelling pretty bad."

"I took a shower at Mike's!" Paul exclaims.

"Did you use soap?" I ask.

Paul just chuckles at that. He pulls the van back on the road and we weave towards the interstate. We pass yet another coffee shop.

"What is it with coffeehouses, man? They are everywhere."

"Welcome to the Pacific Northwest, Don. This is the coffee capital of the world."

"There's a shop on every block," I say in wonder.

"You haven't seen anything, Don. Wait till we get to Portland."

We slide down a ramp onto the interstate, enter the flow, and find our little spot in the rat race. Surprisingly, there are a lot of cars for a town this size. Must be all those university students and professors.

We are out of Eugene pretty quickly. Back into farm land. Oregon agriculture is not just fruit and vegetables, it's also Christmas trees. There are perfect rows of five-foot pines that stretch down flat valleys and up onto the hills. They keep their rows regardless of the slant of the earth. Beyond the hills I can see the outline of the mountains. I ask Paul if these are still the Sierra Nevadas and he answers with an emphatic no. They are the Cascades. It's a volcanic range.

"Volcanic?" I question.

"You've heard of Mt. St. Helens," he says.

"Mt. St. Helens is around here?"

"Just across the border, really. Just up into Washington state about ninety miles. You can see it from Portland. But the big mountain around here is Mt. Hood. It stands in the distance and is visible from the city. You can see it from almost anywhere."

Soon we are out of the valley and into the foothills. The interstate thickens with cars and buses, trucks and minivans. South of Portland, the land rises and turns green. Businesses rest in the shadows beneath clumps of trees.

Right of the highway, the earth dips into a river. It is a large river. I noticed it on the map earlier. The Willamette, it is called. The interstate follows along the river and then before us is downtown Portland. Despite its western status, it appears old and settled. The river wears the skyline like a crown.

We discuss our itinerary and agree on a shower. But where? I suggest we find a university and use the athletic facility. I am not one who can easily pass himself as an athlete, but a confident stride will get you far and Paul tells me Portland State University is somewhere in the downtown area. We drive up and down one-way streets till we see tennis courts and a large adjoining building. We ask a passerby if this is the university. He tells us that it is so we park the van.

We wander around campus and find the athletic facility. With a confident stride, we march in through the doors, through the gym, and into the locker room. A man in a caged room hands us towels and we thank him and take showers. Pretty simple.

Squeaky-clean, the world has a new feel. The sky is bright. This is uncommon, Paul tells me. The weather is all London until July, when it warms up and feels like Florida for about eight weeks.

"What do you want to do now?" I ask my clean friend.

"You want coffee?" he questions.

"When in Rome..."

We wander down to a little coffee shop with green trim. It's called Starbucks and is filled with students poring over open books, wealthy businessmen dressed in suits, and homeless people listening to headphones. They are playing Frank Sinatra over the speakers.

The fellow in front of me seems to be ordering in French, but the lady behind the counter understands him. Then the lady beside me orders in French as well, and the fellow behind the counter understands her. Strange. I ask Paul if this is a French coffee shop and he laughs. Lattes, he says. It's not French, Don.

The lady behind the counter asks me what I want and I look at her like she's stupid. She asks again and I tell her coffee, what else?

"You want room?" she asks.

"Room for what?" I say.

"For cream," she clarifies.

"Yes, leave room." Feeling dumb, I grab my cup of coffee and find a table. Paul orders his coffee in French. He's doing it just to spite me.

——— ——— ———

"You know, Don. I was thinking about what you were saying."

"About the place being French?"

"Nobody is speaking French, Don. That's not what I'm talking about. I mean, what we were discussing on the way here. About God and how He guides us."

"Yeah?"

"Well," Paul begins, "I think most of us are just normal people, you know. I think that God wants us to follow Him and live for Him and tell people about Him, but that doesn't mean we're going to be starring on Focus on the Family or anything."

"What are you saying?" I ask.

"I'm saying that a lot of Christians want to be recognized for their godliness, and a lot of people mistake the recognition for godliness itself."

"Are you accusing me?" I smile.

"No," Paul takes a sip from his French coffee. "It's just that godliness is mostly a private thing. You know that verse in Matthew where Jesus tells people how to pray?"

"Yeah."

"Jesus says that when we pray we are supposed to do it in private. It's a private thing. He warns against public showings of, well, of religion."

"He doesn't want us to go public with our faith?" I ask, more as a devil's advocate than a curious questioner.

"That isn't what He's talking about. He's talking about people who pray real loud and people who brag about how much they give and all. I think what Jesus is saying is that religion is about relationship. It used to be about devotion to Law, and now it is about devotion to relationship with Christ. It used to be about rules, now it's about relationship. Do you understand?"

"Yes, but what does this have to do with what we were talking about? What I was saying is that it doesn't feel like God is taking me anywhere."

"Exactly," Paul emphasizes. "That is because you are looking for God to use you or present Himself to you or some other 'sign' of faith. But I think that God does not so much take us from point A to point B in the physical world as He takes us from not knowing Him to knowing Him. Do you remember what Mike prayed for us before we left Visalia? He prayed that we would come to know God and see Him in everything."

"Yeah. I understand. I thought about that too." I take a drink from my coffee. It's not bad. Not worth the dollar I paid for it, but not bad.

"Well, a lot of times we are looking for a sign that tells us we're godly. We want to preach, or be a missionary or whatever, all to help ourselves believe that God is using us. We look everywhere but to God to make us feel godly. We try to convince others we are godly so that we can convince ourselves we are godly. The bottom line is that godliness is about relationship, not about image. I guess what I am saying," Paul pauses in thought, "is that we shouldn't worry about where God is taking us or what God is doing through us. Instead, we should be asking ourselves 'Who is God?' Do you know what I mean?"

"So, you mean that when I was looking for a feeling, or asking what it feels like to follow God, I was asking the wrong question."

"Exactly!" Paul sets his cup down and leans back in his chair. "Instead of asking what it feels like to follow God or be used by God, we should be asking who God is, and whether we really know Him. Everything else will take care of itself."

"Maybe," I respond.

22. Kindness

I am not completely over Kristin, the gal I left back in Houston. I am certain she is over me, but I am not over her, and this is the primary element that allows me to pass my "chance at Danielle" to Paul without thought. Besides, he doesn't have a shot. We will be there for a day at most; enough time for a meal. Nothing can stir that quickly. Cupid is fat and slow and can't hit moving targets.

I follow Danielle's directions precisely, and we are soon off the interstate and onto farm roads. There is agriculture on our left and right, small general-store types of buildings, and burger shops renovated from gas stations.

We turn right, go for a few miles, and look for the sign that marks the road to Mountain View Christian Center, Danielle's church. Passing the church, we take a left at the next driveway. It is a long road that serves several homes, each with an acre or two. We follow the driveway and find a mailbox with the Bjur name printed on the sign. We turn right again and follow another driveway up a small hill where there is a large, white house covered in the front with windows. The yard is landscaped with shrubs and flowers.

Paul parks the van and breathes deep. I look behind me, through the back window of the van as the door of the house slings open and out comes Danielle. She is running and laughing. I look over at Paul and ask what he thinks.

"She's a looker," he says.

Danielle's hair is cut short. She is wearing a tie-dyed shirt, khaki pants, and combat boots. She is brown-bread tan. Her teeth are perfect. Her smile is perfect. Paul and I haven't seen a pretty girl in 2000 miles.

"It is so great to see you," she says.

"It's great to see you, too. How long has it been?"

"Three years, Don. It's been three years!"

Paul rounds the van and stands with his hands in his pockets. I introduce them, and Danielle offers her hand, which Paul shakes gently.

"You two come inside. You must be starving."

Paul plays the strong, silent type but I tell her we could eat a horse. Danielle says they don't have any horse but they do have turkey sandwiches.

"That will do fine," I tell her.

Inside we are greeted by Shirley Bjur, Danielle's mom. She's a small, petite woman and it becomes obvious where Danielle gets her beauty. Shirley is busy in the kitchen. We hardly walk through the door before we are ushered into a small breakfast nook and Shirley has plates on the counter, bread opened, and turkey and lettuce and tomatoes and mayo. Paul and I marvel at her amazing efficiency. Danielle and her mom are talking at once. One will ask me a question and the other will answer.

"Don, what are you guys doing here in Washington?" Shirley asks.

"Mom, I told you. They are traveling around America."

"America! It's a big country. Where all have you been?" Shirley inquires.

"They've been all over, Mom. Don lives in Texas, remember?"

"That's right. I remember Don. You're a Texan. Tell me, do they wear big cowboy hats down there?"

"Mom, you've seen too many movies. Not everybody from Texas is a cowboy!"

"We went to Texas once," Shirley starts into a story. "Remember, Danielle, we were there when you were little. You and Elida argued and fought the entire way, remember?"

"I remember. Elida was being a pest," Danielle exclaims.

"Who is Elida?" I ask.

"My sister." Danielle smiles. "I told you about Elida. Do you even read my letters?"

"Over and over," I tell her.

"Who is my little brother?" she tests me.

"I can't remember his name. I remember you guys adopted him from Colombia."

"Nate," she says. "His name is Nate, Don." She bonks me on the head with a roll of paper towels.

We eat turkey sandwiches and are bombarded by questions. Shirley attempts to include Paul in the conversation, but Danielle doesn't seem to notice him. She keeps asking about Mike and California and the Grand Canyon. She wants to know about Texas and how long we've been on the road and where did we sleep and did we go to San Francisco or Sacramento. Her grandfather lives in Sacramento.

Paul asks where Shirley's husband is and Shirley tells him he's up in the air. Paul takes this to mean that he's dead and offers his apology, but Shirley laughs and clarifies that he's actually in the air. He's on a plane flying home from Germany. He works for Hewlett-Packard. He doesn't have to leave town often, but when he does, he goes to China or Germany or some place exotic like that.

We move into the living room which stands just off the kitchen, and sit down around a coffee table and keep talking. The words never stop. They make it very comfort-able for us.

Shirley goes back into the kitchen to sweep the floor. She raises her voice and projects it through the doors that open into the living room. "You two will just have to stay here until Randy gets home. He'll be glad to meet you. You need to stay for Elida and Nate, too. They will be home from school in a couple of hours. You need to stay for dinner."

I walk into the kitchen where Shirley is hard at work. "Mrs. Bjur..."

"Call me Shirley, Don."

"Well, Shirley, we don't want to put you out."

"You have nowhere to go. You said that. You guys are just driving around. All I'm saying is you are not leaving here till you get a good meal. And turkey sandwiches don't count."

"You're sure it's not too much trouble?" I ask.

"Not at all. Stay here tonight."

"Spend the night?" I question.

"Yes. You can have dinner tonight, and since tomorrow is Saturday, Elida and Nate and Randy will be here for breakfast and you can eat and be on your way."

"Now, Shirley, I know that would be putting you out. That's too much. We should just leave tonight."

"Where are you going to go?" she asks. "You are just going to go up the road a bit and sleep. Might as well do it here."

Danielle comes into the kitchen from behind me. She rests her hand on my shoulder as she walks by. "You're staying here, Donald Miller. I'm not letting you guys sleep out on the road."

"Whatever you say, ladies." I turn back into the living room. "They're not letting us leave, Paul."

"Sounds good," Paul shouts back. That comment gives both Shirley and Danielle a chuckle.

—••— —••— —••—

We take a walk to the end of the driveway where a neighbor has goats in a pen. Paul names one of the goats Dimitrius but calls him Dimitri for short. Danielle thinks he's funny. It is here that we are interrupted by Danielle's sister, Elida. She races up the driveway in her Honda Prelude. She's got her hand on the horn all the way up the driveway and she's swerving left then right. Danielle just laughs at her. She races toward us and slams on the brakes. Rolling down her window, she interrogates Paul and me.

"Who are you?" she asks. No smile.

"We're friends of Danielle's," I answer.

"Is that your hippie van?" she questions.

"It's mine," Paul tells her.

"Are you hippies?"

"No," I say.

"You, the blonde," Elida points at Paul. "Do you do drugs?"

"No," Paul says.

Danielle, who has been pulling petals off a flower, throws them through Elida's window. Elida races her engine, throws it into first and squeals her tires. She waves her arms out the window and screams and laughs.

"She's crazy," Danielle laughs and throws her head back. "You're crazy!" she shouts as Elida makes the turn and disappears behind the house.

"Let me introduce you guys to Elida." Danielle starts running and we follow behind her. Elida is getting some books out of her car. She asks, this time with a smile, who we are. Danielle reminds Elida of Summit and says she met me there and we've kept in touch through letters.

"You're from Texas!" Elida shouts.

"Yes."

"Well, yeeehaw!"

Their personalities are distinct. Danielle will interest you in conversation and Elida will entertain you by goofing off. We head back inside the house and Elida and Danielle do this little song called "Sisters" where they put their arms around each others shoulders and sing. It's cute. Shirley loves it. Now that Elida is home, Shirley changes from hostess to manager. Danielle needs to prepare dinner and Elida needs to go pick Nate up at school. Elida comments that she always has to pick up Nate and Danielle always gets the easy jobs. Danielle volunteers to pick up Nate if Elida will get dinner ready, but Elida says no, she'll do it. Shirley has to run to the airport to pick up Randy, who will be in at 7:00 P.M. He will be hungry, she says. So will Nate and the boys. We are now called the boys.

With everyone in action, Paul and I decide this would be a good time to change the oil in the van. It will make us look manly and avoid the perception that we are bums who don't work. Soon, we are under the van and talking about the girls. Paul says he's in love with Danielle. I tell him to calm down. He asks me if there is anything there between her and me. I tell him no. I don't think she'd be interested and besides, I think of her like a sister. Paul says he doesn't think of her like a sister.

I do most of the work on the van. Paul just lies there, underneath, with a wrench in his hand. He has a worried look and then a smile and then a worried look. Stop thinking about her, I tell him. He says shut up. I pull the bolt and let the oil drop down into a pan we borrowed from the Bjur's garage.

"She doesn't like me," Paul whimpers.

"She doesn't know you yet. We just got here."

"And we're leaving. I'll never see her again," Paul sighs.

"You're serious, aren't you."

"Yes," he says.

Not far into the evening, Randy and Shirley head to bed. Nate went to sleep earlier. Paul, Elida, Danielle, and I have a great conversation about churches in the south. They've never seen a mega church. Like Paul, they consider churches that have 1000 members to be a large church. I tell them about First Baptist Church and Second Baptist Church, both of them with more than 20,000 members. They don't understand how 20,000 people can all go to one church. There aren't even 20,000 people who live in Ridgefield.

Danielle and Elida attend a small church just down the road. It has about 200 members. Danielle asks what I've been reading in the Bible and I tell her Ecclesiastes. I'm fascinated by it, I tell her.

"Solomon wrote that, right?"

"Right."

"What is it about?" she asks.

"Well," I begin "it is more or less a memoir of Solomon's life. But condensed. He talks about all of his accomplishments, all his women and wealth, and says none of it means anything outside of a relationship with God."

"I thought about that a lot while I was in Costa Rica," Danielle says. "Everything came to a head down there. I was really bent out of shape about church and Christianity. I knew I had to make a decision about what I believed."

"Danielle," I begin. "I didn't realize you were going through anything like that."

Danielle tells us that she did some serious thinking while she was there. She was very thankful for the other students (Christians) who were faithful to their friendships even while she was asking some serious, and possibly offensive, questions about her faith. Everything was resolved, she says, when she had to get on a plane and discovered that she'd lost her wallet. They wouldn't let her on the plane without her ID. With only an hour to spare, she took a cab to the club where she had been the night before. She prayed all the way there and told God she was sorry and got really upset. She ended up finding her wallet in the booth where she had been seated, and also found a renewed relationship with God thanks to the honest prayers.

Paul says he had a similar experience in the junkyard in Vegas. He says that he had been asking some serious questions, not about the truth of Christ, but about whether or not he was really living out and experiencing his faith. He says finding the part in the junkyard was an "instrumental happening." That's what he calls it, an "instrumental happening."

Before we know it, it is 2:00 A.M. and we are all yawns. Elida says we can sleep downstairs, but Paul and I both shake our heads. We'll sleep outside, we say.

"Outside!" Elida says.

"Can't sleep inside anymore. We've been in the van for over a month. We're used to the fresh air," one of us comments.

"Well!" Elida proclaims. "If you guys are sleeping outside, we're sleeping outside!"

"What?" Danielle questions.

"We'll all sleep on the lawn. I'll get the family sleeping bags." With that Elida disappears down the stairs. We hear her stirring around in a closet. Danielle tells us she's getting the sleeping bags out and pulling them from the garbage bags that Daddy keeps them in. There is a side door off the breakfast nook that steps out onto a deck which overlooks the font yard. Danielle steps out on the deck to see Elida unrolling sleeping bags. "Looks like we're sleeping outside," Danielle smiles.

"...and when they went back into the house, they saw the ghost of their Aunt Edna. She was holding a knife and a pumpkin." Elida's voice is soft and quiet. She is almost whispering. "They look at Aunt Edna and she begins to sway in the wind. She says (Elida's voice gets deep) 'you never should have slept in the pumpkin patch.' "

Danielle can't help but interrupt. "Elida. Aunt Edna is not a scary name. And your story has no point."

"It's a scary story," Elida says.

"For three year olds!" Danielle tells her.

"Shhh." Paul quiets the girls.

"What is it?" Danielle asks.

"Did you hear that?" Paul says.

"Hear what?" asks Elida.

"The voice."

"What voice?" I question.

"It sounded like the wind. It was a whisper. Someone whispered in my ear. It was a low voice."

Elida pulls her sleeping bag over her head. Through the bag we hear her ask, "What did the voice say?"

"It said," Paul pauses, lowering his voice to speak in a whisper, "four...will...die...tonight."

Elida gasps. Danielle chuckles. Then there is silence.

"The voice could have been talking about anyone," I say. "It probably won't be us."

23. Ranch

Paul makes a call to Black Butte Ranch from the Bjur's house and he secures a job for himself as a lifeguard. He also finds there is an opening in the housekeeping department and sets a time for me to interview. You will be a janitor, he says. You will be working with about twenty women. You will love it, he assures me.

Black Butte Ranch is a large active cattle ranch in the mountains of central Oregon. It is a resort, but it's also a summer home for wealthy people from Portland and cities in California. Paul says you can see the Three Sisters, Mt. Washington, and Mt. Jefferson from the meadow beneath Black Butte. Apparently students come from all over the country to live in the woods and work on the ranch. There are hundreds of miles of bike paths and thousands of miles of forest service roads that slip in and out of the Cascade Range. It's a great place to spend the summer, Paul tells me.

"When is my interview?" I ask.

"First thing tomorrow morning."

Danielle looks upset. We've been at the Bjurs for more than a week. We started out as moochers, but then the Bjurs wouldn't let us go. Shirley kept us there, really. She'd say we should stay for another meal, then another, then we'd get to talking over coffee and sooner or later, we'd end up staying the night, sleeping on the lawn, telling stories, and counting stars.

Something did spark between Paul and Danielle. Whether it works out, and how it could, given the fact that we will be living in the woods for the summer, remains to be seen. But they both seem levelheaded and patient. Randy and Shirley enjoy the unfolding of their romance. They approve of Paul.

Danielle will be leaving for Sacramento soon, where she will live with her grandparents and attend summer school. She is on track to receive her bachelor's degree in a short three-year span. Two of those years are behind her.

We pack the van slowly, taking most of the afternoon. Paul is in no hurry to leave and neither am I. Elida ditched school to spend the morning with us and Randy is dillydallying around, pretending he has things to do at home that prevent him from going to work on time. We said our good-byes to Nate early, before he was taken to school, and Shirley has been busy packing lunches for us. I have never seen such kindness. This is Jesus kindness. It has a grip to it. You can feel it clinging to your arms.

Randy gathers us around the van and says a prayer. Similar to Mike's prayer back in Visalia, Randy prays that God would protect us and teach us whatever it is He wants us to know. Randy thanks God for introducing us to them, and making us a part of the family. There's nothing we can say after that. We just climb in the van with Paul at the wheel, and head down the driveway. I take a long look at St. Helens as we depart. I imagine 2000 feet of mountain blowing off the top, sending a cloud of ash more than a mile high. Paul just thinks about Danielle.

Highway 26 runs through Gresham, a town east of Port-land, then climbs for about 20 miles into the town of Sandy. Beyond Sandy we get into thick forests of evergreen and pass through towns with funny names like Rhododendron, Welches, and Government Camp. The air is clean up here. The terrain dips down into a canyon on our right and lifts to 11,000 feet on our left. Mt. Hood is all snow and ice and it is a sight to see. Truly majestic. Full-white brightness in the midday sun. Rock is exposed here and there, but most of it is snow and ice. It is the brightest white I've ever seen. The evergreens climb till their lungs cannot breathe the thin air. And this is where they stop and the snow begins. Tree-line, as they call it, is a great sight from the road. In places Mt. Hood appears as a perfect cone, but then another mile down the road and you see a jagged spot on top, then another mile and it is a perfect cone again. A photographer could take 20 photos from 20 locations and convince an amateur that he's shot 20 separate mountains.

Leaving Mt. Hood in our rear-view mirror, we begin our descent into Central Oregon. Paul is right about the terrain changing abruptly. From the deciduous landscape of the valley, we climbed into dense forest with little undergrowth, and now we have settled into rocks, sand, and sagebrush. The clouds that roll in off the Pacific are too thick and heavy to pass over the Cascades, so Central Oregon gets much less rain. Paul tells me the winter brings occasional snow, but the summers are perfect.

Black Butte rests in the foreground of at least six visible snow-capped mountains. Paul names them as the North Sister, the Middle Sister, and the South Sister, Mt. Jefferson, Mt. Washington, and Three-Fingered Jack. He says he's climbed them all. The Pacific Crest Trail, he tells me, runs right between them, over to Mt. Hood and then across the Columbia River into Washington before finding Mt. Rainier and then Canada. His lifelong dream is to hike the PCT from Mexico to Canada. It will take him more than six months, he says.

When we find the town of Sisters it is just as Paul described. There are cone lickers and rows of shops. It's a western town with wooden walks in front of the shops. You can see the hills lift to the east. We are at the base of Black Butte now. It is a perfect cone of a hill; 5000 feet high, if not more. It should be called a mountain. It is big and dark with clouds around its head and forest around its feet.

The entrance to Black Butte Ranch is only 20 miles beyond the town of Sisters. The road climbs all twenty of the miles. We have circled back into the Cascade range, and the air is the cleanest I've breathed.

Paul signals a left turn and we slow, downshift, and pull into the entrance of the ranch. There is a guardhouse and a gate, and Paul navigates to the window at the house (about the size of a tollbooth). The fellow asks what we are doing and Paul tells him he is a lifeguard showing up for the summer. The fellow lifts the gate and we enter. The ranch is all I expected and more. Before us is a meadow surrounded by forest and through the meadow (a square mile in size) runs a stream, and near the stream are horses and cattle. We park in the lot closest to the lodge and step out. Above the clouds, in the distance, stand the Three Sisters; three towering peaks. Next to the Sisters are Three-Fingered Jack and Mt. Jefferson. Behind us is Black Butte.

Paul points out the pool he will be guarding. It backs up to the pond and sits in front of the tennis courts. There are three pools, he says. We rotate, but I usually get assigned to this one. It's nice, he says, because he usually has friends who work in the cafe and they bring him food. Went all last summer without buying a meal.

——— ——— ———

"Where are we going now?" I ask.

"To make camp. We need to do it before the sun goes down. We have about an hour."

We round back by the entrance gate but bypass it for a road that swings left. Not long onto it, we come upon another security gate. Paul looks at a little sheet of paper and punches the code, the gate swings open and we drive through. Enormous homes are tucked into the trees that surround the meadow. There is a paved sidewalk that stitches one home to another, but they are each set on an acre or more of land. The road weaves back into the homes and crosses a golf course and a small lake and then back into more homes. Paul points out an empty lot that backs up to a fence and then dips down into a small ravine covered in aspen. He explains that we will make camp across the fence and down into the woods. It's illegal to camp back there, he warns. He says that the forest service would fine us if we were to get caught. It's a stealth operation.

"Here's what we'll do," he explains. "Let's drop our gear off in this ditch; we'll park the van and come back for the gear."

"Whatever," I tell him.

He stops the van, opens the side door and removes his backpack. The ditch is 20 yards off the road, so he slides his backpack down into the ditch, comes back for his sleeping bag and does the same with a few other items. I pull my gear out and imitate Paul. He has one tent. We've not used it the entire trip so I didn't know he had it, but he removes it from the van and slides it into the ditch. Then, in an instant, we are driving away. We round a turn or two and park the van in the parking lot of another community pool. Nobody will bother the van here, he tells me.

"Why don't we just live in the van?" I ask.

"Ranch security will make sure nobody is living in it. It's okay to park it here for a while, as long as we move it every couple of days, but we can't sleep in it. They will make us leave."

I have a hundred more questions, but Paul does not seem to be in the mood to answer questions. He is home, I guess. These are his stomping grounds.

I realize it, now. All this time I've known Paul, he has been the new guy. Now I am the new guy. It's an odd switch. This is clearly his comfort zone: the woods and all.

We are at a quick clip back to our gear, and Paul checks over his shoulder before pacing down the length of the ditch. Follow me, he says, and shoulders his pack and runs. I grab mine and run behind him. He tosses his pack over a fence and it rolls down a ledge built by exposed rock. He heads back for the rest of the gear. We are each two trips apiece to collect our stuff.

We jump the fence, boulder down the ledge, and gather our things. Paul leads the way through the thick forest, through a hundred yards of baby aspen, all growing only a few feet apart, and into a clearing where there is a tent established. Henry, Paul says. Henry has already set up camp.

"Who is Henry?" I ask.

"An old friend," Paul answers. "You'll love Henry, Don. He's great." Paul walks over to the opening of the tent and drops his gear. "Hank!" he yells. Nobody answers. "He isn't here," Paul says, looking in the tent. "Well," he continues, "we should go ahead and set up the tent."

"Small tent," I say.

"We're not going to sleep in it, Don. We'll just put our gear in there during the day. We should put it over here, under this tree. That way nobody will spot it." Paul begins unrolling the tent. I help him but I don't know what I'm doing, so finally I just stand back and watch, handing him things when he needs them.

"Maybe you can go back and get the rest of the gear at the ledge," Paul tells me.

"Sure. Just bring it all back here, right?"

Paul is busy with the tent. He talks to me without looking up. "Here would be the place."

I venture back through the aspen. On the way, I encounter two deer. They are nibbling at grass. I see their graceful brown bodies in splotches through the thick of trees. When they hear me, they become stiff, move in sudden jerks, find my eyes, stare me down, then leap off in majestic bounds. I read that St. Francis of Assisi could talk to animals. Many legends surround St. Francis. Supposedly he was walking down a road on an icy evening, had a lustful thought, and threw himself into a frozen pond. He believed the pain would occupy his mind in place of the lust. High price to be able to talk to animals.

24. The Woods

We are at 4000 feet, and there is not a city for 20 miles, and there are mountains and pines and oh so many stars. At midnight there is more light in the sky than darkness. Brilliant blue clusters spread thick and dense and they sparkle and fade, sparkle and fade. It is silent music, the night sky. Lovers do well to walk under stars. God does well to live atop them. Do angels look down upon that to which we gaze upward? There are so many stars I dream of them. I open my eyes and see stars, then close them and see stars.

The cow jumped over the moon, only to become tangled in stardust, cough and sneeze, and come tumbling back to earth, rolling around on his back, holding his belly, and laughing at his fate. As I lay there last night, and Paul and I hushed our talking, I realized this is the first time I have truly encountered beauty in nature. I've read poems that have made my heart race. I've read scenes in novels that have caused me to close the book, set my head in my hands, and wonder how a human could so brilliantly orchestrate words. But nature has never inspired me until now. My God is an

artist. I have known this for a long time, seeing His brush-
work in the sunrise and sunset, and His sculpting in the
mountains and the rivers. But the night sky is His greatest
work. Do not die without seeing it. Find a stretch of woods
far from your home, bring a sleeping bag, and wait for the
stars to come. They enter the stage one by one, and soon there
is a crowd and then a symphony of sight.

I do not remember falling asleep. As I told you, I dreamt
of stars. I do not remember closing my eyes. But sunlight
tells me I did. And Paul, frantically, shakes my bag and interrupts my slumber. He tells me I am going to be late for my
interview. I tell him I will go tomorrow. He lifts the end of
my bag and I half slip out.

"No, Don. You have to go. We both have to get jobs,"
he reminds me.

"A little more sleep, a little more folding of the hands,"
I quote from Proverbs.

"No!" he shouts. "You have to go. You are going to
be late."

"You should go," a strange voice says.

"Who is that?" I ask.

"Don, this is Henry. Henry, this is Don. He's a friend
from Texas."

"The Lone Star state." Henry says with a smile. He must
have slipped into camp late last night. He is a wiry fellow
with great big blonde hair sticking out in all directions. A
handsome fellow with big teeth.

"Nice to meet you, Henry."

"Good to meet you, Don. I understand you are going to
be a janitor."

"Yes," I say. "And what is it you do?"

"I'm a lifeguard."

"Tough job," I say as I stand to my feet.

"Someone has to do it," he says.

I look back over at Paul who is wearing a worried expression and looking at the sun through the aspen.

"It's 7:30, Don. You better hustle. Your interview is at 8:00."

"You can tell the time by looking at the sun?"

"Yes. It's late. You better go."

"I didn't know you could do that."

"Do what?" Paul questions.

"Tell time by looking at the sun. Native Americans do that, you know."

"We'll talk later, Don. You need to hit the road." Paul looks at the sun while he's talking. "Do you remember how to get there?"

"Just go up the road and take a left. Two miles, right?"

"Two miles," Paul clarifies.

"How do I look?" I ask.

"Terrible," he says. "Do something with your hair before you talk to them."

"You look fine." Henry speaks through his sleeping bag.

"Thanks, Henry. Pleasure to meet you."

"Meet me at the main pool when you are done," Paul tells me. "Do you remember where it is?"

"I'll find it," I say, stepping into my boots and heading off through the aspen.

"Cool guy," Henry says to Paul as I walk off.

"He's going to be late," Paul states.

The woods grow out of a mist this morning. There are patches of cloud hanging thick in the aspen. It is cold. Must be forty degrees, if not colder. I find a good stride and stick to it, more to warm up than to make my interview on time. Not more than a hundred yards from camp I stumble upon the deer I saw yesterday. There are two, one with horns. A boy and a girl, I surmise, although I do not know which is which. I decide that the girl has horns, and I name her Abbey and the boy I name John. John Deer and Deer Abbey.

Fitting names. I check behind me to see if Paul or Henry can see or hear me, and then I try the St. Francis trick.

"Hey, there, John and Abbey."

They quickly look up and freeze. Their muscles locked, their stare containing the essence of fear.

"I'm godly," I tell them. "Like that Francis fellow. It's okay, you can talk to me. Nobody is looking. Nobody will hear."

In an instant, John and Abbey are off through the woods. With balletic grace they fire through the mist like arrows. They turn and twist around pillows of mist, and then jump over some brush and disappear. Obviously they do not recognize my righteousness.

The road to the housekeeping office is windy and hilly, and is lined by trees and houses. There must be a thousand homes here at Black Butte Ranch. Earlier, when Paul suggested working on a cattle ranch, I pictured us roping cows and driving teams of wild horses. But this is a resort. No doubt about it. It may have started as an active cattle ranch, but now it is a giant real estate project.

"Are you Donald Miller?" a dark-haired woman asks as I enter the housekeeping department. She comes out of her office with a clipboard in her hand. She looks to be stressed: pale white face with lips traced in red lipstick and big bushy eyebrows. Her hands are weathered. One hand grips the clipboard and the other holds a walkie-talkie. She barks a command into the walkie-talkie and then tells me to wait in her office. I can hear her dividing up houses. Team one is to take houses 1-40 and team two is to take 41-80 and so on and so on, all the way through team ten. She makes small talk with one of the workers and then comes back into the office.

"You are late," she says.

"Yes, ma'am. I'm sorry about..."

"Do you make it a habit to be late to interviews?"

"No, ma'am. It's just that..."

"I don't need to hear your personal problems. If you want to work here, you need to be on time."

"I understand," I tell her.

"You understand," she says in sarcasm. "If you understood, you would have been on time. But you didn't understand. You understand now, but you didn't understand before or else you would have been on time. Do you understand?"

"Is that a trick question?" I say with a smile.

"Very funny. We've got a smart aleck, do we?"

"No, ma'am. I didn't mean it like that." I'm hesitant with my words. This woman has no sense of humor. "I was just breaking the ice, I guess. I won't be late. I promise you that much."

"You don't have the job yet, Mr. Miller. You may not have the opportunity to show up on time."

The tension in the room is broken when a large woman steps into the office with a pile of folded towels in her hands. I gather that my interviewer's name is Lucy, because this large woman calls her Lucy. And the large woman's name is Laurell. Laurell tells Lucy that she will need more towels if she is going to clean the condos and the houses 1-40. Lucy tells her to take more, but to make sure and write it down so she knows where they are. Before leaving, Laurell looks down at me and says "fresh meat." She smiles as she says it, so I smile back and laugh. Laurell laughs.

"I'll take this one," Laurell says. "We could use some muscle on my team."

"He has a habit of being late," Lucy says to Laurell.

"I'll whip him into shape," Laurell says, and looks at me with a grin. I grin back.

"You've got him," Lucy tells her. "If he gives you any trouble, tell me. I have already found out he has an attitude."

"What's his name?" Laurell asks. Nobody bothers to ask me.

"It doesn't matter," Lucy says, and slaps Laurell on the back. "He won't last long."

Laurell exits and walks back into the laundry room to get more towels.

"Alright, Donald Miller," Lucy begins, "what is your social security number?"

I give her the number.

"And your address?"

I give her my Texas address.

"Coming in all the way from Texas are you? That's a long commute, don't you think?"

I tell her I don't have an address around here.

Lucy leans back in her chair. She sets her pen down and runs her hands through her long, unkempt hair. She looks out the window.

"Donald, you know that people aren't supposed to live in the woods around here, don't you?"

That's it, I guess. I messed up. "I've heard that, yes, ma'am."

Lucy takes a long look at me, shakes her head, picks up her pen, and begins to write an address on the form.

"There is a shower in the back," she says.

"Pardon me?"

Lucy points through her office door toward a door on the other side of the laundry room. "Through that door," she says, "there is a shower. If a person needed to take a shower in the morning, a person could do it through that door."

"I see."

"Be here at 7:30 A.M. tomorrow morning," she says. She doesn't look up, she just writes on my form.

I sit there and look at her. I cross my legs. I uncross my legs.

"You can go," she says.

"Thank you," I tell her.

"Be on time," she says.

"Yes."

"My name is Lucy. Call me Lucy, but I am not your friend. One mistake, and you are gone."

"I understand," I say.

"You did not understand this morning. You may understand now, but you did not understand this morning."

As I walk out of the office, Laurell snickers when she sees me. I begin to understand why the deer did not speak with me this morning.

———   ———   ———

Bike paths line each street on the ranch. The streets are dark asphalt, and the bike paths are half as wide as the street. I weave through the streets, not really knowing where I am going. I decide that if I continue walking north, I will find the main pool where Paul is supposed to be working. So I wander, between and around big expensive homes. Post-yuppie couples in Volvos pass me. None of them wave.

The bike path breaks away from the road and heads off, away from the houses, into a thick of trees. It is here that I see the woman of my dreams. She is riding a bike, alone. A girl this pretty should not be riding alone. She passes me quickly and grins. She's wearing a Black Butte polo-style shirt. She must work on the ranch, somewhere. I bet Paul knows her. I turn around to watch her pedal through the trees and disappear as the bike path weaves right, which is probably the direction I should be walking. She had long brown hair and looked polite and innocent. What's a nice girl like you doing in a forest like this, I think to myself.

The bike path opens up into a meadow where Mt. Washington, Three-Fingered Jack and Mt. Jefferson are visible. They are snowcapped, lit by the mid-morning sun, and simply beautiful. All is silent, but in my mind I hear the cold wind blow furiously across the mountaintops. Clouds are high and scattered. Beyond the clouds is deep, endless blue. The meadow is a mile wide, it seems. The further I walk into the open, the more spectacular the view becomes. Black Butte lifts to my right, and behind me are the Three Sisters and Broken Top. Six mountains, as well as Black Butte, are all visible from the center of the meadow. Stunning. Absolutely stunning.

The primary occupation of lifeguards is to swing a whistle around their palms. They become good at it, like a cowboy with a lasso.

I find Paul sitting up in his chair, twirling his whistle. Henry is preparing chemicals to put into the pool. Paul asks me if I'm hungry.

"I could eat," I answer.

"Henry, would you mind if I took lunch?"

"Bring me some," Henry says.

"Will do." And with that, Paul jumps down.

"See you later, Henry." I tell him.

"Yeah, dude. I'll see you tonight. Are you going with us to the cave?"

"What cave?" I ask.

"I haven't told him yet," Paul says.

I nod at Henry and he turns to watch the pool. He takes his position atop the chair and starts twirling his whistle. He tells one of the kids not to run.

Paul and I cross the lawn and take seats on a deck outside the cafe. I ask him how we can afford to eat, since we don't have but twenty dollars or so. He tells me that the owner of the cafe always takes care of the guys who live in the woods. The kids who live in their parents' houses pay, but the folks who live in the woods eat for free.

"Do we order?" I ask.

"Nope. We just sit here, and sooner or later food finds its way to the table. He gives us only what he has too much of. You know, leftover pizza and that sort of thing."

"I get it."

"So, Don, how much are they going to pay you?"

"I didn't ask."

"You didn't ask!"

"Didn't think of it. She was kinda tough, you know. She was mad because I was late."

"Told you," he says.

"I didn't think they took housekeeping so seriously."

"Oh yeah," he says. "They're like the army. They drive around in those big white vans and almost run people over. They're serious."

"I gathered that."

A young girl comes through the door and says hello to Paul. It's the girl from the meadow. The girl on the bike. Paul gets up and gives her a hug. He calls her Molly. I love that name. Perfect name for a gal, Molly.

"Molly, this is my friend, Don."

"Nice to meet you," she says. She doesn't remember me from the meadow.

"Nice to meet you," I tell her.

"I suppose you guys are hungry."

"Starved," Paul tells her.

"How does a calzone sound? Sound good?"

"Sounds great," Paul says.

Molly walks back into the cafe.

"Where does she live? Is she from Oregon?"

"I don't know where she's from. She goes to school somewhere in Minnesota. But I don't think she is from Oregon. She stays here every summer with Jodie."

"Who's Jodie?" I ask.

"Jodie is who she stays with."

"You said that already."

"She's a friend. Jodie is a friend. Her family has a summer home on the ranch. Jodie is a lifeguard."

"And Molly is her friend."

"Yes," Paul clarifies. A moment later, "Speaking of infatuation..."

"I'm not infatuated."

"Anyway," he begins. "Speaking of infatuation. Guess who called today?"

"Who?"

"Danielle."

"Danielle called you?"

"She called us. She called the lodge and they transferred the call to me at the pool."

"What did she have to say?"

"She's coming here. She's coming by on her way to Sacramento."

"Cool. How long is she going to stay?" I ask.

"Just for the day. She'll drive all night to get down to Sacramento. She's coming this weekend. Friday, possibly."

"What is today, Paul?"

"Today." Paul thinks to himself for a second. "I think it's Tuesday. But I'm not sure."

"Tuesday," I clarify.

Molly comes out with two huge calzones and sets mine down with a smile. She asks if I'm going to the cave tonight. I give her a confused look, and then glance at Paul.

"I haven't told him yet," Paul says.

25. The Cave

Poppycock religion is America's new faith. It is easy. It is quick. It allows a person to feel spiritual, seem intellectual, have a faith to follow, and have something interesting to talk about over coffee. Poppycock is the quick-fix diet of the spiritual industry. It sells. It rarely threatens or confronts the seeker, allowing each to forge his own individual "religion." The poppycock believer changes the rules as he goes. If he misses a basket, he will say that a missed basket is still worth two points. The poppycock believer does not serve his god, rather his god serves him. He has everything to gain and nothing to lose.

But the Christian faith is very different. God is both the creator and the source of the commands by which humans should live. God gives man a choice: He can be his own god, or he can serve and follow the one true God.

It is Christianity, I believe, that truly faces the facts of reality. The Christian does not try to create his or her own reality. Our search for the truth leads us to Christ. Faith costs something (as all things of worth do) and obedience is hard, but God has poured out His love for us and given us the grace that empowers us to obey.

Here's the rub. I believe everything I have just written. Living it out in the heat of every decision is another matter.

It is the occupation of a Christian to glorify God. The sunrise glorifies God; it is beautiful and God made it. The sunset and the starry night do the same. But I am unshaven, unkempt, and carry a peculiar odor. I am certain that it is not my beautiful looks which glorify God, it is my actions. And all I have to do is let Him work through me, right? Easier said than done. The multitude of formulas (for living the Christian life with success) proposed by Christian writers, preachers, conference speakers, and televangelists simply confuse me. They have different ideas about how it is done, offering promises of fulfillment and joy based on three easy steps, four points of action, or the five smooth stones that David threw. My mind swims.

It would be easier if God would have given us a point A and a point B. It would be easier if He were to make it clear. But He hasn't.

Many of us associate the Christian faith with a list of do's and don'ts. And there are do's and don'ts, to be sure. But if the Christian life is to be oriented in relationship, why is there so much talk of formula? Could it be that the reason we are more interested in formula than relationship is that we would like to deal with our need for religion without dealing with the complications of relationship? That even though we have chosen the Christian faith instead of "pop-pycock religion," we ultimately want the same thing as the pagan? And what is that? Easy answers, comfortable senti-ments, beliefs that make us feel good. So we go through the motions. We go to our churches, we read our self-help books, we watch our religious television, and we check each item off our to-do list as if we were doing work for pay. One thing I am sure of. This is not the kind of real-life faith I'm looking for.

We are not sleeping in the woods tonight. Paul tells me that everyone is headed to the cave. Apparently there are long lava tubes that tunnel under these mountains. There is a special one that these guys camp in every year. It holds all sorts of memories.

We have been at the cafe most of the day. I talked with Paul for a while over lunch, then Henry came and joined us, and Paul introduced me to the guys who are going with us to the cave: Eddie, Pat, Brick, and Owen.

Brick takes the van up steep, dark roads lit softly by moonlight through clouds. Brick is commenting to Paul on the handling. He says it's not bad for a van this old. Paul tells him about the mechanic in Nevada and about the junkyard. Brick isn't the spiritual type, so he shrugs it off.

Brick pulls the van over into some trees. Pine scrapes the side of the van and Owen has a tough time getting the door open. Nice parking, Eddie says. Brick thanks him in sarcasm. Outside the van, everyone acts like they know what they are doing. They grab sleeping bags and Brick throws one at me. Eddie asks about matches and Pat says he has some.

"We running?" Eddie asks.

"Sure we are," Paul tells him.

With that, Eddie bolts into the woods as Pat and Owen follow him. Pat runs smooth and fast around small trees and over logs. Owen simply runs through them. He makes his way through the forest like some sort of beast. I am behind them, and Paul and Brick are behind me. Henry is running parallel. It's quite a sight, all of us running in and out of moon shadows. If there were music to the scene, it would be bagpipes. All of us are breathing heavily, and it's cold, so mist rises out of our mouths. Nobody screams or yells, they just run quickly. I don't know why we are running like this. Seems sensible to walk. But I don't want to get lost, so I run. And we run. And we run. About 20 minutes into the forest, we come to the top of a hill.

"This is it," Paul says.

"I don't see a cave," I tell him.

Paul points to a hole in the ground. It's not a large hole, about five feet by five feet. But he says it's the mouth of a cave. Brick takes a flashlight out of his pack and shines it down into the hole. "The ladder is down," he says.

"Happens every year," Eddie grumbles.

Brick takes some tubed webbing out of his pack and ties it around his waist. He has a headlamp that he straps around his head. He ties the rope around his waist and lowers himself down into the cave. His light throws shadows against the rock wall. It flickers like a fire. As I get a glimpse of the inside of the cave, I note that it is large inside. Enormous, really.

Brick picks up a handmade ladder from the floor of the cave and pokes it through the opening. Eddie is the first to descend, then Paul, then me with Henry, Owen, and Pat right behind. Paul and Brick are the only ones with lights, which they shine deep into the cave.

I follow the light about a hundred yards down to where Paul and Brick reveal an old fire pit. There is wood beside it and they begin to make a fire. Pat has matches and Eddie rolls up a little paper to get the thing going. As it comes to life, the fire slowly illumines our cave, and it is something to see. The rock is deep and jagged, but the ground is smooth. The back of the cave extends at least 200 yards, beyond which it is too dark to see.

"You ever been to the back of this thing?" I ask Paul.

"Nope. We've been back about a mile or so, but it's just more of the same, really. Doesn't get any smaller, doesn't get any bigger."

"Any animals in here?" I ask him.

"Never seen any. The opening is kinda tough on animals. I would think if they fell in, they'd die with the fall. If that didn't get them, they'd die of thirst pretty quickly."

"I see," I say.

Eddie, Pat, and Owen lay out their sleeping bags and sit atop them. Owen is writing something and Pat is tinkering with his pocketknife. Eddie pulls out a pipe and fills the air with sweet-smelling smoke. I lean over to whisper to Paul.

"You know I have to be at work at 7:30 tomorrow. Earlier if I want to take a shower."

"Don't worry, I'll get you there. You'll be fine," he assures me.

Eddie overhears us. "Where you working, Don?"

"Housekeeping," I tell him.

"Militant types," Brick says.

"You can say that again," Henry chimes in.

One of the guys asks how long I intend to stay. I tell them it depends on whether I get a job in Colorado or not. I applied for a position at the Summit, but I haven't called them to see if I got the job. If so, I hope to make enough money in housekeeping to get a plane ticket to Colorado Springs. Paul looks surprised at this. We never really talked about what I was going to do when the trip was over. But that's the plan.

"I didn't know you were thinking of Colorado," Paul says.

"It's not final or anything. I just sent an application in before we left. They start sessions in June, so I would be here for a month, no matter what."

"That's cool. I'd just hate for you to miss a summer in the woods."

"I'll be here for a month. You know, you should think about coming out to Colorado at the end of the summer. If I get the job, I'll be there until September. You should think about coming out for the last session at the Summit."

"Sounds good," Paul says.

We talk until we run out of stories and, one by one, we fall quiet. Everyone is in their sleeping bags, so I lie there and watch the shadows slide up and down the rocks. The smoke drifts to the top of the cave and glides out through the opening. Before long I hear the gentle tap of rain and see the droplets of water reflect against the fire. Water pools on the ground beneath the opening of the cave. I wonder to myself whether Paul put my sleeping bag back into the tent before he left aspen camp this morning.

No warning this time. Paul just lifts the end of my bag and I slide out onto the hard floor of the cave. The fire has gone out, but morning light shines in through the opening of the cave.

"It's 6:00, Don. Time for work."

"I don't have to be there till 7:30," I tell him.

"We're an hour away. I have to drop you off and come back for these guys. Come on, it's a good hike back to the van. You can't be late again."

"I'm up," I say. "I'm up, give me a second here." I find my boots and a rock to sit on. I pull my cold boots over my cold feet. I look at my warm sleeping bag and all I want to do is climb back into it. Henry uncovers his head and smiles through his big teeth with his blonde, straight hair going in all directions. "Clean a toilet for me," he says.

"I'll be thinking of you the entire time," I tell him. He has a good laugh at that.

"Off to fight the war," Eddie says.

Paul rolls his bag and stuffs it into his backpack. He does the same with mine and before I can lace my boots, he is on the ladder climbing out through the roof. I follow him up into the sky. Everything on the ground is wet. Rain drips from the trees. Patches of snow have settled on the ground. It's spring, I think to myself. It's spring and there is snow on the ground.

I follow Paul through the forest. There is no trail to speak of, so we head downhill, letting gravity do all the work. I'm getting dirty sliding over fallen logs, covered in moss and dirt. My hands are brown and muddy. I'll look fine for Lucy and Laurell.

26. Ranch Life

Black Butte Ranch began in the early 1900s when a development company decided that the 29,000 families in the state of Oregon who made more than $40,000 might very well be interested in a second home in the mountains. Their aim was to settle five percent of these wealthy families into vacation homes that would sit empty during the winter months. It was a bold move. Today, one might call it absurd. But back then it worked. Homes were sold and a summer village began. Today homes sell for $300,000 or more. There are over 700 properties on the ranch. Some structures are simply two-bedroom cottages and some are nine-bedroom manors. Paul and I have settled in well during the three weeks we've been here. We live for free. We don't even have to pay taxes.

On several occasions, someone from the ranch will offer me a place to stay. But I always refuse. Only last night we were up late at a party where we drank coffee, played Scrabble, and listened to John Prine records when the fellow who owned the house (I do not know his name) offered to let me stay the night in a spare bedroom. It was well below freezing last night, but I turned him down all the same.

I suppose it takes about a week to get used to sleeping outside. But once accustomed to it, a person cannot easily go back to having a roof over his head. It is no wonder that Christ had a conflict with the rich young ruler. I believe that if Christ were to come to the ranch today, and bid us follow, the folks in the woods might go, and the folks in the homes would probably stay to mow their lawns.

If a man's senses are either sharpened or dulled by the way he rubs against time, mine have become increasingly sharp over these last three weeks. I am hungry, so I appreciate food and thank God for it whenever I find ice cream or other perishables in a condo I am cleaning. I appreciate friendship, and need no television to keep me company. I appreciate birds chirping, as there is no radio to seduce my ears. I appreciate God, because I live in the house He has made, as opposed to a house I purchased by my own means. If I found God on the open road, I found Him the same way Solomon did: by process of elimination. I found God because He kindly removed all the distractions.

I have learned that I don't really know very much about God. All that time in Sunday school filling my head with knowledge about God. But the teaching means very little compared to the experiencing. I've spent so much of my Christian life living like I had God in my pocket. What a mistake. He is bigger than I ever imagined.

If I could, if it would be responsible, I would live in these woods forever: I would let my beard grow, hunt my own food, chart the stars, and write poems about mountains. But these days are passing, and I fear they will soon be over. This morning I made a call to Colorado and Summit Ministries offered me a job. I will be leaving Oregon in a week, leaving behind Paul, Henry, and the boys.

--- --- ---

Paul worked the early shift this morning so he could be free when Danielle arrived. We're expecting her some time before lunch. She's only staying the day, then driving south to Sacramento so she can live with her grandparents and attend summer school.

I'm sitting on the deck outside the cafe. The pool is unusually full of children. But it's a Saturday and all the rich folks are here using their summer homes, so Paul has his hands full. He waves from atop his chair and I wave back. From the deck all the mountains are visible above the meadow where a creek divides the landscape in two. A cowgirl is driving horses into a pen where she will saddle them and give people trail rides for a fee.

Out in the distance, I see Molly. She is just on the other side of the pond and heading to the cafe for work. Nothing ever happened between Molly and me. She got word through Henry that I thought something about her but she didn't respond. Henry says she's still hooked on Eddie even though Eddie is hooked on some New York ballerina that we've all heard a dozen stories about. Still, there is something beautiful about the girl that won't have you. Molly is turned sideways now trying to straighten a bow on the back of her dress. You have to love a girl that wears a dress to work.

Paul comes down from his chair and Henry takes his place. Henry offers a wave from the high post. Paul jumps the railing and sits down next to me.

"Any sign of Danielle?" He asks.

"Yeah. She was with some big football player earlier. She said she'd try to make time for you a little later."

"Very funny."

"No," I say. "I haven't heard from her. When is she supposed to get here?"

"Any time now. She should have been here by 11:00, but she is probably running late."

Paul waves at Molly, who is peering through the glass doors. She mouths and asks him whether he is hungry and Paul nods his head yes.

"So," Paul rests easy in his chair. "Where you been all morning?"

"I spent the morning at camp."

"Sleeping?" He asks with a laugh.

"No, actually. If you must know, I was reading."

"The Bible?"

"Yeah."

"What were you reading?"

"Ecclesiastes."

"Still? Don, move on."

"I want to. It's just that it makes me think about this trip."

"What do you mean?"

"Well," I lean forward like I'm starting into a lecture. "You and I have nothing, right?"

"Right," Paul agrees.

"And we're completely happy. At least I am happy."

"I'm happy too," he assures me.

"Well, that's more or less what Solomon is saying. Nothing made him happy except for God."

"I understand," my friend mumbles.

"That's similar to what you were saying back in Portland. That getting to know God is what the Christian journey is all about."

"What does that have to do with having nothing?"

"Well, I don't know if I could have gotten to know God as well as I've begun to without getting all the other stuff out of the way and learning to trust Him."

"What do you mean?"

"He's forced us to get to know Him, Paul. I mean, we took the initiative by hitting the road. But God may have been behind us breaking down, and meeting the mechanic;

getting hungry, and having food given to us. It's as though He lead us all this way, not to bring us to Oregon, but to bring us to Him."

"Sounds like a sermon, Don."

"But you know what I mean, don't you?"

"Yeah, except the trip is still going. You make it sound like you've figured it all out already."

"I understand that it's still going. It never ends. The reason we exist is to get to know God. That's what earth is for, right?"

"I suppose."

"Well, that's all I'm saying then."

"You haven't said anything."

"What do you mean I haven't said anything? I'm saying that the only reason we exist on this earth is to get to know God."

"Yeah?"

"And God has led us to get to know Him better. It's obvious by all that we've seen and done. He is always reaching out to us."

"I understand, Don. But isn't that obvious?"

"Not to me. I don't think I understood this before. I mean, I might have understood it as a theological principle, but I don't think I really understood it. Before we left, my paradigm was that I was supposed to serve God. Follow a list of rules. And if I did, God would make my life go better. But it was just a cultural thing. God was kind of like a genie in a lamp."

"Your faith was cultural? What do you mean?"

"It was about going to church, because that's the way I was raised. I read my Bible because my friends did, because of my upbringing. But now I've taken a second look at God, and I believe that what I've been looking for in terms of the 'Christian journey,' is not the 'Christian journey' at all."

"Explain," Paul says.

"I think that I was expecting God to do something in my life that was supernatural. But I've begun to realize that all of life is supernatural. I mean, what is more miraculous? God healing somebody, or God giving us a sunrise every morning? I think I was differentiating the supernatural from the every day. So, I was worldly. I mean, I still am. It's a process, I think. It takes time to begin to connect the mundane with the eternal. But ultimately, life has no meaning apart from an eternal perspective. Maybe that's what Solomon was getting at in Ecclesiastes. Maybe we just need to learn to open our eyes."

27. Sunrise

We do not understand how time passes. We cannot study it like a river or tame it with a clock. Our devices only mark its coming and going. I dropped an anchor three months back but time did not slow.

Everything plays like an art film tonight. Owen is listening to Bruce Springstein on the jukebox. He says Bruce is as good as Bob Dylan. Danielle is sitting across from me at the table and she's flipping pages in Eddie's literature book. Molly is making everybody yogurt. She closed the cafe several hours ago, but let us in to hang out because Paul told her I was leaving and everyone decided to throw a "going away" celebration. We've been sitting around for hours. It's late, and Danielle has a look of frustration because she knows every minute she waits will make for a longer, more weary drive down to Sacramento. Henry and Jodie are arm wrestling and laughing because Henry keeps letting her win.

"When you leaving?" Eddie asks me.

"The end of the week," I tell him.

Molly comes over with yogurt. Paul told Danielle about my crush so Danielle offers a gentle smile when Molly hands me my cup. Molly rounds the tables and gives everyone as they'd asked: chocolate or vanilla or both swirled together.

"I think you should stay," Henry says.

"Stay, Don," Jodie offers.

"He's already made up his mind," Paul tells them.

"Where are you going again?" Molly asks.

"Colorado," I tell her.

"Last I checked, we had mountains here," Owen says, dropping another quarter into the jukebox.

"Well, Don," Danielle begins. "I'm jealous. I'd love to be going back to Colorado. I think you're making the right decision."

Paul looks over at Danielle like she's crazy. Danielle just shrugs her shoulders and grins.

Molly swipes the table with a wet cloth. She laughs at us but then tells us she needs to get going. She has to work in the morning and it's already four o'clock. She's not going to get much sleep.

"It's four in the morning!" Danielle exclaims.

"Sure is," Paul says.

"Oh, heavens. I've got to get going."

"Danielle!" Paul gives her a confused look. "You can't drive. You haven't slept."

"I've had about seven cups of coffee. I have to get to Sacramento. I'll be fine."

"Stay here," Paul tells her. "Stay here and camp for the night. You can get started tomorrow."

"I have to go," she says into Paul's lovesick eyes.

"I don't think that is a good idea, Danielle. Stay here for a few hours and get some sleep." Danielle thinks to herself for a second, but shakes her head no. She gets up and gathers her things.

"You can sleep at my place," Jodie tells her.

"No. I need to go. I'm good about driving at night. I'll pull over and sleep if I need to. Besides, the sun will be up in an hour or so. Don't worry. I'll be fine."

"Famous last words," Eddie says.

Paul and I walk Danielle out to her car and they exchange a close hug. Danielle gives me a hug too, but it's one of those "old friend" types of hugs, not like the "I can't wait to see you, my heart is aglow with passionate fire" hug she gave Paul. Oh well. Maybe there's a gal waiting for me in Colorado.

Danielle gets into her car and closes the door. Paul does not blink or shift his eyes while she fastens her seat belt.

"Pull over as soon as you get tired," he tells her.

"I will," she says. Then she tells us that she loves us. Paul grins when she says it.

"She said she loves *us*, not just you," I tell him under my breath.

Danielle's brake lights lay their glow on the asphalt and she sputters around the parking lot, down the road and out toward the main gate. Paul watches her all the way out, never taking his eye from the little head above the driver's seat.

"You think she'll be all right, Don?"

"I think so. She's a smart girl."

"You know, Don. I think she's the one."

"What are you talking about? You haven't known her one month."

"One month is a long time," he says.

"One month is one month."

"That's a long time. Besides, it's been longer than that. It's been one month and a few days."

"Oh, I see. That makes a difference."

"Sure it does," Paul says, shifting his weight around and kicking a little rock. We walk across the parking lot toward the road without saying a word. Black Butte is visible in the fading moonlight. The sun will be coming up in an hour or so and the earth is beginning to ready itself. Distant birds chirp and clouds are perching themselves on the backs of mountains.

"You want to catch sunrise?" Paul asks.

"Sounds good. It's not like we're going to get any sleep tonight."

"Where?" Paul asks.

"How about the meadow. We can see the entire horizon from the meadow."

"Sounds good," he says.

I trail Paul to the center of the meadow.

"This one's going to be a good one." I'm walking with my hands in my pockets, watching closely at his feet, being careful not to step off the dark trail. "See those clouds, Paul? Those will light up."

The earth around the meadow is heavy in anticipation. The mountains are silhouetted like sleeping dragons. There is a deep, blue coolness at the western edge of the land-scape, where a few stars linger, their last flickered flames shimmering.

Paul wraps his arms around his chest, unfolds them, blows warm air into his cupped hands then slides them into his pockets. He's shifting his stiff weight from foot to foot and squinting his eyes, breathing thick mist into the air around him.

"Thanks, Don."

"Thanks for what?"

"Just thanks. I'm going to miss you around here."

"You should come to Colorado, Paul. You'd love it."

"I'll think about it," he says.

"You'll think about it. I thought you said you'll miss me."

"Won't miss you that bad."

"I see," I tell him.

Had these mountains eyes, they would wake to find two strangers in their fences, standing in admiration as a breathing red pours its tinge upon earth's shore. These mountains, which have seen untold suns rise, long to thunder praise but stand reverent, silent so that man's weak praise should be given God's full attention.

It is a great wonder that those exposed to such beauty forfeit their obedience in the face of this miraculous evidence. Had these mountains the gift of logic, they might very well contemplate both the majesty of God and the ignorance of man in one bewildering context.

Their brows are rumpled even now.

Acknowledgments:

I owe heartfelt thanks to Paul Harris for giving me the sort of friendship a guy could write a book about.

And to Terry Glaspey, my editor, who opened the windows in the book and let the fresh air in. Please take the cost of one box of red pens from my first royalty check. You'll have to cover the cost of the second box yourself. I still have my pride.

This true story would not have been written without the real-life characters who make my life more interesting than television. Kind thanks to Randy and Shirly Bjur, Danielle, Elida and Nate, Wes and Maja, Grampa and Grandma Bjur, and the whole Ridgefield/Sacramento clan. Also, Ben Bonham, Betty and Bob from the truck stop, and Mrs. Tucker and Mike from California.

A number of people read the early stages of the manuscript and gave criticism that helped the book like medicine. Kim Moore proofread the project and made me look smart by correcting my rotten grammar and spelling. John and Terri MacMurray read and praised every chapter, and I would not have sent it to a publisher save their kindness and encouragement. Also Mary Miller, Evelyn Hall, Nathan and Sara Pylate, Shelly Burke, Andy Whipps, Amy Martin, Missy Tygert, Adam Rehman, Jamie Bushek, Sara Mathews, Matt Jacobson, Don Jacobson, Jeff Baldwin, Ross Tunnell, Michaela Frick, Kim Kemper, Dave Beitler, Lonnie Hull-Dupont, Gregg Harris, Matt and Julie Canlis, Randy and Jan Demlow, Angie Rabatin, Scott Armstrong, and David Gentiles. Special thanks to Curt Heidschmidt and Rick Crosser for their friendship and encouragement. Much gratitude to Jeff Olson for countless conversations and for giving me the opportunity to read portions of the manuscript to the college group and Mosaic. I owe a debt of gratitude to Fred "one page a day" Willis for giving me Robert Pirsig's book with a little note on the inside cover. And to Chad Hicks and Stephanie Storey for their early encouragement and excitement about the book. Many thank-you's to the MMT at GSCC for being real and being role models. Big Texas thanks to my family whom the mountains do not replace. I miss you like a pain. And lastly, to my dearest friend Emily who was called back in her fifty-sixth year. Tough to trust the heavens...kindly exclude me from the world that never wrote to you.

Contact and Further Information:
www.roadsearching.com

Photo of the author (right) with Paul on the occasion of Paul's marriage to Danielle.